#7.13

1964-65

Great
Aspirations

norc

NATIONAL OPINION RESEARCH CENTER
MONOGRAPHS IN SOCIAL RESEARCH

Great Aspirations

The
Graduate School Plans
of
America's College Seniors

By

JAMES A. DAVIS

ALDINE PUBLISHING COMPANY
Chicago

The research reported herein was supported through
The Cooperative Research Program of the Office of Education,
U.S. Department of Health, Education and Welfare

First published 1964 by
ALDINE Publishing Company
64 East Van Buren Street
Chicago, Illinois 60605

Library of Congress Catalog Card Number 64-15603
Designed by Greer Allen
Printed in the United States of America

Preface

Colleges and universities are charged with the important task of preparing young men and women for professional, technical, and managerial occupations. Undergraduate schools and the undergraduate divisions of universities certainly perform the major part of this task, each year over the past few years conferring more than a third of a million undergraduate degrees.

For many career fields the bachelor's degree is an important step on the way to entry into those occupations, but, for better or for worse, postgraduate training either in the traditional liberal arts and sciences graduate schools or in professional schools is the educational experience that will make such an entry finally possible. Postgraduate training is no longer confined to a small minority of college graduates—nearly a third of each year's new bachelors of arts and science go on to such training the year of their graduation. We expect that by the time these college graduates reach the midpoint of their careers, in their forties, this proportion will be nearly doubled.

The research embodied in this monograph is concerned with this increasingly important part of educational training. It uses a large sample of the classes graduating from American colleges and universities in June, 1961, as an entry point into the more general problem of how postgraduate training plans are formed.

Manpower issues are among the more important aspects of today's headlines and public discussions: "satellites," "teacher shortage," "population explosion," "electronic computers," "the two cultures," "new nations," "cancer research," "why Johnny can't (or can) read," "automation," "equality of opportunity." A moment's reflection of any of these topical issues leads very quickly to unanswered questions about the selection, allocation, and training of the specialists needed to grapple with the problems involved. Some of the more critical specialists are in very short supply; some careers are not drawing enough of the very talented; and still others need new kinds of training.

Social scientists have a more academic interest in such manpower questions. The intricate complexity of the occupational systems of a modern industrial society raises the general social science question of how such societies manage to fill their sets of diverse occupational niches with persons of at least sufficient competence and skill to keep the system going. Educational institutions are of critical importance to the student of modern society since they are the organizational means through which such societies attempt to solve their highly complicated manpower problems.

The intersection of these two interests — social science and social policy — has given rise to the present research and to other studies currently underway at the National Opinion Research Center and elsewhere. The formation of career preferences and the choice of occupation are research themes that run through a number of studies presently underway, each to contribute knowledge and understanding concerning the workings of our society generally and towards the formation of social policies designed to minimize social costs and maximize the ability of our society to meet its critical manpower issues.

Properly to design policy that would make our educational system and our college-educated youths more sensitive to the manpower needs implicit in the topical issues of the day, we need more information on a variety of questions concerning college graduates. Some of these quite specific questions are as follows:

Who goes on to postgraduate training?

What are the numbers of graduating seniors planning to enter various critical occupations?

How do the various occupations fare in competing for the top academic talent in the graduating class?

How many talented students are lost to postgraduate training?

What are the social and personal characteristics of students planning postgraduate study in particular fields?

In order to seek answers to these questions about graduating seniors, three government agencies — the Cooperative Research Program of the U.S. Office of Education, the National Institutes of Health, and the National Science Foundation — in early 1961, joined to provide funds for a large scale national survey[1] to be administered through the Cooperative Research Program. Drs. Herbert H. Rosenberg of the National Institutes of Health, Robert Cain of the National Science Foundation, and Drs. Alice Scates and Herbert Conrad, both of the Office of Education, constituted a vigorous and effective sponsoring committee that succeeded in the complicated task of administering the grant and providing important guidance and advice to the research group.

The research itself was conducted by the National Opinion Research Center of the University of Chicago. At various times and in various capacities more than 100 persons participated in the survey at NORC; space limits us to naming only those staff members who played key roles. While I served as principal investigator for the project and provided over-all administrative and policy direction, Dr. James A. Davis was the social scientist most directly responsible for the design of the study and the preparation of this monograph. Dr. Davis' skills and sensitivity are clearly evident throughout this monograph. Jacob J. Feldman, Director of Research at NORC, designed the sample and served as technical consultant throughout the study. Richard McKinlay, Assistant Study Director, supervised the extremely difficult process of machine-editing and tabulation of the large number of questionnaires. NORC Field Director Galen Gockel and Mrs. Ruth Boorstin guided data-gathering operations. Norman Bradburn, Study Director, contributed heavily to the preliminary stages of the analyses, particularly in the construction of measures of academic performance. Joseph Zelan, Assistant Study Director, was responsible for preparation of the final tables. Harold Levy, Machine Room Superintendent, and Sanford Abrams, Assistant Machine Room Superintendent, directed the formidable task of IBM processing. Of the many student assistants involved in the survey, Judy Schick, Dorothy Pownall, and George Hesslink made especially important contributions. Mrs. Nella Siefert again displayed her unique craftsmanship in the typing of endless text and complex statistical tables, ably assisted by Mrs. Joanne Hesslink. And the superb performance of Elroy

[1]The National Institutes of Health had supported an exploratory phase of the research during the 1960 calendar year.

Parker, who first multilithed and supervised the assembling of this huge report, should not be forgotten.

Outside of NORC, we wish to acknowledge a special indebtedness to the National Merit Scholarship Corporation and, in particular, to John Holland, Alexander Astin, and Robert Nichols, who provided us with ideas, encouragement, and important sets of data.

PETER H. ROSSI
Director
National Opinion Research Center

Contents

LIST
OF
TABLES

TABLE

Illustrations

Introduction

THE SAMPLE

Data for this report are based on self-administered questionnaires (a copy of which is appended to this report) completed in the spring of 1961 by 33,982 June graduates sampled from 135 colleges and universities. The sample was designed to be representative of June, 1961, graduates receiving degrees from either accredited or very large non-accredited institutions granting bachelors degrees.

A detailed analysis of the sample and a list of the sample institutions appear in Appendices 4 and 5. For introductory purposes, however, we may note that: (a) All of the 135 sampled schools agreed to cooperate with the study, (b) Approximately 85 per cent of the eligible students completed a questionnaire, (c) The large size of the sample makes sampling error very small for figures based on the total number of cases.

Four qualifications and restrictions must be noted:

a. Because the sample was designed to be representative of *students,* not *institutions,* the 135 schools are not a random sample of American colleges and universities, for large institutions are greatly over-represented.

b. In recent years approximately one-fourth of each year's college graduates finished their undergraduate work at a time other than the spring terms. To the unknown extent that they differ from June graduates, the sample is not representative of 1961 graduates as a whole.

c. Because many students enter graduate school after a period of a year or more out of college, and others enter professional schools after less than four years of college, the sample is not designed to be representative of students entering graduate training in the fall of 1961, although students from our universe constitute a high proportion of those entrants.

d. At many points in the analysis, it is important to remember that the sample was not designed to be representative of college students in general. About 60 per cent of college freshmen survive to graduation, and it is these "survivors" who constitute the population sampled.

THE TABLES

Some of the tables in this report are based on the total sample and others are based upon a representative sub-sample, the latter being employed to reduce when possible the data-handling burden of the research staff. Thus, the tables come from two different series:

a. Most of the data are based on a "Total Weighted Sample" (TWS) of 56,664 cases. Such computations are actually based on 33,982 individual questionnaires. Because the sample design deliberately over-represents some schools and under-represents others, the cases have been multiplied by various weighting factors to make the total weighted N of 56,664 representative of the universe as a whole.

b. A number of tables are based on a representative sub-sample (RSS) of 3,397 cases, drawn from the total to facilitate speed in analysis. The representative sub-sample was drawn in such a fashion that it is equivalent to a two-stage sample of 3,397 cases drawn from the universe.

Proportions based on the entire 3,397 cases in the sub-sample should be quite reliable. Proportions computed for small sub-groups are subject to considerable sampling error and should be treated only as suggestive rather than conclusive.

THE QUESTIONNAIRE

Each student in the sample was asked to complete the same 19-page self-administered questionnaire (reproduced in Appendix VI). Because of the unusually large sample size and the limitations of time and budget, the questionnaire was designed to meet the following restrictions:

a. Except for the student's name, the entire questionnaire was "pre-coded," i.e., the respondent answered by circling the IBM code number of a particular alternative, rather than answering in his own words.

b. The questionnaire was designed so that the same instrument was applicable to a variety of fields, schools, career plans, etc.

c. The questionnaire was designed so that no coding or editing took place prior to key punching. The completed cards, however, were subjected to extensive machine-editing ("cleaning") to resolve discrepancies, detect erroneous punches, etc.

The following topics were covered in the questionnaire:

a. Intentions for postgraduate study.

b. For students planning postgraduate study in 1961: application and acceptance status, stipend applications and offers, and expected financial resources.

c. Intended career field and type of employer.

d. Occupational interests and values.

e. Undergraduate activities and associations, place of residence, employment, etc.

f. Reactions to academic courses, faculty relationships, and the college or university itself.

g. Academic performance and honors.

h. Self-rated personality characteristics and social values.

i. Background information: sex, parental family characteristics, religion, marital status, residence, etc.

THIS REPORT

Because of the unusual size and strategic importance of this sample, this report is but the first of several to be produced by NORC from this project. In particular, a monograph treating the field of law in more detail than is possible here has been prepared by Seymour Warkov, and it is hoped that other specific occupations can be added to the list. In addition, Father Andrew Greeley of NORC has completed a book entitled *Religion and Career: A Study of College Graduates* in which he analyzes religious differences in the sample. The book was published by Sheed and Ward, Inc. in 1963.

Even more important, NORC has received since the completion of this report a grant from the National Institute of Mental Health to conduct follow-up studies of the sample during their initial years after graduation. In the spring of 1962 the total sample received a questionnaire to determine whether their anticipated occupational and educational plans worked out in reality. Norman Miller, Senior Study Director, was responsible for the analysis of these materials. In the spring of 1963 a follow-up questionnaire went on its way to the total sample, and additional waves of questionnaires are anticipated in the next two years.

Since the data treated in this report were all collected in the weeks shortly before graduation, the materials have a special time perspective. Our major concern was the past and future of these students rather than their immediate situation. Although their past decisions were subject to the distortion of memory, their true futures were unknown. It is our belief that the materials catch these young people at a crucial point in their occupational and academic lives.

1

A
Senior Class
Portrait

Who are these graduates? Where did they come from? Where are they going? What did they think of college? What do they want out of life? What do they think about themselves? These questions must have occurred to the people who sat through the graduation addresses in June of 1961. Everyone has some impressions of the graduate who emerges after sixteen years in the American educational system, but impressions can be wrong. In this chapter we will present a profile of the June, 1961, class; our data, though extensive, are fragmentary for there are still many things about the class we do not yet know. What we do know, however, confirms some popular ideas and casts doubts on others.

The modal graduate of June, 1961, was more likely to be a man than a woman, was in his early twenties, came from a family where he was neither the youngest nor the oldest nor the only child, was unmarried, and was a white, native-born American from a city of over 100,000. He was a member of the middle or upper middle class; his father and mother had graduated at least from high school and had an income of over $7,500. His father was a manager or professional. The graduate had held at least a part-time job during his final year of college and was still a member of the Protestant religion in which he had been reared.

He had warm and positive feelings toward his school and professors, planned to continue his education in graduate school (at least eventually), planned to be a professional of some kind (if one counts education trom elementary to university as a profession), did not particularly like businessmen, had at least a B minus average, thought of himself as being in the top one-fourth of his class and would look for intellectual and service values in his career. While he was in school he had lived in a dormitory or in off-campus housing; he was within four hours' driving time from his family.

He thought of himself as conventional, religious, and politically liberal, and was inclined to describe himself as co-operative, ambitious, happy, fun-loving, easy-going, idealistic, athletic, and cautious.

Such, then, is a description of the "typical" June, 1961, graduate, but such a modal profile overlooks many interesting details in the portrait of the senior class as a whole. In this chapter we will group some simple descriptive items under five headings— demography, social class, college experience, future plans, and self-description—and then proceed to a more detailed analysis using various "background indices."

DEMOGRAPHY

Table 1.1 summarizes the pertinent demographic information about the 1961 graduates.

Six out of ten graduates were male, four out of ten were female (Table 1.1a), a fact that had continual implications for career decisions. The students were very heavily concentrated in their early twenties (1.1b). About two-thirds were twenty-one or twenty-two; five per cent were under twenty-one and thirty per cent were older than the more or less standard graduating age of twenty-two (18 per cent were over twenty-five). The clear suggestion is that part-time or postponed studies are far from rare in American higher education.

Despite the increase in youthful marriages, three-fourths of the graduates were still unmarried according to Table 1.1c. Furthermore, almost two-thirds planned to be single at least beyond the fall after their graduation. If a graduate was married, however, he (or she) was very likely to have children or to be expecting a child.

Tables 1.1d and 1.1e show that the vast majority of graduates were white, native-born Americans. Even though the Negro population of the country is some 10 per cent of the total, only three per cent of the graduates were Negro. (Just as the social experiences of American Negroes are unique, the career plans and choices of the 1,778 Negro students were found to be distinctive. Throughout this report we shall treat them as a special group.)

Table 1.1. Selected Demographic Characteristics of the Sample (Representative Sub-sample)

a. Sex		b. Age (at last birthday)		
	PER CENT		PER CENT	CUMU-LATIVE
Male	60			
Female	40	19 or younger	—	—
	100%	20	5	—
		21	39	95
N = 3,397		22	26	56
		23-24	12	30
		25-29	12	18
		30 or older	6	6
		Total	100%	
		N	3,355	
		NA	42	
		Total N	3,397	

c. Marital Status		d. Race		
	PER CENT			PER CENT
Single	75	White		94
Expect to be married		Negro		3
before Fall, 1961	13	Oriental		2
Other	62	Other		1
Married	24	Total		100%
Child or expecting a				
child	16	N	3,328	
No children	8	NA	69	
Ex-married	1	Total N	3,397	
Total	100%			
N	3,356			
NA	41			
Total N	3,397			

(Table 1.1 continued)

Table 1.1. *Continued*

e. Nativity

	PER CENT	
U.S. born	97	
Foreign born	3	
Naturalized		2
Other, expect to stay in U.S.		1
Other, do not expect to stay		1
Total	100%	
N	3,327	
NA	70	
Total N	3,397	

f. Hometown During High School

	PER CENT	
Central city	44	
More than 2 million		9
500,000 – 2 million		5
100,000 – 499,999		8
50,000 – 99,999		4
10,000 – 49,999		10
Less than 10,000		8
Suburb in a metropolitan area	35	
More than 2 million		10
500,000 – 2 million		9
100,000 – 499,999		8
Less than 100,000		9
Farm or open country	22	
Total	101%	
N	3,307	
NA	90	
Total N	3,397	

Although originally included as a routine demographic item, the size of "the community that you think of as your home town during high school days" turned out to be an important correlate of career decisions. The answer categories were framed to classify a "hometown" along two dimensions: a) whether it was a central city, a suburb, or a rural area, and b) what size it was. Table 1.1f shows the distribution of the respondents: 44 per cent came from a central city, 35 per cent from a suburb, and 22 per cent from a farm or open country. (Because only eight per cent of the sample reported "farm" as the occupation of the head of their parental household, it appears that a substantial number of those from the last category ought to be classified as "rural, non-farm.") One-half of the graduates were from cities over 100,000 or their suburbs and about one-fifth of them were from rural areas.

SOCIAL CLASS

Table 1.2 furnishes us with information on the socio-economic background of the June, 1961, seniors.

By the socio-economic status of a family we mean its possession or lack of possession of those characteristics that are preferred in a given society. In modern America, the characteristics that largely determine one's status are income, occupation, education, and religion. (The first three elements are highly intercorrelated, while the last element is to some extent correlated both with the first three and with hometown size. In this study two indices are used to control the operation of these variables — a socio-economic status index and an index of background characteristics. Later in this chapter we discuss the construction of these indices as well as the relationships existing between the indices and other variables.)

Table 1.2a presents data on the income of the families of the 1961 graduates. One-third reported family incomes of more than $10,000 a year, while one-fifth reported incomes of less than $5,000 a year. The validity of these figures is unknown, but the suggested pattern — a concentration in the "middle-income levels" with a larger minority from high-income families and a smaller minority from low-income families — appears intuitively reasonable.

From Table 1.2b we learn that about one-half of the wage earners in parental families were considered by their children to be professionals or proprietors, about six out of ten had white collar jobs, a little less than one-third had urban working-class jobs, and less than one-tenth were farmers. Table 1.2c completes

Table 1.2. Selected Social Class Characteristics of the Sample (Representative Sub-sample)

a. Annual Income of Parental Family

	PER CENT	CUMU-LATIVE
Less than $5,000	20	—
$ 5,000 – $ 7,499	29	80
$ 7,500 – $ 9,999	19	51
$10,000 – $14,999	15	32
$15,000 – $19,999	6	17
$20,000 and over	11	11
Total	100%	

N	2,882
"I have no idea"	400
NA	115
Total N	3,397

b. Occupation of Head of Parental Family

	PER CENT
Professional	24
Mgr. or Prop.	25
Sales	7
Clerical	5
Skilled	17
Semi-skilled	7
Service	3
Unskilled	4
Farmer, farm worker	8
Total	100%

N	3,271
NA	126
Total N	3,397

c. Father's Education

	PER CENT	CUMU-LATIVE
8th Grade or Less	22	22
Part High School	17	39
High School Graduate	21	60
Part College	14	74
Bachelor's	12	86
Graduate or Professional Degree	13	
Total	99%	

N	3,309
NA	88
Total N	3,397

d. Original Religion

	PER CENT
Protestant	60
Roman Catholic	25
Jewish	8
Other	3
None	3
Total	99%

N	3,320
NA	77
Total N	3,397

e. Employment During Academic Year

TYPE	PER CENT
None	47
Part Time	45
Full Time	9
Total	101%

N	3,348
NA	49
Total N	3,397

the picture of the income-occupation-education trinity by demonstrating that 25 per cent of the graduates' fathers were college graduates, 39 per cent had attended some college, 60 per cent had graduated from high school, while one-fifth had not progressed beyond eighth grade. Clearly college graduation represented upward mobility for a considerable number of graduates. The mobility is not as great, however, as a comparison with parental education alone would suggest, since many of the parents obviously had jobs whose income and status were obtainable in the past without college education but are not so today. Thus, even though only one-fourth of the fathers had graduated from college, one-half were managers or professionals and 30 per cent were earning over $10,000 a year. On the other hand, it is possible for the children of poorly-educated working-class wage earners to make it to college commencement day. It is no secret, of course, that it is much easier for those who are higher on the socio-economic scale.

The exact nature of religion as a predictor variable is not clear; whether religion and ethnicity are status or social-psychological factors is by no means settled, although in all probability they are both. The operation of the "religious factor" in the career choices of the 1961 graduates was not at all surprising in some instances, and quite unpredicted in others. The main line of religious difference seemed to be along the Jew-Gentile dimension, rather than the Protestant-Catholic one, despite the predictions of the Protestant Ethic hypothesis. Table 1.2d gives the distribution of the sample according to original religion. Protestants were somewhat underrepresented and Jews somewhat overrepresented in comparison with their proportions in the national population (as reported in the 1957 Federal Census study). The one-fourth of the college population that was Catholic was the same as the Catholic population in the national population. The small proportion of "others" turned out to be quite heterogeneous. In examining a sample of the "others," Greeley found that 24 per cent of them were Fundamentalist Protestants, 18 per cent Greek Orthodox, 12 per cent Greek or Polish Catholic, and 10 per cent Mormon.

Religious affiliation was quite stable for the 1961 seniors. Even though there were some shifts from original religion to present religion, notably a nine per cent increase in the "nones," 85 per cent of the seniors were in the same religion at graduation as that in which they were reared.[1]

In summary, even though college does make some upward mobility possible and serve as the occasion for some religious change, the vast majority of college graduates belong to the same broad religious, social, and economic groups as their parents.

COLLEGE EXPERIENCE

What did the 1961 graduates think of their years in college? It is clear that they liked their schools. Table 1.3a shows that one-third reported a very strong attachment to their schools, while almost another half were willing to say that they liked the school but were not enthusiastic. Only 6 per cent admitted to disliking it.

They did not personally believe that the purpose of college was "vocational"; however, they suspected that their classmates were not inclined to be so "liberal." As we observe in Table 1.3b, two-thirds of them thought that getting a basic education and gaining an appreciation of ideas was their own goal in college, but only 38 per cent were willing to credit the "typical student" with their own objectives. Since they were obviously talking about each other, we have a case of confused perceptions. It is especially interesting that only 3 per cent said they thought the purpose of college is to have a good time, but one-fourth of them thought that the *typical* student had this frivolous attitude.

Table 1.3c presents another phenomenon in the matter of subjective rank. One-fourth of the students thought of themselves as being in the top 10 per cent of their class, one-half rated themselves in the top quarter, and only 4 per cent admitted to being in the lowest quarter. This "selective misperception" (it is unlikely that 4 per cent could constitute one-fourth!) does not seem to apply to the reporting of grade point averages. Table 1.3d shows that the grades cover a rough normal curve with 68 per cent being in the B to C+ brackets.

[1] Andrew Greeley and Joseph Zelan are engaged in an analysis of the correlates of religious apostasy. Their work suggests that college may be the occasion of apostasy but is probably not the cause.

Table 1.3. College Experience (Representative Sub-sample)

a. Attachment to Present College

	PER CENT
Very strong attachment	32
Like it, but not strongly	43
Mixed feelings	19
Don't like it, but not strongly	4
Thoroughly dislike it	2
Total	100%

N = 3,397

b. Perceived Purpose of College

	MYSELF	THE TYPICAL STUDENT HERE
A basic general education and appreciation of ideas	67%	38%
Having a good time while getting a degree	3	25
Career training	32	39
Developing the ability to get along with different kinds of people	16*	9*
N	3,334	3,294
NA	43	103
Total N	3,397	3,397

*Totals more than 100 per cent because of multiple answers.

c. Self-ranking Among Graduates in Same Field		d. Self-reported Grade Point Average	
	PER CENT		PER CENT
Top ten per cent	25	A	1
Top quarter, but not top ten per cent	26	A−	6
		B+	11
Second quarter	30	B	14
Third quarter	14	B−	27
Lowest quarter	4	C+	26
Total	99%	C	13
		C− or lower	2
N	3,249	Total	100%
NA	148		
Total N	3,397	N	3,345
		NA	52
		Total N	3,397

(Table 1.3 continued)

Table 1.3. *Continued*

e. Feelings about Occupation "College Professor"

	PER CENT
This sort of work would be very interesting.	42
I don't have the ability to do this kind of work.	65
I probably couldn't make as much money at this type of work as I'd like to make.	6
One would have to devote too much time and energy to this work. I want to be able to spend more time with my family and friends.	22
One would have to invest more time and money in preparing for this occupation than I feel I could afford.	22
I know as a personal friend or family friend, one or more people in this field.	30
My parents would disapprove of my going into this field.	2
My personality isn't suitable for work in this field.	31
People with my religious, racial, or family background don't have much chance of success in this field.	1
It wouldn't be challenging enough for me.	2
I wouldn't like the life I'd have to lead outside the job.	5
This is my father's occupation.	1

N	3,222
NA	175
Total N	3,397

f. Importance of Faculty Members and Parents for Career Advice

	FACULTY MEMBERS	PARENTS
Very important	19%	20%
Fairly important	38	40
Unimportant	27	26
Never received any	16	12
Total per cent	100%	98%
N	3,283	3,297
NA	114	100
Total N	3,397	3,397

Two items on the questionnaire indicate what the students thought of their professors. Table 1.3e shows the response to the idea of college teaching as a career occupation; two-thirds of them thought it an interesting profession and two-thirds reported having a friend in the field. One is forced to conclude that some students actually look on their professors as friends. Of the six occupations presented for evaluation on this item (research chemist, business executive, high school teacher, M.D., college professor, and engineer), the professor proved to be by far the most popular.[2]

A second indication of the student's affection for his professor is to be found in Table 1.3f. The members of the college faculty appeared to be almost as important in helping the student make a career choice as were the student's parents. Perhaps the despair faculty often feel about their contribution to the lives of the young is not altogether justified.

FUTURE PLANS

Perhaps the biggest compliment that the graduating seniors paid to higher education was that they wanted more of it. Table 1.4a shows the graduate school plans of the 1961 class. Only one-fourth had no plans to go to graduate school at any time,

[2]The writer, in collaboration with Richard McKinlay and Andrew Greeley, is engaged in a study of the comparative images of the college professor and the business executive in the minds of the June, 1961, seniors. The college professor is an easy winner.

Table 1.4 Future Plans (as of Spring, 1961)
(Representative Sub-sample)

a. Graduate or Professional School Plans for Fall, 1961	
	PER CENT
Going to graduate or professional school, and accepted by one or more schools	19
Going to graduate or professional school, and not yet accepted by one or more schools	12
Going to graduate or professional school after fall, 1961, and have a definite date in mind	30
Going to graduate or professional school after fall, 1961, but no definite date in mind	15
Not going to graduate or professional school, but would like to if there were no obstacles	6
Not going to graduate or professional school and would not like to	18
Total	100%

	N	3,254
	NA	143
	Total N	3,397

(Table 1.4 continued)

Table 1.4. *Continued*

b. Anticipated Career Field	
	PER CENT
Science	8
Social Science and Humanities	11
Medicine	3
Law	4
Engineering	9
Education	33
Business	18
Other Professions	15
Total per cent	101
N	3,151
NEC, Non-labor Force, NA	246
Total N	3,397

c. Characteristics Which Would Be Very Important in Picking a Job or Career	
	PER CENT
Opportunities to be helpful to others or useful to society	65
Opportunity to work with people rather than things	56
Opportunity to be original and creative	51
A chance to exercise leadership	41
Living and working in the world of ideas	39
Opportunities for moderate but steady progress rather than the chance of extreme success or failure	33
Making a lot of money	24
Freedom from supervision in my work	18
Avoiding a high pressure job which takes too much out of you	16
Getting away from the city or area in which I grew up	13
Remaining in the city or area in which I grew up	7
N	3,387
NA	10
Total N	3,397

while almost one-third were planning to go the next fall. A college graduate is more likely to go on to graduate school than a high school graduate is to go to college.

What kinds of careers did these graduates plan for themselves? Tables 1.4b, c, d, and e indicate the highly "professional" orientation of the graduates. Eighteen per cent were headed

Table 1.4. *Continued*

d. Anticipated Career Employer

	PER CENT
Private company with 100 or more employees	27
Private company with fewer than 100 employees or professional partnership	11
Family business	2
Self-employed	8
Research organization or institute	7
College, university, or junior college	12
Elementary or secondary school or school system	33
Other educational institutions	1
U.S. Federal Government	14
State or local government	6
Hospital, church, clinic, welfare organization, etc.	8
Other	3

N	3,144
No answer and not applicable	253
Total N	3,397

e. Anticipated Career Activities

	PER CENT
Teaching	50
Research	24
Administration	33
Service to patients or clients	24
None of these	7

N	3,139
No answer, not applicable	258
Total N	3,397

for the arts and sciences, 7 per cent for the traditional professions of law and medicine, and 33 per cent for education. Only 18 per cent were inclined to the business world.

One of the major reasons for the choice of "professions" is the preferred occupational values of the students, as described in Table 1.4c. Despite the fears expressed by people who have read *The Man in The Grey Flannel Suit,* security and money do not seem to be among the important occupational values of young college graduate Americans. Indeed, the most important value was the "opportunity to be useful to others or helpful to society"; the "opportunity to work with people instead of things" was second and the "opportunity to be original and creative" was third. All three were checked by half of the respondents. "Money" was checked by one-fourth, "security" by one-third, and the "avoidance of pressure" by 16 per cent. One is tempted to suggest that, at least in terms of occupational values, the June, 1961, college graduates seemed to be an extraordinarily idealistic lot.

Tables 1.4d and e complete the picture of the future plans of the respondents. In Table 1.4d we see that 21 per cent of the students hoped to be independent entrepreneurs (self-employed, small company or family business). Most thought they would work for organizations—large companies, educational institutions or governmental agencies. In Table 1.4e we note that half of the graduates saw teaching as one of their major career activities and one-fourth saw research as a major part of their career plans. Once again it would appear that the four years of academic life left the graduate well disposed toward this life.

SELF-DESCRIPTION

We now have some idea of who the June, 1961, senior was, and what he wanted out of life. But what did he think of himself? A detailed answer to this question would take much further research; however, one of the items on the questionnaire asked the respondent to rate himself on a list of 24 self-descriptive adjectives. Table 1.5a shows the results. The graduating senior refused to restrict himself to being either an inner-directed man or an other-directed man, insisting that he was both co-operative and ambitious, and at the same time happy, fun-loving and easygoing. Nor was he willing to describe himself as lazy or shy, rebellious or sophisticated.

Table 1.5b takes up four scales of self-description that were in the questionnaire. Only one-fourth were willing to take a stand against modern art and only one-third admitted that they were conservative politically. (Only 6 per cent described themselves as very conservative; one wonders if the New Conservatism

Table 1.5.   Self-Description

a. Self-descriptive Adjectives

	PER CENT
Eight most frequently mentioned adjectives:	
Cooperative	62
Ambitious	56
Happy	49
Fun-loving	46
Easy-going	36
Idealistic	33
Athletic	32
Cautious	31
Seventeen adjectives of Intermediate Frequency:	
Calm, Cultured, Energetic, Good-looking,	
Hard-driving, High-strung, Intellectual,	
Methodical, Middle Brow, Moody, Obliging,	
Outgoing, Poised, Quiet, Reserved,	
Talkative, Witty	
Eight least frequently mentioned adjectives:	
Dominant	12
Shy	10
Impetuous	10
Lazy	9
Forceful	9
Rebellious	9
Sophisticated	7
Low Brow	1

	N	3,380
	NA	17
	Total N	3,397

b. Attitude toward Modern Art

	PER CENT
Very favorable	14
Fairly favorable	34
Neither	26
Fairly unfavorable	17
Very unfavorable	9
Total	100%

N	3,323
NA	74
Total N	3,397

c. Political Orientation

	PER CENT
Very liberal	11
Fairly liberal	37
Neither	18
Fairly conservative	28
Very conservative	6
Total	100%

N	3,307
NA	90
Total N	3,397

(Table 1.5 continued)

Table 1.5. *Continued*

d. Conventionality	PER CENT	e. Religiousness	PER CENT
Very conventional	8	Very religious	20
Fairly conventional	47	Fairly religious	50
Neither	15	Neither	13
Fairly unconventional	24	Fairly non-religious	10
Very unconventional	6	Very non-religious	6
Total	100%	Total	99%
N	3,319	N	3,338
NA	78	NA	59
Total N	3,397	Total N	3,397

about which the press is so concerned really has much campus support.) Although almost one-half thought of themselves as politically liberal, a much smaller proportion described themselves as either unconventional (30 per cent) or unreligious (16 per cent). Indeed, almost three-fourths thought of themselves as religious.[3]

INDEX OF BACKGROUND CHARACTERISTICS

As was mentioned before, many of the background variables are quite closely related. In this section we propose to develop several indices of these related variables which will facilitate analysis of the huge amount of data generated in this study.

Family position on the three measures of socio-economic status was, of course, strongly related (Table 1.6). The per cent of families with incomes of $10,000 or more ranged from 5 per cent among the semi-skilled, service, and unskilled group to 62 per cent among the professionals; from 14 per cent among the fathers with less than a high school education to 66 per cent among the fathers who graduated from college. Similarly, the percentage of college graduates ranged occupationally from 1 per cent among the semi-skilled, service, and unskilled to 72 per cent among those reported as professionals.

[3]In an analysis of materials from a second phase of this study, Greeley found that this perceived religiousness was carried over into very high rates of church attendance when the graduates were a year out of college.

Table 1.6. Socio-Economic Status Index: Parental Income, Father's Education, and Parental Occupation (Representative Sub-sample)

a. Parental Income and Parental Occupation (per cent reporting parental income of $10,000 a year or more)

Professional	62	(666)
Proprietor, Manager	52	(649)
Sales, Clerical	21	(352)
Skilled	10	(524)
Semi-Skilled, Service, Unskilled	5	(450)
Farm, Farm Laborer	15	(207)
Total N	2,848	
NA Parental Occupation	34	
NA Parental Income	515	
Total	3,397	

b. Parental Income and Father's Education (per cent reporting parental income of $10,000 a year or more)

Bachelors or More	66	(691)
Part College	40	(408)
High School	25	(609)
Less than High School	14	(1,159)
Total N	2,867	
NA Father's Education	15	
NA Parental Income	515	
Total	3,397	

c. Parental Occupation and Father's Education
(Per cent with given education level)

Parental Occupation	Father's Education				Total	
	Bachelor's or More	Part College	High School	Less than High School	Per Cent	N
Professional	72	14	8	7	101	777
Proprietor, Manager	21	21	28	30	100	803
Sales, Clerical	16	24	27	33	100	386
Skilled	2	10	30	58	100	565
Semi-Skilled, Service, Unskilled	1	4	19	76	100	469
Farm, Farm Laborer	5	10	19	65	99	252

Total N		3,251
NA Father's Education		15
NA Parental Occupation		131
Total		3,397

(Table 1.6 continued)

Table 1.6. *Continued*

d. Income by Occupation and Education (Per cent $10,000 or more)

Parental Occupation	Education		
	High School or Less	Part College	Bachelor's or More
Professional	36 (94)	51 (91)	70 (476)
Proprietor, Manager	41 (383)	64 (137)	71 (128)
Sales, Clerical	16 (216)	23 (82)	40 (53)
Other*	8 (1,054)	13 (92)	30 (27)

Total N	2,833
NA Parental Occupation	34
NA Father's Education	15
NA or DK on Income	515
	3,397

e. Education by Occupation and Income (Per cent part college or more)

Occupation	Income	
	Under $10,000	$10,000 or More
Professional	76 (250)	92 (411)
Manager, Proprietor	28 (311)	53 (337)
Sales, Clerical	34 (276)	53 (75)
Other*	9 (1,067)	19 (106)

Total N	2,833
NA Parental Occupation	34
NA Father's Education	15
NA or DK on Income	515
	3,397

*Skilled, Semi-Skilled, Service, Unskilled, Farm.

Partial correlation tables (1.6d, 1.6e) show that any two of the variables contributed independently toward predicting the third. Thus, among professionals twice as many college graduate families as high school-educated families had high incomes; similarly, in the part-college group, the per cent reporting $10,000 or more ranged by occupation from 13 to 64.

The tables show patterns known to be characteristic of American society, increasing our confidence in the validity of the measures. Although professionals in general make more than managers (Table 1.6a), within an educational level managers

Table 1.6. *Continued*

f. Construction of Index of Socio-Economic Status (SES)
I. Distribution of Cases

Occupation of Family Head	Father's Education	Parental Income	
		Under $7,500	$7,500 or More
White Collar*	Part College or More	206 (b)	761 (a)
	High School or Less	312 (d)	381 (c)
Blue Collar**	Part College or More	67 (f)	52 (e)
	High School or Less	782 (h)	272 (g)

N = 2,833

*White Collar = Professional, Proprietor or Managerial, Sales and Clerical.
**Blue Collar = Skilled, Semi-Skilled, Service, Unskilled and Farm.

II. Assignment of "No Answer" and "Don't Know" on Family Income

Occupation	Education	Per cent with Income of $7,500 or More Among Those Answering	N	N DK or NA	Cell Assignment
Professional	AB or More	85	476	82	a
	Part College	71	91	15	a
	High School or Less	61	94	19	c
Manager, Prop.	AB or More	84	128	39	a
	Part College	81	137	30	a
	High School or Less	64	383	85	c
Sales, Clerical	AB or More	57	53	8	None
	Part College	52	82	11	None
	High School or Less	37	216	16	d
Blue Collar	Post High School	45	121	15	f
	High School	30	274	30	h
	Part High School	27	307	21	h
	8th Grade or Less	23	471	47	h

N	2,833
NA Income Only	418
NA Parental Occupation Only	34
NA Father's Education Only	15
NA Two or More	97
Total N	3,397

III. Distribution of Cases by Index Scores

Score	N	Per cent
3	927	29
2	743	23
1	682	21
0	880	27
N = 3,232		100
NA	165	
Total N = 3,397		

31128

have higher incomes (Table 1.6d). Sales and clerical families have about the same educational levels as managers (1.6c), but their incomes are less (1.6d); there is a considerable gap in income and education between the white-collar and the blue-collar farm occupations.

It would be extremely interesting to study the independent contribution of each of these variables. What, for instance, is the effect of variations in parental education level on children's career plans among families with similar incomes and occupations? Are those families with discrepant characteristics (e.g., high income, low education) different in their influence? However, in comparison with their association with outside variables, these characteristics are so strongly associated with each other that it is inefficient to use them individually in complex tabulations. It is a well-known principle that the best strategy for multivariate prediction is to assemble predictor variables, each of which is associated with the dependent variable but is weakly or randomly associated with the others.

Therefore, a pooled Index of Socio-Economic Status (SES) was constructed as follows:

1. Each variable was dichotomized:

Variable	Categories	
	High	Low
Family income	$7,500 or more	Less than $7,500
Father's education	Part college or more	High school graduate or less
Parental occupation	Professional, Manager-Proprietor Sales Clerical	Skilled Semi-skilled Service Unskilled Farm

2. Because of the high non-response rates on income (10 per cent circled "I have no idea" and 3 per cent didn't answer the question [RSS]) and the high relationship between the other two variables and income, incomes were estimated for non-respondents who reported both of the other variables. Twelve per cent of the total cases were successfully assigned this way (Table 1.6f).

3. Scores on SES are the number of high scores on the constituent items.

4. The index has a range from 0 to 3 and each score includes about one-fourth of the cases (Table 1.6f).

5. For most analyses the only distinction made is between high (scores 2 and 3) and low (scores 0 and 1).

Family SES varied considerably with the student's race, religion, and hometown.

Although the Negro college students were undoubtedly recruited disproportionately from the highest SES levels among Negroes, they were characterized by much lower SES scores than other students. Fifteen per cent of the Negroes, in comparison with 54 per cent of the whites, were scored high on SES! (See Table 1.7a.)

Table 1.7. Correlates of Race, Religion, Hometown, and SES (Representative Sub-sample)

a. Race and SES

Those Who Are	Among Whites		Among Negroes	
	Per cent	N	Per cent	N
High SES	54	(3,047)	15	(100)

N	3,147
NA SES	98
Race: Other & NA	85
NA Both	67
Total N	3,397

b. Race and Hometown

Those Who Are	Among Whites		Among Negroes	
	Per cent	N	Per cent	N
From larger cities	48	(3,116)	30	(104)

N	3,220
NA Hometown	24
Race: Other & NA	87
NA Both	66
Total N	3,397

(Table 1.7 continued)

Table 1.7. *Continued*

c. Race and Religion

Those Who Are	Among Whites Per cent	N	Among Negroes Per cent	N
Protestant	52		70	
Roman Catholic	26		15	
Jewish	8		0	
None	11		5	
Other	3		11	
	100	(3,117)	101	(102)

N	3,219
Race: Other & NA	86
NA Religion	25
NA Both	67
Total N	3,397

Among the white respondents, SES, hometown, and religion were associated in a complex fashion (Table 1.8). In general, high status was associated with larger cities, 62 per cent of those from larger hometowns being high on SES in comparison with 46 per cent of those from smaller cities. Jewish students came from higher status families (69 per cent high SES) than Protestants (54 per cent) and Catholics (49 per cent). The Catholic-Protestant difference was small and somewhat exaggerated by the removal of Negroes from the tabulation, although Protestants were a little more likely to be high.

As in the general population, there was a striking association between religion and hometown (Table 1.8c). Among the white students 37 per cent of the Protestants, 59 per cent of the Roman Catholics, and 87 per cent of the Jews were from the larger cities. Viewing it the other way, three-fourths of the students from the smaller cities were Protestant, but only one-half of the students from larger cities were Protestant.

Because religion is strongly associated with city size, it is necessary to examine religion, SES, and hometown simultaneously. When this is done (Table 1.8a), a pattern of relationships appears:

1. Among Jews, the hometown difference was reversed, for Jewish
students from small towns had higher status origins.

2. Among students from larger cities, Protestants and Jews showed
no SES difference, although there was a considerable one among those
from smaller cities.

Table 1.8 SES, Religion, and Hometown Among Whites
Who Are Protestant, Catholic, or Jewish

a. Per cent High SES

Hometown	Religion			Total	
	Protestant	Roman Catholic	Jewish	Per cent	N
Larger	68 (11,246)	53 (7,766)	68 (3,765)	62	22,777
Smaller	46 (19,159)	44 (5,438)	77 (541)	46	25,138
Total	54 (30,405)	49 (13,204)	69 (4,306)	54	47,915

b. Per cent with Given Religious Preference

Hometown	SES	Religious Preference			Total	
		Protestant	Roman Catholic	Jewish	Per cent	N
Larger	High	53	29	18	100	14,232
	Low	43	43	14	100	8,545
Smaller	High	76	21	4	101	11,686
	Low	76	23	1	100	13,452

c. Per cent from larger cities — pop. ≧ 100,000

Religion	Per cent	N
Protestant	37	(30,405)
Roman Catholic	59	(13,204)
Jewish	87	(4,306)

N	47,915	
Negroes	1,778	
Excluded from IBC	6,971	
Total: Weighted N	56,664	

3. Among students from smaller cities, there was no Protestant-Catholic SES difference, although there was a considerable one for students from larger cities.

These findings are a reflection of a basic fact of American social structure, one that has continuing importance for the nation's politics, economy and education. Because of the immigration into the larger cities of low-status, non-Protestant Europeans, this country has changed during the last 100 years from an essentially rural, Protestant nation to a heterogeneous urban society. The rapid upward mobility of the Jews has left a sizeable urban Roman Catholic working class which is, we think, the best single explanation of the asymmetries in Table 1.8. While Catholic students made up 21 per cent of the smaller city—high SES category, 23 per cent of the smaller city—low SES group, and 29 per cent of the larger city—high SES cases, they comprised 43 per cent of the larger city—low SES category. Metaphorically speaking, the urban Catholic working class "pushed up" the SES levels of big city Protestants toward those of the Jews, the highest status ethnic group in the country. Conversely, in smaller cities that have no Catholic working class—there the working class is essentially Protestant—Protestants showed about the same class levels as Catholics and, as a group, were lower in status than Catholics from big cities.

We must remember that we are dealing only with the college graduate sons and daughters of these social groups, and differentials in college attendance rates must be considered in interpreting the data. Nevertheless, it is clear that the variables of SES, religion, and hometown are so intricately interrelated that they must be considered together. In order to do so, an Index of Background Characteristics was developed (Table 1.9). White Protestants, Catholics, and Jews were divided by SES and hometown, making twelve categories. Negroes made up the thirteenth category and, because of the small number of cases, are not subdivided by SES, hometown, or religion. Because Negro students are essentially low status, Protestant, and from smaller cities (Table 1.7), we will use smaller-city, lower-status, Protestant whites as their comparison group. Eighty-eight per cent of the cases fell into one of the thirteen categories on the Index of Background Characteristics, the remainder being Orientals, "Other" on race, "Other" or "None" on religion, or "No answer" on one or more of the constituent items.

Having reviewed race, hometown, religion, and SES and their interrelations, let us turn to a very important characteristic, sex.

When we examine the sex composition of the various groups in the Index of Background Characteristics (Table 1.10), two consistent differences turn up.

In each religion and each hometown grouping, high status groups had a greater per cent of co-eds. Among the total group of whites, 44 per cent of the high status students were female in comparison with 35 per cent of the low status students. Attrition during college may play a part in this differential, but our guess is that the disproportion results from the fact that high status families value and can afford higher education for all their chil-

Table 1.9. Index of Background Characteristics (IBC)
(Percentage Distribution of Cases — Total Weighted Sample)

Hometown	SES	Race				Total
		White			Negro	
		Religion				
		Protestant	Roman Catholic	Jewish		
Larger	High	15.3	8.2	5.1		28.6
	Low	7.3	7.4	2.4		17.1
Smaller	High	17.8	4.8	0.8		23.4
	Low	20.7	6.1	0.2		27.0
					3.6	3.6
Total per cent		61.1	26.5	8.5	3.6	99.7

N   49,663
Excluded from the Index:
　NA on any of the above and other races
　　and other religions   6,971
Total Weighted N   56,664

dren while lower status families value and can afford it for their children who "need it," more often a son than a daughter.

Among Negroes, however, the group with the greatest obstacles to college graduation, we find the highest proportion of women (54 per cent), 18 per cent more than among low status, smaller city Protestants. We have no ready explanation for this fact save that Census data on the per cent of the population enrolled in school for ages 18-19 and 20-24 show a roughly similar pattern.

ACADEMIC PERFORMANCE INDEX (API)

As might be expected, academic performance, the record of achievement in course work during the four years of college, turns out to be the single most important variable in the analysis of career plans, and is involved in many of the relevant questions analyzed: Are the brightest students going on for postgraduate training? How many of the brightest students are lost to graduate

Table 1.10. Sex By Index of Background Characteristics (Per cent Female)

Hometown	SES	Race			Negro
		White			
		Religion			
		Protestant	Roman Catholic	Jewish	
Larger	High	47 (7,596)	39 (4,081)	38 (2,555)	
Smaller	Low	37 (3,650)	28 (3,685)	33 (1,210)	
	High	46 (8,863)	44 (2,404)	48 (419)	
	Low	36 (10,296)	37 (3,034)	38 (122)	
					54 (1,778)

N	49,693
NA or Excluded from IBC	6,971
Total Weighted N	56,664

and professional school? Are different fields of work and study getting equal shares of the better students?

Because these questions are very important, it is necessary to begin with a description of the measure of academic performance used in this research. Perhaps it would have been desirable to administer intelligence or aptitude tests to the entire sample. Such a procedure was impossible, and even if it could have been done, enormous problems would have arisen in the choice of dimensions to measure. Therefore, we employed a global measure of intellectual performance—the student's cumulative grade point average. It offered a number of advantages: (a) The data were easy to collect without extracting records or administering tests; (b) Pre-test results indicated that student reports of GPA's are highly accurate when compared with registrars' records; (c) Graduate and professional schools often make use of GPA's as a selection criterion; (d) GPA's tap actual achievement rather than potential and thus get at what a student has "delivered," as well as what he might be able to do.

There are two drawbacks to the measure, however. First GPA's are a composite measure rather than a pure measure of any psychological dimension because both native ability and motivation contribute to grades. Second, GPA's are very much school-bound, and research evidence, as well as folklore, tells us that a "B" at such-and-such a school is probably worth an "A" at so-and-so and is equivalent to a "C" at some other school. The first problem was ignored, on the assumption that what was wanted was a global measure of performance rather than a measure of pure psychological factors.

In order to meet the second objection, the following steps were taken:

a. For 114 of 135 sample schools, the research staff of the National Merit Scholarship Corporation[4] made available average scores for entering freshmen who had taken the test administered throughout the nation by that organization to select candidates for its scholarships. This test correlates strongly with similar

[4]Alexander Astin, John Holland and Donald Thistlethwaite of the National Merit Scholarship Corporation were unusually helpful in this, as well as in many other aspects of the research.

tests such as the Scholastic Aptitude Test administered by the College Entrance Examination Board.

b. For the 21 schools with no National Merit data available, average National Merit scores were estimated on the basis of available data (Phi Beta Kappa chapters, library expenditures, etc.) that correlated with National Merit scores among the other schools in the sample.

c. On the basis of these scores, the schools were ranked in one of four classes:

Class	Number of schools	Per cent of students in representative sub-sample
I	11	6
II	12	8
III	71	54
IV	41	32
Total	135	100%
	N = 3,397	

d. In each class an arbitrary cutting point on GPA was established as follows:

School Class	GPA							
	A	A−	B+	B	B−	C+	C	C−	D+
I								
II	*Top Fifth*			*Above Average*			*Bottom Half*	
III								
IV								

The effect was to divide the students into three groups:

"Top Fifth": 19 per cent of the students. This group consists of straight A students from group IV schools, A and A− students from group III schools, B or better students from group II, and B− or better students from group I. Thus, this high performance group consists of the A students from the schools that graduated 86 per cent of the sample and B and B− students from the small group of highly selective institutions.

"Above Average": 37 per cent of the sample. This group consists of B to A− students in group IV, B− to B+ students in group III, C to B− students in group II, and C to C+ students in group I.

"Bottom Half": 45 per cent of the sample. This group comprises those whose grade averages were below that of the two groups defined above.

It was, of course, inevitable that such a gross index would do injustice to particular students and particular schools, but it is assumed that for comparisons among groups of students, it showed differences similar to those that would have been found if a test had been administered to the entire sample. The validity of API is supported by the evidence presented in Appendix 3.

Whether the disproportions were due to selection, motivation, native ability, or grading biases is unknown, but academic achievement varied with each of the social characteristics discussed so far (Table 1.11). To take each comparison: a) Women got better grades than men,[5] b) Students from high SES families did better than those from low SES families, c) Students from larger cities surpassed those from smaller ones, d) Jews surpassed Protestants and Catholics. In addition, Negro students fell below low SES Protestants from smaller cities. Whether Protestants and Catholics varied in academic performance (API) is less clear. In most comparisons, Protestants were more likely to be high, but among high status women there was no difference.

No one of these differences is terribly strong, but their cumulative effect is to produce a range from 78 per cent in the "above average" category among high status, big city Jewish girls to 39 per cent among Negro males.

These differences have a number of implications for career decisions. For example, any profession that tends to attract high status, big city students will get better academic performers on the average, even if API is not part of the formal selection criteria. Conversely, any profession that discriminates against Jews

[5]When all three categories of API are considered (Table 1.12), it turns out that the big difference is in "above average" and "bottom half." That is, about the same percentage of men and women are in the "top fifth." Very roughly speaking, this supports the general impression that while there is little sex difference in very top grades, "women get the B's while men get the C's."

Table 1.11. Sex and Academic Performance Index by Index of Background Characteristics (Per cent High Academic Performance)

			Sex					
			Male			Female		
			Religion			Religion		
SES	Hometown		Roman Catholic	Protestant	Jewish	Roman Catholic	Protestant	Jewish
High	Larger		51	61	67	73	70	78
	Smaller		43	53	61	66	66	71
Low	Larger		47	51	56	55	63	66
	Smaller		40	42	*	56	57	*
	Negro		39			46		

*Base N's too small to compare percentages.

Base N's for above table

			Male			Female		
			Religion			Religion		
SES	Hometown		Roman Catholic	Protestant	Jewish	Roman Catholic	Protestant	Jewish
High	Larger		2,444	4,010	1,563	1,578	3,520	954
	Smaller		1,339	4,686	218	1,035	4,051	198
Low	Larger		2,614	2,278	802	1,013	1,313	394
	Smaller		1,890	6,452	71	1,107	3,621	46
	Negro		792			938		

N: 48,927
NA or Excluded from IBC: 7,737
Total Weighted N: 56,664

necessarily pays in a loss of high performers. Or again, men (who will stay in the labor force) and high performers (who will presumably continue to do well) are preferred for many careers, but only 53 per cent of the top half were men, in contrast to 66 per cent of the bottom half. There was, therefore, a relative scarcity of brighter men.

Because college students as a group are highly selected, and because the students in the sample were the survivors of four academic years of winnowing, the sample as a whole represents an intellectual elite. Nevertheless, there was considerable variation in academic performance within the group, and, as measured by the API, the social groupings into which the students fell showed variation in their average level of performance.

OCCUPATIONAL INTERESTS AND VALUES

Perhaps the longest and most fruitful tradition of research on occupational choice is that concerned with the relationship between generalized interests or values and the choice of specific fields of work. From Strong's pioneering and continued research[6] to the recent Cornell values study,[7] strong and stable relation-

[6]Cf. E. K. Strong, Jr., *Vocational Interests of Men and Women* (Stanford University Press, 1943).

[7]Cf. Morris Rosenberg, with the assistance of Edward A. Suchman and Rose K. Goldsen, *Occupations and Values* (Glencoe, Illinois: Free Press, 1957).

Table 1.12. Sex and Academic Performance Index

Sex	Academic Performance				
	Top Fifth	Above Average	Bottom Half	Total	
				Per cent	N
Male	17.0	33.0	50.0	100.0	32,957
Female	21.2	42.1	36.7	100.0	22,802

N	55,759
NA API	905
Total Weighted N	56,664

ships have been found between values and occupations. The sources of these values are still obscure and it is not clear whether, over time, values affect occupational choice or occupational choices affect values or both.[8] However, it is clear that data on such values and interests are exceedingly important in analyzing career plans.

Our measure of these values[9] is a slightly modified version of the Cornell questionnaire items and is based on answers to the following question: "Which of these characteristics would be very important to you in picking a job or career? (Circle as many as apply.)" The items and frequency of endorsement (ranging from 65 per cent to 7 per cent) were given in Table 1.4c.

Since there were 2^{11} (two to the eleventh power) possible combinations of answers to the items, it became necessary to find a simplification or summary of the information. To do this, the intercorrelations of answers to the nine most frequently circled responses (RSS) were computed (Table 1.13), using Yule's Q as the appropriate statistic for attribute data. After inspecting the results, three items essentially independent of each other but each associated with one or more of the remaining items were selected as tapping four manifest independent dimensions of values. They are:

People: "Opportunity to work with people, rather than things" was endorsed by 56 per cent. The item is quite strongly related to "Opportunities to be helpful to others or useful to society" (Q = .55), and moderately related to "A chance to exercise leadership" (Q = .35), and essentially independent of the remaining items.

Original and Creative: "Opportunities to be original and creative" was endorsed by 51 per cent. The item is strongly related to "Living

[8]Rosenberg concludes from his panel data on college students that "values have a greater effect on change of occupational choice than the other way around." (Cf. Rosenberg, *op. cit.,* p. 22.) A reanalysis of his data, however, shows that among students whose 1950 value and occupational choices were "inconsistent," 27 per cent had, by 1952, arrived at consistency by changing their values, 26 per cent had arrived at consistency by changing their job preference, while 6 per cent had changed both and thus remained inconsistent. This suggests a trend toward consistency, but no clear priority between the two variables.

[9]We shall use interests and values interchangeably, although there is some difference in the theoretical overtones of the two words.

Table 1.13. Intercorrelations of Occupational Values (Representative Sub-sample) (Q Values)

Values*	Per cent Checking...	People	Original	Money	Steady	Helpful	Ideas	Avoid	Lead.	No Super.
People	56		-.01	-.06	.04	.55	.09	.09	.35	-.10
Original	51	-.01		.06	-.17	.11	.68	-.09	.27	.36
Money	24	-.06	.06		.06	-.25	-.05	.14	.41	.39
Steady	33	.04	-.17	.06		.05	-.13	.46	.12	-.05
Helpful	65	.55	.11	-.25	.05		.22	-.09	.10	-.13
Ideas	39	.09	.68	-.05	-.13	.22		.00	.22	.23
Avoid pressure	16	.09	-.09	.14	.46	-.09	.00		-.16	.38
Leadership	41	.35	.27	.41	.12	.10	.22	-.16		.21
No supervision	18	-.10	.36	.39	-.05	-.13	.23	.38	.21	

N = 3,397

*People = Opportunity to work with people rather than things
Original = Opportunities to be original and creative
Money = Making a lot of money
Steady = Opportunities for moderate but steady progress rather than the chance of extreme success or failure
Helpful = Opportunities to be helpful to others or useful to society
Ideas = Living and working in the world of ideas
Avoid pressure = Avoiding a high-pressure job that takes too much out of you
Leadership = A chance to exercise leadership
No supervision = Freedom from supervision in my work
("Remaining in the city or area in which I grew up," endorsed by 7 per cent, and "Getting away from the city or area in which I grew up," endorsed by 13 per cent, are excluded.)

and working in the world of ideas" (Q = .68), and is moderately related to "Freedom from supervision in my work" (Q = .36), and "A chance to exercise leadership" (Q = .27).

Money: "Making a lot of money" was endorsed by 24 per cent of the sample. It is positively associated with "A chance to exercise leadership" (Q = .41), "Freedom from supervision in my work" (Q = .39), and negatively related to "Opportunities to be helpful to others or useful to society" (Q = −.25).

A case could be made that "Opportunities for moderate but steady progress rather than the chance of extreme success or failure" (endorsed by 33 per cent) constitutes a fourth dimension, but since it does have a slight negative relationship with original and creative (Q = −.17) and because inspection of the data indicated that the discriminations it provides are less interesting in terms of the professions given high priority in this research, it was ignored.

Precisely because the items are independent, they provide a classification of the students' occupational values into eight cells provided by the possible combinations of responses to the three items. These value configurations, as we shall see, are quite strongly related to preference for specific occupations and to changes in occupational preference from freshman to senior year.

Although independent of each other, the three value dimensions are correlated with the variables discussed in this chapter. We can conclude this introductory description by examining the relationships between race, religion, SES, hometown, sex, API and occupational value preferences.

"People," or the service dimension is strongly related to sex, but otherwise independent of the other personal characteristics (Table 1.14). Among the white graduating seniors, regardless of API, SES, city size, or religion, two-thirds or more of the women circled this item, while the proportion of men who circled it was nearer one-half, ranging from 42 per cent to 57 per cent in various cells of the table. Negro men seemed little different from white men, but for some unknown reason Negro women had very low rates of endorsement for this item. Because Negro students were low on endorsement of any of the three values, it is impossible to tell whether Negro females are less people-oriented or whether the entire group of occupational values is less important to them. The only other finding on "People" is negative. Despite the suggestion of Stanley Schachter's *The Psychology of Affiliation*,[10] it is unrelated to birth order.

The occupational value, "Original and creative," which, we remember, is strongly associated with "Living and working in the world of ideas," was consistently correlated with the Academic Performance Index. The better the student's academic per-

[10]Stanley Schachter, *The Psychology of Affiliation* (Stanford University Press, 1959).

Table 1.14. Sex, Academic Performance Index, and Values by Index of Background Characteristics (Per cent Checking "People")

Religion	Hometown	SES	Academic Performance Index			
			High		Low	
			Male	Female	Male	Female
Protestant	Larger	High	43 (2,446)	67 (2,463)	48 (1,547)	72 (1,038)
		Low	42 (1,152)	70 (825)	46 (1,119)	66 (485)
	Smaller	High	47 (2,494)	71 (2,667)	48 (2,176)	69 (1,376)
		Low	43 (2,679)	69 (2,047)	44 (3,746)	70 (1,561)
	Negro		49 (305)	47 (427)	40 (487)	48 (507)
Roman Catholic	Larger	High	48 (1,244)	66 (1,149)	47 (1,196)	67 (427)
		Low	43 (1,215)	66 (553)	48 (1,393)	66 (456)
	Smaller	High	48 (571)	72 (680)	47 (764)	69 (350)
		Low	44 (753)	71 (619)	42 (1,133)	72 (481)
Jewish	Larger	High	50 (1,045)	68 (739)	51 (515)	67 (213)
		Low	48 (451)	61 (261)	44 (348)	71 (133)
	Smaller	High	57 (132)	72 (141)	45 (84)	86 (57)
		Low	— (37)	— (25)	— (34)	— (21)

N	48,767
NA, API	755
NA, Values Only	160
NA on Both	11
Excluded from IBC	6,971
Total Weighted N	56,664

formance, the more likely he was to endorse this item (Table 1.15). While no other variable made a consistent difference, the association between API and "Original and creative" varied with sex. In each comparison in Table 1.15, the endorsement of this value among men varied more widely according to API than it did among women. Consequently, while there was no consistent relationship between sex and this value, low API men, in each cell of the table, were least likely to endorse the item. An equivalent formulation would be that while there was no sex difference in this response among the higher performers, there was among those in the bottom half, where men were less likely than women to value originality.

While "People" and "Original-Creative" showed simple one-variable relationships, "Making money" had a complicated pattern. To begin with, it was a sex-differentiated trait (Table 1.16). Women were much less likely to select this value; among women, endorsement of the item was unrelated to the other variables. Among the men, however, making money was associated with *all* of the other variables. The differences were somewhat small but entirely consistent — making a lot of money was associated with high SES, larger cities, lower academic performance, and with religion (Jews were higher than Catholics, who were, in turn, higher than Protestants). At the extremes, 64 per cent of the lower API, high SES, larger city, Jewish men endorsed the item, while 23 per cent of the high API, small town, low status, Protestant men circled it. As with the other two items, Negroes showed lower rates of endorsement.

While most of these findings — the greater interest "People" had for women, the greater interest "Originality" had for the academically superior, the greater interest "Making money" had for the more urban and sophisticated males — appear intuitively sensible, our aim is not to untangle the origins of these values, but to show how patterns of occupational values, alone and in combination with the other variables, relate to career choice.

SUMMARY

This chapter has described the June, 1961, college graduates in terms of their distributions on measures of race, size of home-

Table 1.15. Sex, Academic Performance Index and Values by Index of Background Characteristics (Per cent Checking "Original and Creative")

Hometown	SES	Sex	Protestant API High	Low	High Minus Low	Roman Catholic API High	Low	High Minus Low	Jewish API High	Low	High Minus Low
Larger	High	F	62 (2,463)	52 (1,038)	10	52 (1,149)	50 (427)	2	74 (739)	61 (213)	13
		M	64 (2,446)	48 (1,547)	16	53 (1,244)	46 (1,196)	7	66 (1,045)	47 (515)	19
	Low	F	56 (325)	45 (485)	11	51 (553)	39 (456)	12	63 (261)	58 (133)	5
		M	63 (1,152)	44 (1,119)	19	54 (1,215)	42 (1,393)	12	60 (451)	52 (348)	8
Smaller	High	F	58 (2,567)	46 (1,376)	12	51 (680)	52 (350)	−1	61 (141)	63 (57)	−2
		M	58 (2,494)	44 (2,176)	14	51 (571)	40 (764)	11	67 (132)	48 (84)	19
	Low	F	45 (2,647)	40 (1,561)	5	55 (619)	41 (481)	14	48 (25)	86 (21)	−38
		M	49 (2,679)	35 (3,746)	14	58 (753)	36 (1,133)	22	62 (37)	26 (34)	36

Academic Performance Index

		High	Low	High Minus Low
Negro	F	33 (427)	34 (507)	−1
	M	43 (305)	30 (487)	13

N	48,767
NA, API only	755
NA Values only	160
NA on Both	11
Excluded from IBC	6,971
Total Weighted N	56,664

Table 1.16. Sex, Academic Performance Index, and Values by Index of Background Characteristics (Per cent Checking "Money" Among Males Only)

| SES | Hometown | White — Protestant | | White — Roman Catholic | | White — Jewish | | Negro | |
| | | Academic Performance Index | | Academic Performance Index | | Academic Performance Index | | Academic Performance Index | |
		High	Low	High	Low	High	Low	High	Low
High	Larger	32 (2,446)	35 (1,547)	36 (1,244)	37 (1,196)	46 (1,045)	64 (515)		
	Smaller	29 (2,494)	32 (2,176)	34 (571)	35 (764)	43 (132)	61 (84)		
Low	Larger	26 (1,152)	30 (1,119)	31 (1,215)	35 (1,393)	34 (451)	47 (348)	18 (305)	20 (487)
	Smaller	23 (2,679)	24 (3,746)	30 (753)	28 (1,133)	38 (37)	32 (34)		

N (Male)	29,066
Excluded: Female	19,701
NA, API Only	755
NA Values Only	160
NA on Both	11
Excluded from IBC	6,971
Total Weighted N	56,664

town, socio-economic status, religion, sex, academic performance, and three occupational values—people, originality, and
money. In addition, the patterns of correlation among these
characteristics have been presented, both to add to the description of the students and to set the stage for future analyses using
various combinations of these variables. The interrelationships
of these characteristics are summarized in Table 1.17.

Race

Three per cent of the sample are Negroes. The Negro students,
in contrast with the whites, come from smaller cities, are more
likely Protestant, show lesser academic accomplishment, are
less likely to endorse any of the three occupational values, and
include proportionately more females.

Hometown

About one-half of the sample comes from cities of 100,000 or
more or from the suburbs of such cities. The students from larger
cities are characterized by higher SES, a lower proportion of
Protestants, higher API scores, and, among males, more interest
in making money.

SES

The students are scored on socio-economic status on the basis
of family income, occupation of the head of the household, and
father's education. High SES students (those possessing two or
three of the following: white collar heads of families, parental
incomes of $7,500 or more, fathers with part college or more
education) comprise about one-half the sample. High SES is
associated with being Jewish or being a larger city Protestant,
with being female, with higher academic performance and, among
men, with valuing making money.

Original religion

Protestants are the largest group, comprising 60 per cent of
the total sample (RSS). Protestants are disproportionately from
smaller cities and, among men, less interested in making money.
Catholics comprise 25 per cent of the sample, are disproportion-

ately from larger cities, lower SES families, and, among males, are more likely to value making money in comparison with Protestants. Jews, who make up 8 per cent of the sample, are almost all from larger cities, come from high SES families, show superior academic performance, and, among males, are more interested in making money than are Christians.

Sex

Six out of ten of the graduates are male. The woman student is characterized by high SES origins, superior academic performance, more interest in working with people, and less interest in making money.

Academic performance

Academic performance is measured by the student's reported cumulative grade point average, with a small correction for variation among the schools in the ability levels of their students. Women, high SES students, and Jews are more likely to be high on API. The higher performing student is more likely to value opportunities to be original and creative.

People

Fifty-six per cent of the sample endorsed "Opportunity to work with people, rather than things," as important in choosing a job or career. Women are much more likely to endorse the item.

Original and creative

Fifty-one per cent endorsed "Opportunities to be original and creative." Low API students were less likely to choose this item, particularly among the men.

Money

Twenty-four per cent of the sample endorsed "Making a lot of money." Men were much more likely to pick this value, and among men it was more frequently chosen by those lower on API, higher on SES, and from larger cities. Among men, Jews were most likely to choose this value, Protestants least likely. No consistent relationships were found among women students.

Table 1.17.   Intercorrelations (Q) of Sex, Academic Performance Index, Values, and Background

Inter-Correlations	People	Original and Creative	Money	Sex	API	SES*	Hometown*	Prot.+*	R.C.+*	Jewish+*	None
People		-01	-08	-43	04	09	-02	02	-03	02	-18
Original and Creative			07	03	27	17	16	-02	-08	24	-34
Money				48	-11	10	15	-22	12	30	-27
Sex					-27	-20	04	-11	10	05	-29
API*						25	16	01	-11	24	-22
SES*							34	-04	-07	32	—
Hometown*								-56	35	79	—
Protestant*+									—	—	—
Roman Catholic*+										—	—
Jewish*+											—
None											

* = "Q" computed only among whites who are Protestant, Catholic, or Jewish.

+ = for Protestant the coefficient is based on the dichotomy Protestant vs. Catholic and Jewish; for Catholic the coefficient is based on the dichotomy Catholic vs. Protestant and Jewish; for Jewish the coefficient is based on the dichotomy Jewish vs. Protestant and Catholic.

2

Plans for Postgraduate Study: An Overview

One of the greatest recent social changes in America has been the revolution in college attendance; the resultant consequences for social mobility, national intellectual level, and personal values have been the source of considerable scholarly and popular discussion. According to the United States Census, 19 per cent of the 18- and 19-year-olds were enrolled in college in 1900, 25 per cent by 1930, 32 per cent in the post-World War II spurt, and by 1960, 42 per cent.

The similarly explosive increase in graduate education has received less attention, and statistical documentation for it is actually difficult to find. It was only in 1960 that the Census first distinguished between college graduation and the enrollment in postgraduate studies in its schedule and tabulations. However, it is clear that each higher level of education must increase as those below it swell, so it is hardly surprising that the number of graduate degrees awarded has risen phenomenally in this century. Prior to the early 1920's, for example, fewer than 1,000 Ph.D.'s were awarded each year, while the current figures are near 10,000. What is less obvious is the major finding of this research, that *acceptance of study beyond the bachelor's degree is so great that the vast bulk of June, 1961, graduates anticipated further study.* Putting it another way, our evidence will be that a *bach-*

elor's degree recipient is more likely to anticipate postgraduate study than a high school student is to anticipate college.

Because we wanted to pin down as accurately as possible how many and what kinds of students planned to go on to postgraduate work, several items in the questionnaire were designed to probe intentions in this area. From a combination of questions about plans for the fall of 1961, plans for later years, and attitudes toward further study, developed a classification of the seniors into three major groups, with two subgroups in each. The resultant Plans Index is presented in Table 2.1.

The six groups and their percentages are as follows:

a. Expecting to go on next year (32.6 per cent)
   1. Planning to go on in the fall of 1961, and accepted by at least one school by the spring of 1961 (20.2 per cent)
   2. Planning to go on in the fall of 1961, but not yet accepted by spring, 1961 (12.4 per cent)
b. Planning to attend later (44.6 per cent)
   3. Planning to attend in 1962-1963 or some later *specific* date (29.9 per cent)
   4. Planning to attend sometime in the future, but with no specific date in mind (14.7 per cent)

Table 2.1 Plans for Graduate or Professional Study

Group	Per cent		Cumulative Per cent
Plan to attend graduate or professional school, fall, 1961	32.6		
Accepted by one or more schools		20.2	20.2
Other		12.4	32.6
Plan to attend after 1961–1962	44.6		
Specific year given		29.9	62.5
No specific date in mind		14.7	77.2
Do not plan to attend	22.8		
Yes on "If there were no obstacles. . .would you like to attend?"		5.4	82.7
Maybe or no		17.4	100.1
Total	100.0%		

N	54,236
NA on one or more items in index	2,428 (= 4.3% of Total)
Total Weighted N	56,664

c. Planning never to go on (22.8 per cent)

5. Not planning to attend, but answered "Yes" to "Would you *like* to go on if there were no obstacles?" (5.4 per cent)

6. Not planning to attend and answered "No" or "Maybe" to question on preference (17.4 per cent)

The six groups order the students as follows: those already accepted for the next year, those planning to attend in the fall of 1961 but not yet accepted, those with definite plans for later study, those with indefinite plans, those who would like to go on but did not expect to, and, finally, those who neither expected nor preferred to go on.

In the wording of the questionnaire and in the editing of schedules,[1] postgraduate study was deliberately defined quite inclusively; the reader should bear in mind that night school study and study in technical and commercial courses, as well as full-time enrollment in arts and science or professional school, are considered "postgraduate work" or "advanced study."

The following inferences may be drawn from the distribution of cases:

1. College seniors had a favorable orientation toward postgraduate study. Assuming that all those going on were favorable and adding to them the 5.4 per cent who would have liked to go on but did not ever plan to, we find that 83 per cent "favor" advanced study.

2. College seniors had high aspirations for postgraduate study. Seventy-seven per cent expected to undertake advanced study eventually.

3. Of those seniors who were "positively oriented" toward graduate study, very few felt they could not accomplish their goal. Only 7 per cent of the oriented group did not expect further study; three-quarters of the oriented group had a specific plan (at least in terms of a date) to attend.

4. Of the students oriented toward graduate study, only 24 per cent had been admitted for study in the fall of 1961; 15 per cent of the oriented

---

[1]Although the high volume of schedules prohibited editing of the schedules prior to key punching, the entire set was subjected to an elaborate "cleaning" process in which cases with discrepant responses (e.g., students who said they were going on next year and also answered the question on reasons for not going on) were reconciled by reference to the original schedules.

group expected to attend but hadn't been admitted, and 54 per cent of the oriented group planned to attend after being out of school for some period of time.

5. The data present an ambiguous category—more than half of the students (57 per cent) anticipated graduate study sometime, but were not admitted to a graduate school for fall, 1961.

The two most important conclusions to be drawn from the figures are these: An extraordinarily high proportion of graduating seniors anticipated postgraduate study, but in June, 1961, the majority of these had fairly indefinite plans. Considering only anticipations, it appears that postgraduate study had almost universal acceptance for 1961 college graduates. If it is true that "everybody plans to go to college these days," it is just as true that "everybody with a bachelor's degree plans to go to graduate school," for the 77 per cent expecting advanced study was well above the 40 per cent of high school seniors, reported by Natalie Rogoff for 1955 data, who expected to go to college.[2]

What about those who were postponing graduate work or who hadn't yet been accepted, however? Were they merely wishful thinkers? Did the 20 per cent who had been accepted really constitute the body of graduate students produced by the class of 1961? While it might appear more "objective" to write off the "later" group, the following indirect evidence leads us to conclude that this would be inaccurate:

1. A recently completed NORC survey of the financial problems of arts and science graduate students[3] showed that a little more than 40 per cent of them began their studies after being out of undergraduate school one or more years.

2. In some fields, such as education and social work, entry to graduate study after a period of practical experience is the norm rather than the exception.

3. The Bureau of the Census reported that in 1959, 41 per cent of the nation's college graduates had completed some work

[2]Quoted in Burton R. Clark, *Educating the Expert Society* (San Francisco: Chandler Publishing Company, 1962), p. 61.

[3]James A. Davis, with the assistance of David Gottlieb, Jan Hajda, Carolyn Huson, and Joe L. Spaeth, *Stipends and Spouses: The Finances of American Arts and Science Graduate Students* (University of Chicago Press, 1962), p. 28.

beyond the BA (or equivalent).[4] This percentage ranged from a low of 23 per cent among those aged 20 – 24 to a high of 52 per cent among those 65 and over, figures quite consistent with the assumption that many of the "middle" group on the index will eventually take up advanced study.

4. Considering the pattern of closing dates for application to postgraduate studies, it would appear that the 12 per cent of the sample who planned to begin in the fall of 1961, but had not been admitted by June, had unrealistic expectations. However, tabulations on this group in the representative sub-sample showed that 63 per cent of them expected to be employed full-time while going to school, in contrast to nine per cent of the accepted group. Thus, those in group 2 on the index might have been prospective night students who had not yet picked a school because their job situations were not yet settled.

NORC has received a grant for a follow-up study to determine the actual outcomes for these students, but at this writing all the data are not available. It is undoubtedly safe to conclude, however, that although American college students have "great aspirations" for advanced study, the realization of these hopes and plans is often complicated and difficult.

FIELD OF SPECIALIZATION

Postgraduate education has a vocational focus that is not characteristic of lower levels of study. (Even though American colleges are often damned for their emphasis on "practical" studies, 67 per cent of our sample checked "a basic general education and appreciation of ideas" as the most important purpose of college, while 32 per cent checked "career training," [Table 1.3].) Whether the field is philosophy or forestry, studies beyond the bachelor's degree are organized to prepare young people for entry into particular lines of work.

It is hardly surprising, therefore, that the single most important factor in predicting a student's category on the Plans Index is his anticipated career. Very few people expect to succeed in medicine without attending medical school; 89 per cent of those

[4]*Current Population Reports*, P–20, No. 99, Bureau of the Census, Washington, D.C., February, 1960.

aspiring to be physicians fell into the group who planned to go on in 1961. At the opposite pole, it would be difficult to persuade a young woman that she will fail in the career of housewife without advanced training; among those girls who planned to be housewives exclusively (a very small proportion of the women, by the way), one per cent anticipated going on in 1961. Most career fields lay between these extremes, and the relationship between career and postgraduate study is more complicated than these polar examples would indicate. The fact remains, however, that the findings on the large numbers planning on advanced study make a lot more sense when we realize that so many of the students were aiming for careers where advanced study is either a ticket of admission or a very useful asset.

In Table 2.2 we have assembled for comparison data on undergraduate major, graduate study, and career plans.

There are some interesting trends in the figures. Arts and science fields declined from 38 per cent of the undergraduate majors to 30 per cent of the graduate majors to 18 per cent of the future careers. Education increased from 28 per cent of the undergraduate majors to 32 per cent of the careers.

On the whole, however, the figures are quite similar in each column. The generalization is rough and there were some clear exceptions (e.g., you cannot study law or medicine as an undergraduate), but the broad tendency was for undergraduate majors, graduate fields, and careers to show very similar distributions. Just as modern America has provided a rich choice of undergraduate fields for its youth, it also has made available graduate studies no longer limited to the old-line professions or Ph.D. tracks, but spread across the wide spectrum of interests and specializations of the graduates.

The fact that the distribution of career fields is so similar to the distribution of anticipated graduate fields might appear to contradict our statement that career field is the best predictor of graduate plans, for the similarity might suggest that about the same per cent plan graduate study regardless of the career field. The deceptive appearance of small percentages is a partial explanation. Thus, the facts that physical scientists amounted to 7.4 per cent of the graduate students and 5.4 per cent of the ca-

Table 2.2 Distribution in Sample of Undergraduate Major, Graduate Field of Study, and Career Field

Field	Undergraduate Major For Total Sample	Graduate Field For Those Planning Advanced Study	Career Field For Total Sample
Arts and Science	38.5	30.1	18.0
Physical Science	7.6	7.4	5.4
Biological Science	3.9	3.4	2.1
Social Science	10.7	7.0	4.0
Humanities & Fine Arts	16.3	12.3	6.5
Professional Fields	45.0	56.6	59.3
Education	27.6	29.4	32.2
Engineering	9.2	7.7	8.3
Law (Pre-Law)	0.3	6.1	3.9
Medicine (Pre-Med)	0.9	3.4	2.8
Social Work	0.4	1.9	1.8
Other	6.6	8.1	10.3
Other	14.7	12.2	19.7
Business and Administration	13.3	11.4	18.2
Agriculture & Related	1.4	0.8	1.5
Respondent Checked "No near equivalent on this list."	1.3	1.0	2.8
Total	99.5%	99.9%	99.8%
N	55,546	N 39,726	N 54,172
NA Field	1,118	No Grad School 12,383	Do Not Expect To Work 901
Total Weighted N	56,664	NA Field 2,127	NA Field 1,591
		NA Plans 2,428	Total Weighted N 56,664
		Total Weighted N 56,664	

reers and that businessmen totaled 11.4 per cent of the graduate students and 18.2 per cent of the careers do not seem particularly noteworthy. Yet they are really indicative of sharp differences in plans for scientists and businessmen. More important, however, is the difference between "next year" and "later." The figures on graduate field included both students who planned to begin in the fall of 1961 and those with the less definite intentions of going on sometime in the future. Because almost 80 per cent planned to go on sometime and because there is continuity from under-graduate major to graduate field to career field, it would be surprising to find tremendous differences in the three sets of figures. We gain a new perspective on the relationship between careers and graduate study, however, when we treat separately the three groups: a) Those expecting to go on next year ("Next Year"), b) Those planning to attend later ("Later"), and c) Those not ever planning to go on ("Never").

The plans of the three groups are listed in a detailed breakdown of the fields in Table 2.3a. Because the case bases are rather small for some of the detailed fields, we shall treat only the grouped data (Table 2.3b). The most convenient way to analyze trichotomous data employs "triangular coordinate paper," the data in Table 2.3b being presented in graph form in Chart 2.1. The graph has three axes allowing for a range from zero to 100 per cent on "Next Year," "Later," and "Never"; for each point one can read off the percentages, which must total 100.

Examining the distribution of career fields on the graph, one sees that the career fields fall into four clusters determined by the pattern of the plans for advanced study:

1. Medicine, dentistry, and law were heavily concentrated toward the "Next Year" pole with virtually no students in "Never."
2. The arts and science fields (physics, social sciences, chemistry, other physical sciences, mathematics, biological sciences, humanities) and the "other professions" were low on "Never," but tended to have only slight majorities going on next year.
3. Engineering, social work, and education were low on per cent saying "Never," as were the fields in group 2, but more students said they were going later than were going next year.
4. Business and administration, agricultural fields, and health pro-

Table 2.3. Anticipated Long-Run Career Field and Plans Index

a. Ungrouped Fields

Code†	Field	Next Year	Later	Never	Total Per cent	Total N
21	Medicine	89	11	0	100	1,484
30	Anatomy	86	14	0	100	14
20	Dentistry	79	20	1	100	270
40	Physiology	78	16	6	100	51
01	Astronomy	77	23	0	100	30
95	Law	76	23	1	100	2,010
34	Biophysics	75	25	0	100	24
33	Botany	73	18	9	100	55
89	Theology, Religion	72	22	6	100	60*
36	Genetics	71	29	0	100	41
03	Physics	69	28	2	99	643
70	Clinical Psychology	68	26	5	99	19*
82, 84	Foreign Languages	66	16	19	101	32*
41	Zoology	63	24	13	100	105
07	Metallurgy	63	33	4	100	24
06	Oceanography	62	31	7	100	29
3X	Biology, Other	61	28	11	100	100
81	English	58	28	14	100	36*
83	History	58	34	8	100	38*
75, 76, 79, 7X	Social Science	58	36	6	100	36*
05	Geology	57	30	13	100	98
39	Pharmacology	57	39	4	100	23
66, 67	Educational Psychology	57	37	6	100	30*
78	Political Science	55	30	15	100	40*
32	Biochemistry	54	41	5	100	152
88	Library	53	27	20	100	15*
94	Foreign Service	52	38	10	100	21*
02	Chemistry	51	37	12	100	960
12	Chemical Engineering	50	17	33	100	18*
52, 53	Secondary Languages	44	41	15	100	27*
37	Microbiology	44	37	19	100	144
09	Mathematics	42	41	17	100	825
13	Electrical Engineering	40	50	10	100	89*
35	Entomology	40	50	10	100	48

Code†	Field					N
04	Geography	40	49	11	100	110
68	Ed. Administration	39	59	3	101	38*
55	Secondary Science	38	55	8	101	40*
08	Meteorology	38	48	14	100	42
0X	Physical Science, Other	37	48	15	100	46
80	Fine Arts	37	43	20	100	92*
60	Ed. of Exceptional Children	36	59	5	100	22*
31	Biology	35	39	26	100	327
1X	Engineering, General	34	44	22	100	32*
54	Secondary History, Social Studies	33	57	10	100	79*
93	Public Administration	32	50	18	100	22*
23, 25, 26, 28, 2X	Other Health	30	40	30	100	40*
61, 62, 63, 64, 65	Vocational Education	28	50	22	100	108*
96	Social Work	27	53	20	100	49*
51	Secondary English	27	59	14	100	90*
10, 14, 15, 17, 18	Engineering, Other	27	48	25	100	48*
97	Secretarial	25	25	50	100	28*
72	Industrial Psychology	24	48	28	100	21*
71, 73, 74	Psychology, Other	23	46	31	100	13*
56	Secondary Mathematics	23	70	7	100	43*
11	Civil Engineering	22	38	40	100	45*
86	Architecture, City Planning	22	35	43	100	23*
27, 45, 46, 47	Agriculture	22	29	49	100	753
98	Home Economics	20	52	28	100	25*
57	Physical Education	19	75	6	100	72*
50	Elementary Education	17	67	16	100	278*
91	Business	17	41	42	100	353*
58, 59	Art-Music Education	15	72	13	100	60*
5X	Housewife-Teaching**	14	46	40	100	87*
16	Mechanical Engineering	14	59	27	100	37*
87	Journalism	14	42	44	100	43*
38	Pathology	14	43	43	100	7
92	Accounting	13	47	40	100	102*
6X	Education, Other	10	75	15	100	20*
22	Nursing	9	45	46	100	56*
90	Advertising	7	51	42	100	43*
24	Pharmacy	5	32	63	100	19*
9X	Military	5	70	25	100	20*
99	Housewife	1	26	73	100	811

(Table 2.3 continued)

† = Code refers to the numbers on pages 6 and 7 of the appended questionnaire.

* = N based on representative sub-sample.

** = This group emerged after a re-coding of the "housewife" group (99) when it became apparent from other data that some women intending to be housewives intended also to teach at some time.

Table 2.3. *Continued*

b. Grouped Fields (TWS)

Career Field	Plans			Total	
	Next Year	Later	Never	Per cent	N
Medicine	89	11	0	100	1,484
Dentristry	79	20	1	100	270
Law	76	23	1	100	2,010
Physics	69	28	2	99	643
Social Sciences	52	36	12	100	2,084
Chemistry	51	37	12	100	960
Biological Sciences	51	34	15	100	1,091
Other Physical Sciences	50	39	11	100	379
Humanities	48	38	14	100	3,382
Mathematics-Statistics	42	41	17	100	825
Other Professions	41	39	20	100	3,253
Engineering	32	45	23	100	4,393
Social Work	28	49	23	100	961
Education	25	60	15	100	16,683
Business and Administration	16	43	41	100	9,545
Other Health Professions	18	37	45	100	1,837
Agriculture and Related	22	29	49	100	753

N		50,553
NA Plans		2,098
Respondent circled "Job which has no near equivalent on this list"		1,521
Do not expect to work after graduation		901
NA on future career		1,591
Total Weighted N		56,664

fessions other than medicine were very low on "Next Year," and relatively high on "Never."

Our general finding, that acceptance of advanced training beyond the bachelor's degree was almost universal in the class of 1961, is also supported by this analysis. In no field in the table did a majorityof students fall into the "Never" group; even in the agricultural fields 51 per cent anticipated some advanced study. (Seventy-three per cent of the housewives did fall into the "Never" category, as is seen in Table 2.3a, but the data in Chart 2.1 are limited to fields of employment.) Except for business and administration, other health professions, and agriculture, more than 75 per cent of the students in every other field anticipated eventual graduate work. The variation between "Next Year" and "Later" is considerable, however; the four groups delineated above may be interpreted as follows:

Group 1 may be characterized as the "licensed" professions in which advanced study is prerequisite for employment. Because students aspiring to careers in fields such as law and medicine are barred from entry until they receive graduate degrees, they had overwhelming majorities in "Next Year."

Group 2 comprises the arts and science fields in which advanced degrees are an eventual necessity, but in which a low level of employment is possible with a bachelor's degree. Almost all the students in these fields planned some graduate work, but about one-half intended to postpone their studies.

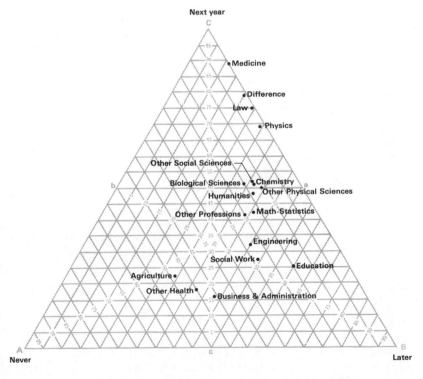

Chart 2.1. Grouped Fields: Graph of Table 2.3b

Group 3 may be characterized as the fields in which advanced study is very desirable for promotion and upgrading after entry into the field, but in which there is little resistance to employment of B.A.'s. Thus, students in education knew that a Master's degree would be very useful after they had worked a while, but they saw it coming after a year or so of practical experience.

Group 4 includes the fields in which graduate training is optional. Thus, about one-half of the students aiming for careers in business and administration did plan advanced study even though entry into the field and promotions are not barred to the student who stops at the bachelor's degree.

It appears that for some fields advanced study is an immediate necessity, in some it is an eventual necessity, and in some it is a luxury; but in every case there is general acceptance of its desirability.

Those students who were aiming for arts and science careers appeared to be exceptions to the generalization that graduate plans are in harmony with the career structure of a given occupation. While the fact that the majority of students in education intended to postpone their studies until they had some practical experience "makes sense," the fact that only about one-half of the arts and science students planned to go on the next year does not appear so "natural." As was noted before, both this research and NORC's previous survey of arts and science graduate students suggest a major problem in the recruitment of arts and science personnel—the slow rate at which these people tend to begin and complete their advanced training.

The description of the relationship between career field and graduate field can be completed by examining the match between the two. Table 2.4 gives the per cent of students who planned graduate study in the same field as their future career. The correlation between career field and graduate field was naturally very high, but there was some variation. Among students who planned to do advanced study in chemistry, for example, 91 per cent gave it as their career field. However, for those planning graduate work in history, less than one-half (41 per cent) named history as their ultimate career field. Why? Because 42 per cent who were going to study history planned eventually to go into primary or secondary education.

Table 2.4. Graduate Major and Future Career Field (Per cent in Given Future Career Field When the Career Field Is Not Identical[a] to Their Graduate Major)

Graduate Major	Per cent with Identical Future Career Field	Nat. Sci.	Bio. Sci.	Soc. Sci.	Hum.	Eng.	Med.	Edu.	Bus.	Law	Soc. Work	Other Health	Other Profs.	Total Per cent	Total N
Chemistry	91	1	0	0	0	0	0	5	0	0	0	0	2	99	861
Physics	81	3	1	0	0	6	0	4	1	0	0	1	4	101	721
Geology & Geography	65	1	0	3	2	1	0	19	1	0	0	0	8	100	271
Mathematics	68	3	0	0	0	6	1	15	4	0	0	0	4	101	898
Other Physical Sciences	65	2	1	0	0	12	1	13	1	1	0	0	4	100	156
Engineering	85	1	0	0	0	8	0	0	3	0	0	0	3	100	3,041
Medicine	97	0	0	0	0	0	0	1	0	0	0	1	1	100	1,431
Nursing	98	0	0	0	0	0	0	1	0	0	0	0	0	99	400
Other Health	88	0	0	1	2	0	4	4	0	0	0	4	2	99	663
Biology	46	0	6	0	0	0	4	40	0	0	0	1	1	101	360
Biochemistry	71	9	2	0	0	0	4	1	1	0	0	13	2	102	182
Botany	48	1	21	0	0	0	0	21	0	0	0	0	9	100	103
Microbiology	79	0	3	0	0	0	2	2	0	0	0	11	2	99	131
Other Biology	62	0	9	0	0	2	1	10	0	0	0	7	8	99	287
Physiology	46	0	21	0	0	0	16	7	0	0	0	10	0	100	96
Zoology	48	1	14	0	0	0	3	26	0	0	0	1	8	101	157
Other Professions	80	0	0	1	1	1	0	9	2	0	0	1	4	99	2,988
Clinical Psychology	84	0	0	1	0	0	1	10	2	0	1	1	2	101	366
Other Psychology	61	1	0	5	0	1	0	12	13	1	0	1	4	99	281
Economics	52	0	0	2	1	2	0	5	25	2	0	0	10	99	455
Political Science	53	1	0	1	1	0	0	10	6	1	0	0	28	101	676
Sociology	49	0	0	1	0	0	0	21	7	0	12	0	9	99	362

[a] In some cases (e.g., Education) it is possible to find that people "changed" from a given graduate major to the identical category on "Future Career Field." This seeming inconsistency is explained by the fact that those categories frequently include sub-categorizations (e.g., 25 per cent of those with graduate majors in one educational field actually expect to teach in another).

(Table 2.4 continued)

Table 2.4. Continued

Graduate Major	Per cent with Identical Future Career Fields	Nat. Sci.	Bio. Sci.	Soc. Sci.	Hum.	Eng.	Med.	Edu.	Bus.	Law	Soc. Work	Other Health	Other Profs.	Total Per Cent	Total N
Other Social Sciences	41	1	0	8	11	0	0	27	2	0	0	1	8	99	270
Fine Arts	62	1	0	0	3	1	0	24	3	0	0	0	5	99	1,407
English	55	0	0	0	2	0	0	31	4	0	0	0	7	99	1,172
Languages	48	1	0	1	3	0	0	30	4	1	0	1	10	99	700
History	41	0	0	2	1	0	0	42	3	1	1	0	10	101	1,121
Philosophy	62	1	0	1	3	0	0	13	4	0	0	0	16	100	193
Humanities, Other	28	0	0	1	14	2	0	30	6	1	0	9	11	102	176
Education	68	0	0	0	1	0	0	25	1	0	0	1	3	99	11,469
Business	74	0	0	0	0	6	0	2	10	0	0	0	7	99	4,526
Law	79	0	0	2	0	1	0	1	11	0	0	0	6	100	2,434
Social Work	86	0	0	0	0	0	0	9	2	0	0	0	1	98	705

N   39,059
NA Future Career Field or Unclassifiable   667
NA Graduate Field only   1,622
NA both Future Career Field and Graduate Major   505

Total   41,853
Excluded:
  (a) Not Planning Grad. School Ever   12,383
  (b) NA Plans Index   2,428

Total Weighted N   56,664

History is not alone in attracting graduate students whose long-run careers lie in primary and secondary education. Listed below from Table 2.4 are all the graduate fields where more than 10 per cent of the students planned on careers in education.

GRADUATE FIELD	PER CENT EXPECTING CAREER IN EDUCATION
History	42
Biology	40
English	31
Humanities, Other	30
Languages	30
Social Sciences, Other	27
Zoology	26
Fine Arts	24
Botany	21
Sociology	21
Geology, Geography	19
Mathematics	15
Philosophy	13
Physical Sciences, Other	13
Psychology, Other than Clinical	12

Other discrepancies between graduate field and career field are less striking, but the following are all the examples from Table 2.4 where more than 10 per cent of the students who planned to do graduate study in a given field anticipated careers in a particular different field:

GRADUATE FIELD	CAREER FIELD	PER CENT
Political Science	Other Professions	28
Economics	Business	25
Botany	Bio. Sci. Other than Botany	21
Physiology	Bio. Sci. Other than Physiology	21
Physiology	Medicine	16
Philosphy	Other Professions	16
Zoology	Bio. Sci. Other than Zoology	14
Humanities, Other	Different Humanities Field	14
Biochemistry	Health, Other	13

Psychology, Other than		
Clinical	Business	13
Physical Science, Other	Engineering	12
Sociology	Social Work	12
Microbiology	Health, Other	11
Social Sciences, Other	Humanities	11
Humanities, Other	Other Professions	11
Law	Business	11

Even though the percentages are small, they are in some in-stances cumulative. The result is that graduate fields vary widely in the proportion of students who reported the same field as their long-range career plan. Of the 33 fields listed in Table 2.4, nine show more than 80 per cent "matches," while nine show less than 50 per cent. Furthermore, a distinct pattern emerges when the fields are grouped (Table 2.5).

As common knowledge would suggest, the overtly professional fields have relatively high proportions of matches, while the arts and science fields are lower. Within the arts and science group, however, there is considerable variation by division. In the physical sciences, the proportion of matches is high, but in the social sciences and the humanities (except for clinical psycho-logy, an essentially professional field housed in arts and sciences by historical accident) the proportion of matches is relatively low. Aside from clinical psychology, there is no field in the social sciences or humanities where as many as two-thirds of the prospective graduate students anticipated long-run careers in their field of study.

A low rate of matches need not mean that graduate study in a given field is non-vocational. The high school teacher seeking a master's degree in English or the government administrator working toward a graduate degree in political science undoubt-edly has an essentially occupational motivation. What is sug-gested, however, is that those fields with low percentages of matches have a dual training function, to train individuals who plan to enter the field and also to provide supplemental training for others whose long-range plans lie in other occupations. Later analyses will reveal a number of otherwise puzzling findings which become more meaningful when the idea of "dual function" fields is remembered.

CONCLUSIONS

In this introduction to the analysis of the 1961 seniors' plans for postgraduate studies we have examined the distribution of the sample on the Plans Index, the distribution of fields of anticipated graduate study, and the relationships between career plans and plans for advanced study.

The major conclusions may be summarized as follows:

1. Although the graduating seniors have a strikingly high orientation toward further study, 83 per cent being favorable toward it and 77 per cent expecting to go on themselves, only 20 per cent had been accepted

Table 2.5. Per Cent Identical in Table 2.4

	Professional	Graduate Field			
		Arts and Sciences			
		Phy. Sci.	Bio. Sci.	Soc. Sci.	Hum.
00 –					
98 –	Nursing				
96 –	Medicine				
94 –					
92 –		Chemistry			
90 –					
88 –	Health, Other				
86 –	Social Work				
84 –	Engineering			Clin. Psych.	
82 –		Physics			
80 –	Other Prof.				
78 –	Law		Microbiol.		
76 –					
74 –	Business				
72 –					
70 –			Biochem.		
68 –	Education	Math.			
66 –		Geol.-Geog; Oth. Phy.			
64 –					
62 –			Bio., Other	Other Psychol.	Fine Arts, Philos.
60 –					
58 –					
56 –					English
54 –				Pol. Sci.	
52 –				Economics	
50 –				Sociology	
48 –			Botany, Zoology		Languages
46 –			Biol., Physiology		
44 –					
42 –				Other Soc. Sci.	History
40 –					
38 –					
36 –					
34 –					
32 –					
30 –					
28 –					Other Hum.
26 –					

for graduate study in the fall of 1961, at the time of their graduation in June of 1961; 57 per cent of the sample has less definite or immediate plans for advanced study.

2. Indirect evidence suggests that the high proportion "Later" is not merely due to wishful thinking, but that delay in entry to postgraduate studies is characteristic of American higher education.

3. While there is hardly a career field in which expectations of advanced study are not surprisingly high, detailed tabulations suggest that the generally high rate of "interest" in graduate study conceals considerable variation in the function of graduate study in different occupations. In terms of timing, it appears that, depending on the occupation, graduate study serves as a ticket for admission, an eventual necessity, or a desirable luxury. In terms of content, where the study field is identical with the career field, graduate study implies a direct training function, but the common case of graduate training in a field different from the career field suggests that much graduate training is supplementary "broadening."

3

Who Plans
to Go
to Graduate School?

While Chapter 2 revealed the great aspirations of the June, 1961, graduates, it also documented the fact that only a minority intended to realize their educational plans immediately after graduation. Even though differences in career field helped to explain much of the variation in plans, there remain differences in plans among students within a career field that are not yet accounted for. It is the aim of this chapter to discover the factors that explain these differences.

Unexplained variation is, of course, an intellectual problem that always challenges the research worker, but this problem also has considerable practical importance. Granted that engineers and business administrators can be quite effective without advanced degrees or that school teachers may actually benefit from having practical experience before they begin their master's degree work, the advantages of immediate and extensive graduate training for the major professions and the arts and science fields are overwhelming. Without graduate training, entry into the major professions is barred and work in the arts and sciences can be only at a low level.

Even postponement of advanced training takes a toll. From the viewpoint of the student, the older he is when he begins graduate study the fewer working years he will have as a thoroughly-trained professional and the greater the chance that he will have a family to support during his studies.[1] When one considers that in most arts and science fields (physics and chemistry constitute conspicuous exceptions) the median age on receiving the doctoral degree is over 30,[2] these considerations take on additional significance. Assuming the individual receives his Ph.D. when he is 30 and retires at the age of 65, each year of postponed graduate study subtracts three per cent from the working life of the doctoral recipient, and any reform that would enable the great bulk of future Ph.D.'s to begin their studies sooner would probably add several percentages to the supply of doctoral-level man years available to the nation.

Not all of this "waste" is modifiable. At the same time, Appendix 2 (National Projections on Graduate School Attendance) estimates that about 1,000 June graduates from the top fifth in API are postponing studies in the physical sciences, as are about 4,000 high API students in the humanities and social sciences.

We shall want to examine the relevant factors most carefully, beginning with the reasons reported by the students themselves and then considering objective measures associated with delay or abandonment of plans for advanced study.

THE SUBJECTIVE REASONS

In examining the reasons why otherwise-qualified students did not intend to undertake graduate study immediately, it is useful to distinguish between two broad classes of reasons. On the one hand was the motivation of the students — the extent to which they really wanted to go on to school. Even though the writer is fully persuaded of the advantages of immediate advanced study, students did not necessarily share these ideas. To the extent that there were other things they would rather do, to the extent that they saw plentiful opportunities that did not require the time, money, and work of immediate training, and to the extent they believed that practical experience should come first, we can say that they were low on motivation to continue.

[1]Cf. James A. Davis, with the assistance of David Gottlieb, Jan Hajda, Carolyn Huson, and Joe L. Spaeth, *Stipends and Spouses: The Finances of American Arts and Science Graduate Students* (Chicago: University of Chicago Press, 1962), p. 170.

[2]*Ibid.*, p. 29.

External obstacles constitute a second and strategically important class of factors. The student whose finances prohibited further study, the young man who faced obligatory military service, and the student whose undergraduate record was of low quality had formidable obstacles to further study regardless of their motivations. In particular, financial obstacles deserve special attention. Certainly anyone has the right to decide against advanced study of his own free will, but if qualified students are prevented from going on because of financial problems, we can say that a clear-cut social problem exists. Furthermore, the solution to the problem of finances is simple compared to the difficult task of affecting the motivations of the college graduates.

We shall begin, then, by attempting to separate the motivational factors from the external obstacles, paying particular attention to financial barriers.

Although it is commonly believed that survey analysis is particularly adept at analyzing "reasons," these are actually quite difficult to treat scientifically. NORC's experience in this and other surveys is that respondents almost unanimously try to "tell the truth" as they see it, but the human being's capacity for rationalization is almost endless. We shall see that only 2 per cent of the graduating students did not think they had the ability to go on for graduate work—a statistic that is a pretty poor objective measure of ability but *is* important for what it reveals about students' views of the situation.

All students who did not fall into the "Next Year" group in the Plans Index were asked, "Which of the following best explains why you do not anticipate going to graduate or professional school next year? (Circle any which apply.)" The students selected from a list of twelve possible reasons ("I want to get practical experience first," "Family responsibilities," and so on). We put into a single group all those who chose the same reason for not going on and tabulated the percentages for those not going on and for the total sample (Table 3.1). The group who said, "I want to get practical experience first" is the largest, comprising 22 per cent of the total sample and 33 per cent of those not going on. Other reasons, in order, were "Financial obstacles," "I'm tired of being a student," "Can get a desirable job without further schooling," and "No desire to do so." At the opposite end, "I lack the necessary undergraduate course prerequisites," "I don't think I have the ability," and "Low grades in college," were each checked by less than 10 per cent of the total sample.

Lack of motivation and the external obstacle of finances were most frequently given as reasons; from the point of view of the

Table 3.1. Distribution on Reasons for Not Attending Graduate or Professional School Next Year

Specific Reasons
(Per cent circling item as answer to "Which of the following best explains why you do not anticipate going to graduate or professional school next year?"

Response	Per cent of. . .*	
	Total Sample	Those Not Going
I want to get practical experience first	22	33
Financial obstacles	20	30
I'm tired of being a student	18	27
Can get a desirable job without further schooling	16	23
No desire to do so	15	22
Family responsibilities	12	19
I would rather get married	8	12
Military service	7	11
Low grades in college	7	10
I will be in a company training program which provides the equivalent	2	4
I don't think I have the ability	2	4
I lack the necessary undergraduate course prerequisites	1	2
N	53,665	36,010
NA, Reasons Not Going On	571	571
Plan to Attend School Next Year	–	17,655
NA on Plans	2,428	2,428
Total Weighted N	56,664	56,664

*Percentages total more than 100 because of multiple answers.

students, the obstacle of academic barriers presented itself only rarely.

Later evidence will show that whether they realized it or not, the students with lower academic performance were much less likely to go on. However, the low percentage of those who chose not to go on because of a mediocre or poor college record suggests that the graduating seniors did not define advanced study as the prerogative of the "Phi Bete," but assumed rather that a bachelor's degree is sufficient qualification for advanced study. This in turn may reflect a widely-held attitude that further study is a continuation rather than a selected process, an academic "step up."

We learned more from the list when we examined the interrelations of the items (Table 3.2), the Q coefficients telling whether students who circled a given reason were disproportionately likely or unlikely to circle another particular reason. We considered the nine items circled by 10 per cent or more of those not going on and found the following groupings:

A. Motivational

1. "I'm tired of being a student," "No desire to do so," "Can get a desirable job without further schooling," and "I would rather get married" all have positive Q interrelations of .21 or more and generally negative relations with other items.

2. "I want to get practical experience first," tends to be independent of or negatively related to all the other items.

B. External Obstacles

3. "Family responsibilities" and "Financial obstacles" are associated with each other ($Q = .29$) and have generally negative associations with the other items.

4. "Low grades in college" is essentially independent of all other reasons, except for a negative association ($Q = -.31$) with "I want to get practical experience first."

5. Military service is negatively related to all the other items except that it is independent of low grades.

There are apparently two components to the motivational factors. The first (Cluster 1) is simply lack of interest in attending. The second, "I want to get practical experience first," is

Table 3.2. Intercorrelations of Reasons for Not Going to Graduate or Professional School Next Year (Representative Sub-sample) (Q Values)

Values	Tired	No Desire	Good Job	Prefer Marriage	Military	Experience	Grades	Family	Money
Tired		.50	.34	.24	-.23	.17	.10	-.24	-.11
No desire	.50		.50	.21	-.36	-.37	-.02	-.27	-.57
Good job	.34	.50		.27	-.60	-.05	-.16	-.04	-.18
Prefer marriage	.24	.21	.27		-.38	-.02	-.14	-.60	-.20
Military	-.23	-.36	-.60	-.38		-.42	.01	-.53	-.15
Experience	.17	-.37	-.05	-.02	-.42		-.31	-.55	-.12
Grades	.10	-.02	-.16	-.14	.01	-.31		-.07	.11
Family	-.24	-.27	-.04	-.60	-.53	-.55	-.07		.29
Money	-.11	-.57	-.18	-.20	-.15	-.12	.11	.29	

Notes:
1) Item wordings are as follows:
Tired = "I'm tired of being a student"
No Desire = "No desire to do so"
Good Job = "Can get a desirable job without further schooling"
Prefer Marriage = "I would rather get married"
Military = "Military service"
Experience = "I want to get practical experience first"
Grades = "Low grades in college"
Family = "Family responsibilities"
Money = "Financial obstacles"
2) The following items in the schedule, circled by 10 per cent or less of those not going on next year, were excluded from this table:
   "I don't think I have the ability"
   "I lack the necessary undergraduate course prerequisites"
   "I will be in a company training program which provides the equivalent"

different. It is unrelated to the "Interest" cluster and has a strong negative relationship with low grades. This was presumably the characteristic motive of the "Later" group in the Plans Index who were definitely interested in advanced study and felt qualified, but preferred to postpone study until they had worked a while.

Within the external obstacle group, family responsibilities and financial obstacles go together reasonably enough, and military service and grades are separate of finances and of each other. By considering a positive answer to any one of the "low interest" reasons as positive for the general type, we can arrange the two types of motivation and the external factors of financial obstacles and military service as follows: (data recomputed from Table 3.3).

a. Per cent of Total Sample (RSS)

Low Interest	Practical Experience	Financial Obstacles No	Financial Obstacles Yes	Total
+	−	17	7	24
+	+	7	4	11
−	+	9	3	12
Total Motivational		33	14	47
−	− Military Yes 4 / No 4		14 }	22
Total		41	28	69%

b. Per cent Among Students Not Going On Next Year

Low Interest	Practical Experience	Financial Obstacles No	Financial Obstacles Yes	Total
+	−	26	11	37
+	+	10	6	16
−	+	12	5	17
Total Motivational		48	22	70
−	− Military Yes 5 / No 5		21 }	31
Total		58	43	101%

We may draw the following inferences, remembering that these are reported reasons, not necessarily "real ones."

1. Motivational reasons are common. Forty-seven per cent of the total sample and 70 per cent of those not going on reported one or more items from the motivational group.

2. Low interest is more common than a desire for practical experience. Thirty-five per cent of the total sample and 53 per cent of the group not going on in 1962 indicated one or more items from the low interest

Table 3.3. Index of Reasons for Not Going to Graduate or Professional School Next Year

Reasons Index				Per cent of Sub-sample	Per cent of Those Not Going Next Year
Expect to go on next year				32	—
Do Not Expect to Go On*					
Low Interest	Money	Practical Experience	Military		
+	+	+	+ or −	4	6
+	+	−	+ or −	7	11
+	−	+	+ or −	7	10
+	−	−	+ or −	17	26
−	+	+	+ or −	3	5
−	+	−	+ or −	14	21
−	−	+	+ or −	9	12
−	−	−	+	4	5
−	−	−	−	4	5
		Total per cent		101	101
	N			3,221	
	NA on Plans Only			85	
	NA on Reasons Only			33	
	NA on Both			58	
	Total N			3,397	

*Low Interest: + = positive response to one or more among Tired, No desire, Good job, Prefer marriage.
Money: + = "Financial obstacles."
Practical Experience: + = "I want to get practical experience first."
Military service is considered only for those not giving a response to any of the three other items in the index, and is to be interpreted as "military service only."

cluster. At the same time, it should be noted that the majority of students in the sample and 48 per cent of those not going on immediately did not circle any of the items in this cluster, and hence the majority may be considered "interested."

3. Four per cent of the total sample and 5 per cent of those not going on indicated "Military service" and did not check a motivational or financial reason. Thus, only a small number cited military service as the "single" obstacle.

4. Although 28 per cent of the total sample and 43 per cent of those not going on reported financial obstacles, only 14 per cent of the total and 21 per cent of those not going on reported financial obstacles and no motivational reasons. Half of those reporting financial obstacles also reported a motivational reason for not going on immediately.

To summarize, the students may be seen as falling into four groups: 1) One-third of the total and about half (48 per cent) of those not going on reported only motivational reasons; 2) 14 per cent of the total and 22 per cent of those not going on had a motivational reason and financial obstacles; 3) 14 per cent of the total group and 21 per cent of those not going on next year cited a financial obstacle, but no motivational hesitations; 4) 8 per cent of the total group and 10 per cent of the students not going on in 1962 reported neither motivational nor financial obstacles. Within this last group, half (4 per cent of the total sample) gave military service as their reason.

As the students viewed it, those who were not going on generally had a motivational reason; only a minority saw themselves as motivated for immediate study but blocked by external obstacles. However, 14 per cent of the total and one out of five among those not going said that although they were motivated to go on, they could not because of financial problems. This figure is not far from the percentages arrived at in a direct question, "To what extent did immediate financial obstacles (not doubts about the long-run economic value of further study) affect your decision regarding graduate or professional school next year?" (Table 3.4.) Here 12 per cent of the total sample and 18 per cent of those not going on in 1962 circled, "Financial obstacles are the major reason I am not going on for further study next year." Thirty-one per cent of the total group and 47 per cent of those not going on circled "Financial obstacles had nothing to do with it," and the remainder (24 per cent of the total, 35 per cent of those not going on) indicated that "Financial obstacles played some part in my decision."

So far we have been treating the situation as a unilateral decision by the student. But since decisions on the part of graduate and professional schools are also involved, it is necessary to consider the subjective data in combination with data on application status before the picture is complete. Table 3.5a arranges the students according to how far they had proceeded along the following steps: application to a school, acceptance by a school, application for a stipend, and offer of a stipend. The index forces somewhat greater consistency onto the process than really exists (Woodrow Wilson Fellows, for example, apply for a stipend without applying to a school; some students may have

Table 3.4. Financial Obstacles as Reason for not Attending Graduate or Professional School Next Year

Percentage Distribution of Answers to . . . "To what extent did immediate financial obstacles (not doubts about the long-run economic value of further study) affect your decision regarding graduate or professional school *next* year?"

Response	Per cent of	
	Total Sample	Those Not Going
Financial obstacles had nothing to do with it	31	47
Financial obstacles played some part in my decision	24	35
Financial obstacles are the major reason I am not going on for further study next year	12	18
Total	67	100
N	54,075	36,420
NA	161	161
Plan to Attend School Next Year	–	17,655
NA on Plans	2,428	2,428
Total Weighted N	56,664	56,664

Table 3.5. Application Status and Financial Obstacles, Controlling for Sex and Academic Performance (Representative Sub-sample)

a. Application Status

Stage	Applied to a School	Accepted by a School	Applied for Stipend	Offered a Stipend	Per cent of Sample	Per cent of Previous Row
I	Yes				25	—
II	Yes	Yes	Yes		21*	84*
III	Yes	Yes	Yes		12	58
IV	Yes	Yes	Yes	Yes	9	73

$$N \qquad 3,315$$
$$\text{NA on Applications} \qquad \underline{82}$$
$$\text{Total N} \qquad 3,397$$

*The "21" and the "84," for example, are to be interpreted as follows: "21 per cent of the sample applied to a graduate or professional school for study next year and were accepted by one or more schools"; "84 per cent of those who applied were accepted by one or more schools."

(Table 3.5 continued)

Table 3.5. Continued

b. Financial Obstacles and Application Status,
Controlling for Sex and Academic Performance

Sex	Academic Performance	Outcome[a]	Stage on Application Index				
			Didn't Apply to School	Not Accepted by School	Stipend Refused	Didn't Apply for Stipend	Stipend Offered
Male	High	Next	18	71	73	94	96
		No, $	47	23	21	3	4
		No, Other	36	5	5	4	1
		Total N =	101% (491)	99% (39)	99% (56)	101% (154)	101% (190)
	Low	Next	13	42	80	85	100
		No, $	50	37	20	8	0
		No, Other	37	21	0	7	0
		Total N =	100% (799)	100% (43)	100% (15)	100% (71)	100% (27)
Female	High	Next	15	58	72	97	99
		No, $	38	38	16	0	1
		No, Other	47	4	12	3	0
		Total N =	100% (646)	100% (24)	100% (32)	100% (39)	100% (69)
	Low	Next	9	50	–	81	–
		No, $	42	14	–	14	–
		No, Other	49	36	–	5	–
		Total N =	100% (440)	100% (14)	– (2)	100% (21)	– (2)

N 3,174
N.A. on Application 31
N.A. on API 49
N.A. on Plans 143
Total N 3,397

[a] Next = Those who plan to go on to graduate or professional school
No, $ = Those who do not plan to go on next fall and who indicated that financial obstacles played some part or are the major reason

c. Data in Table 3.5b Percentaged Across the Rows

Sex	Academic Performance	Outcome	Stage on Application Index					Total	
			Didn't Apply to School	Not Accepted	Didn't Apply for Aid	Stipend Refused	Stipend Offered	Per cent	N
Male	High	Next	18	6	30	9	38	101	481
		No, $	88	3	2	5	3	101	261
		No, Other	94	1	3	2	*	100	188
	Low	Next	46	8	28	6	12	100	218
		No, $	94	4	1	1	0	100	423
		No, Other	96	3	1	0	0	100	314
Female	High	Next	41	6	16	10	28	101	242
		No, $	94	3	0	2	*	99	258
		No, Other	98	*	*	1	0	99	310
	Low	Next	59	10	25	3	3	100	68
		No, $	97	1	2	0	0	100	189
		No, Other	97	2	*	0	0	99	222

N 3,174
NA on Application 31
NA on API 49
NA on Plans 143
Total N 3,397

*Less than one-half of 1 per cent.

(Table 3.5 continued)

Table 3.5. Continued

d. Financial Obstacles and Application Status,
Controlling for Sex and Academic Performance

Academic Performance	Sex	Outcome	Stage on Application Index			N
			Applied to a School	Applied and Accepted	Applied, Accepted, and Applied for a Stipend	
High	Male	Next	82%	76%	47%	481
		No, $	12	9	8	261
		No, Other	6	5	2	188
	Female	Next	59	53	38	242
		No, $	6	3	2	258
		No, Other	2	1	1	310
Low	Male	Next	54	46	18	218
		No, $	6	2	1	423
		No, Other	4	1	0	314
	Female	Next	41	31	6	68
		No, $	3	2	0	189
		No, Other	3	1	0	222

N 3,174
NA on Application 31
NA on API 49
NA on Plans 143
Total N 3,397

e. Outcome for Students Who Applied to a School, Were Accepted, and Applied for a Stipend, by Outcome of Stipend Application (RSS)

Academic Performance	Sex	Stipend Offer	Student Status			Total	
			Next Year	No, $	No, Other	Per cent	N
High	Male	Yes	96	4	1	101	190
		No	73	21	5	99	56
	Female	Yes	99	1	0	100	69
		No	72	16	12	100	32
Low	Male	Yes	100	0	0	100	27
		No	80	20	0	100	15
	Female	Yes	—	—	—	—	2
		No	—	—	—	—	2

N   393
Excluded:
Didn't apply to school   2,376
Not accepted by school   120
Didn't apply for stipend   285
NA, Application   31
NA, API   49
NA, Plans   143
Total N   3,397

received informal word that they would be accepted for graduate school without making formal applications, etc.), but the index does approximate the main outline of the decision process.

Table 3.5a indicates what the June graduates as a whole had done by the time of graduation. One-quarter had applied to a school; 84 per cent of the applicants had been accepted by one or more schools (of the remainder, many had applications pending and should not be considered as turned down by all the schools to which they applied); 58 per cent of those accepted had applied for a stipend; and 73 per cent of the stipend applicants reported some offer of financial aid. These figures suggest that the decision not to apply at all was a greater screening factor than refusals of applications or stipends. The majority of those applying to schools were accepted and the majority of stipend applicants received some financial offer; yet only a small proportion of students applied for either.

We can see the effect of stipends on financial obstacles when we consider the application status of various types of students. Table 3.5c shows the application status for three types of students: a) those expecting to go on for advanced study next year; b) those in the "Later" and "Never" categories who indicated that financial obstacles "played some part" or were "the major reason"; c) those in "Later" and "Never" who said "Financial obstacles had nothing to do with it."

In Table 3.5d the data from 3.5b are repercentaged. Here the trend is very clear. The decision of students not to go on for study immediately was not a result of running into barriers in the application process. Regardless of sex and API, almost 90 per cent of those not going on immediately had not even applied to a school. This was true whether or not they cited financial reasons as an obstacle.

Data from Table 3.5b, as rearranged in Table 3.5e, do indicate, however, that for the minority of students who did proceed far enough on the application route to be affected, stipend offerings did make a difference. Regardless of sex or API, the student who was refused financial aid was considerably less likely to anticipate immediate graduate work. Ninety-six per cent of the high API males with stipends expected to go on the next year, in contrast to 73 per cent of those who were refused. Putting it another way, students who received a stipend offer very seldom fell in the group constituted of those who were not going on for financial reasons, while about one-fifth of those who had been denied assistance were not going on immediately, citing a financial reason for their decision.

Perhaps all that is going on here was self-selection. If the non-applicants were merely saving the admissions and fellowship committees the trouble of making a negative decision, we have seriously underestimated the impact of perceived external obstacles. As far as academic admission is concerned, we doubt that this is the case, since so few of the students *believed* they could not be admitted. As for stipend applications, our only information is as follows: Students who expected to go on immediately were asked "Did you apply (or were you nominated) for financial support (scholarship, fellowship, assistantship, etc.) for this fall?" Those who circled "No" were then asked, "Did you not apply because . . . ?" The distribution of answers from the representative sub-sample is as follows:

	PER CENT
Did apply for a stipend	44
Did not, because	
I wouldn't need any support of this type	21
I didn't think I could get any	17
It didn't occur to me to apply	9
I had no intention of going to school at the time applications were due	4
The amount I would get would have been too little	2
The duties attached would have been unsatisfactory	2
Other	8
*Total	107
	N = 1,210

*Total is greater than 100% because of multiple answers on reasons.

The reasons scatter, but we note that 17 per cent of those going on next year said they did not apply because they did not think they would receive any aid, in contrast with 65 per cent who either applied or said they did not need any financial aid.

The core of the problem, however, is the low rates of application. When we assume that those who were refused stipends would behave like those who were offered one and repercentage the data in Table 3.5b accordingly, we get the following results:

			Per cent "Next Year" (RSS)	
API	Sex	As is	If all stipend applications were accepted	N
High	Male	52	53	930
	Female	30	31	810
Low	Male	23	23	955
	Female (insufficient applicants to percentage)			

Our data suggest that if every stipend application made by the class of 1961 (including a number of clearly unqualified and undesirable applicants) had been accepted and all other things were equal, about 1 per cent more of the higher API students would have gone on the next year and there would have been no increase among the students with lesser academic performance. The implication here is not that stipend programs should be abolished or that stipends do not affect attendance, but rather that attendance rates might rise if a stipend program were accompanied by a wide-spread publicity campaign aimed at encouraging the rate of applications. The importance of this idea grows when we note in Table 3.5b that the rate of expected enrollment among those who were refused stipends was many times greater than among those who did not apply to a school.

A number of qualifications must be made. Undoubtedly the students who did not apply to a school differed in their abilities and motivations in ways which can only be crudely controlled by our API measure and question on financial obstacles. At the very least, the evidence indicates that the reluctance of the student to apply was the major deterrent to immediate entry into advanced study. It may well be that the non-applicants would have been refused, but unless they were motivated to apply there was no chance of selecting the promising ones from among them.

While those students who gave financial reasons as barriers to graduate study were so pessimistic about their immediate chances that few of them took even the initial steps toward enrollment for the fall of 1961, they showed a definite long-range optimism (Table 3.6). A large majority of them expected to attend school later, in contrast with those whose barriers were nonfinancial. Among high API men, 83 per cent of those citing financial obstacles expected to study later, compared with 64 per cent of those with no financial barriers. Among women and lower API men respectively, the comparable figures were about 75 per cent and 50 per cent. As the students saw it, financial obstacles lead to the postponement and not the abandonment of studies.

Table 3.6. Plans for Future Graduate and Professional Study Among Students Who Do Not Expect to Attend Next Year by Sex, Academic Performance, and Financial Obstacles (Representative Sub-sample)

Sex	API	Financial Obstacles*	Plans			Total	
			Later		Never		
			Definite Date	Indefinite		Per cent	N
Male	High	Yes	62	21	17	100	263
		No	49	15	36	100	191
	Low	Yes	51	23	26	100	428
		No	28	18	53	99	317
Female	High	Yes	52	28	19	99	262
		No	34	20	46	100	313
	Low	Yes	52	28	20	100	189
		No	23	25	52	100	224

N	2,187
Expect to Attend Next Year	1,018
NA on API	49
NA on Plans	143
Total N	3,397

*Yes = "played some part" or "the major reason"
No = "had nothing to do with it"

SUMMARY:

1. The reasons reported by students not planning to go on for advanced study immediately have been analyzed in terms of two broad types of perceived factors, internal motivation and external obstacles.

2. Of the two, internal motivations appear the more common, 70 per cent of those in the "Later" and "Never" categories citing lack of interest or preferring to get practical experience first.

3. Concerning external obstacles, financial barriers are seen by the students as the major external problem, 43 per cent of those not going on citing a financial reason. Depending on the measure used, between 12 and 14 per cent of the total group and 18 and 20 per cent of those not going on believe that financial obstacles are the major factor preventing immediate advanced study.

4. As the students view it, very few believe that academic deficiency or inappropriate undergraduate training is an obstacle to further study.

5. About 5 per cent of the total sample appear to be barred from immediate study by military service.

6. Although students who have been refused stipends have less frequent expectations of immediate study, so few of the students had applied for either schools or stipends that actual rejection plays a small role in affecting plans.

OBJECTIVE CORRELATES: ACADEMIC PERFORMANCE AND SEX

If one were to take the students at their word, the conclusion would be that academic performance is not a major factor in plans for postgraduate study. Low motivation and financial obstacles were the common reasons given by those who were not planning immediate graduate study. However, when the Academic Performance Index (API) is introduced into the tabulations, things are seen in a different light. The reader will remember that each student's reported cumulative grade point average was weighted by the average academic ability of students at his school to give an index of academic performance, which is our basic measure of intellectual achievement in the study since mass testing of the respondents was precluded on practical grounds.

When the Plans Index is cross-tabulated against API (Table 3.7), strong differences emerge:

1. Among the top fifth, 54 per cent expected to attend graduate or professional school immediately; among those who were above average, 35 per cent planned to do so; among the bottom half, the figure dropped to 22 per cent.

2. Forty-four per cent of the top fifth had been accepted when they filled out the schedule, in comparison with 21 per cent of those above average and 10 per cent of the bottom half.

3. Of the group who expected to attend school immediately, 41 per cent were from the top fifth, 38 per cent from the above average category, and 21 per cent from the bottom half.

4. Although there is a continuous falling off in API as one moves through the categories on the Plans Index, the big difference is between those accepted for next year and the remainder. The students who expected to attend in the fall of 1961 or later, but who had not been accepted by the spring of 1961, were not conspicuously higher in academic performance than students in general.

5. Among those who did not ever plan to go to postgraduate school, the "frustrated" (those who said they would like to go) were distinctly lower in API than the others. Thus, they were barred from advanced study as a result of low academic performance.

Students whose academic performance was high were considerably more likely to be aiming for postgraduate training, and students who expected to enter advanced study immediately were by and large high in academic performance. The relationship is far from perfect, and it is important to note that:

1. Ten per cent of those accepted and 22 per cent of those planning to attend were from the bottom half, academically.

2. Almost one-third of the highest API group were postponing their studies. Projecting the total June graduates from our universe of schools at 265,000, this implies that somewhere around 16,000 of the students in the top fifth postponed their studies and approximately 7,000 did not plan further study beyond the bachelor's degree.[3]

[3]See Appendix 2 for detailed projections of plans by API and field of study.

Table 3.7. Academic Performance Index and Plans Index

Plans	Top Fifth	Above Average	Bottom Half	Per cent from Top Fifth	Above Average	Bottom Half	Total Per cent	Total N
Next Year	53.6	35.3	21.5					
Accepted	43.9	21.1	9.5	40.8	38.2	20.9	99.9	10,807
Other	9.7	14.2	12.0	14.7	42.0	43.3	100.0	6,617
Later	32.2	44.9	49.6					
Definite date	22.9	30.4	32.5	14.4	37.2	48.4	100.0	15,975
Indefinite	9.3	14.5	17.1	11.9	36.2	51.9	100.0	7,855
Never	14.3	19.8	28.7					
Like to	2.4	3.9	8.0	8.3	26.3	65.4	100.0	2,920
Other	11.9	15.9	20.7	12.9	33.7	53.4	100.0	9,232
Total	100.1	100.0	99.8					
N	10,057	19,573	23,776	55,759				
NA	369	905	1,079	905				
Total N NA, API	10,426	20,478	24,855	56,664				
Total Weighted N								

Do both of the components of API, school quality and grade point average, contribute to the relationship? Table 3.8 indicates that both do. Among students with grade point averages (GPA) of B+ or higher, 63 per cent of those from the highest quality schools planned immediate graduate work in comparison with 41 per cent of those from the lowest group of schools. Similarly, within a school quality level there was a progressive variation with GPA. The school difference remains, interestingly, when sex and career type are also controlled (Table 3.9). When career fields are divided into those where generally half or more anticipated going on next year ("High Go" career fields) versus those where less than one-half had such plans ("Low Go" career fields), the relationship remains within each career type. Thus, among men in careers with high rates of graduate school attendance (essentially the major professions and the arts and sciences), 94 per cent of those with B+ or better averages from the top institutions planned to go on immediately, in contrast with 43 per cent of those with C+ or lower averages from the least distinguished institutions. We shall not speculate on whether this was simply a result of the calibre of students recruited to the

Table 3.8. Student's Reported Cumulative Grade Point Average, Classification of School on National Merit Scholarship Index, and Plans Index (RSS) (Per cent Expecting to Attend Graduate or Professional School Next Year)

GPA	School Type		
	I – II	III	IV
B+ or higher	63 (84)	49 (307)	41 (199)
B	58 (59)	43 (247)	31 (155)
B–	49 (147)	32 (449)	27 (264)
C+ or lower	34 (147)	19 (751)	16 (399)

N	3,208
NA, Grade Point Average	46
NA, Plans	143
Total N	3,397

Table 3.9. Sex, Career Type, Grade Point Average, School Quality, and Plans (RSS) (Per cent Expecting to Attend Graduate or Professional School Next Year)

Career Type	GPA	Men			Women		
		School Group			School Group		
		I–II	III	IV	I–II	III	IV
"High Go"	B+	94 (18)	84 (61)	72 (36)	75 (16)	72 (39)	40 (15)
	B, B–	91 (56)	72 (131)	61 (49)	64 (14)	55 (44)	50 (14)
	C+	66 (29)	53 (113)	43 (47)	– (6)	30 (27)	– (9)
Other	B+	62 (24)	45 (89)	45 (49)	36 (25)	26 (106)	26 (88)
	B, B–	45 (73)	30 (212)	32 (180)	18 (50)	23 (285)	18 (152)
	C+	30 (61)	13 (348)	12 (208)	22 (45)	15 (223)	12 (91)

N	3,033
N.A. Career Type Only	172
N.A. Grade Point Average Only	45
N.A. Plans Only	121
N.A. Two or More	26
Total N	3,397

schools or whether exposure to a "high quality" institution enhanced the probability of going on, for this question is the subject of extensive analyses to be reported elsewhere. We reiterate that both components of the Academic Performance Index contributed, however, independent of sex and general career type.

While API was a major predictor of plans, sex was almost as important (Table 3.10); the combination of both factors produced a striking range in plans (Table 3.11). Among the men 39 per cent expected to attend immediately; among women the figure was 24 per cent. You will remember that women were more likely to be high academic performers, 63 per cent of the women being in the top half in comparison with 50 per cent of the men (Table 3.11a). Because API and being a male were negatively associated but both were positively associated with plans to go on immediately, the combination of sex and API made a powerful predictor of plans (Table 3.11b). Without considering career field at all, we find that plans to go on the next year ranged from 68 per cent of the men in the top fifth to 16 per cent of the women in the bottom half. There was also an apparent "interaction" between sex, API, and plans, which can be put alternatively as:

Table 3.10. Sex and Plans Index

Plans	Male		Female		Per cent Male	
Next Year	38.8		23.6			
Accepted		25.9		11.9	76.0	(10,933)
Other		12.9		11.7	61.3	(6,722)
Later	41.4		49.2			
Definite date		29.7		30.2	58.7	(16,218)
Indefinite		11.7		19.0	47.1	(7,980)
Never	19.8		27.1			
Like to		6.0		4.7	64.8	(2,972)
Other		13.8		22.4	47.2	(9,411)
Total per cent	100.0		99.9			
N	32,071		22,165			
NA	1,435		993			
Total N	33,506		23,158	= 56,664 Total Weighted N		

API made more difference among the men (OR) sex made a greater difference among those high on API. Thus in the bottom half the sex difference in the per cent "Next Year" was a modest 8 per cent, while in the top fifth the difference amounted to 32 per cent.

Is the obvious reason why women were less likely to anticipate further study that most of them were planning to get married and raise families instead? Apparently it isn't quite that simple. To begin with, less than 5 per cent of the women indicated that they did not plan to work after college, and two-thirds of the women did not expect to be married by the fall of 1961 (Table 3.12a). The question of the relationship between marital status and postgraduate plans is important and deserves careful analysis because the trends are complicated.

Table 3.12b gives the relationship between family status and the Plans Index, controlling for sex and API. The differences are not clear-cut, but the important trends are these:

The fact of being married had little impact on the plans of men who were high on API. Fifty-six per cent of the single men expected to go on the next year, and 50 per cent of those expect-

Table 3.11. Sex, Academic Performance Index, and Plans Index (Plans Index by Sex and Academic Performance)

Sex	Academic Performance	Plans			Total	
		Next Year	Later	Never	Per cent	N
Male	Top Fifth	68.4	23.3	8.4	100.1	5,416
	Above Average	45.3	40.1	14.6	100.0	10,387
	Bottom Half	24.4	48.5	27.1	100.0	15,769
Female	Top Fifth	36.3	42.6	21.2	100.1	4,641
	Above Average	24.0	50.3	25.7	100.0	9,186
	Bottom Half	16.0	52.0	32.0	100.0	8,007

N		53,406
NA, API		830
NA, Plans		2,428
Total Weighted N		56,664

Table 3.12. Marital Status and Plans Index, Controlling for Sex and Academic Performance (RSS)

a. Marital Status by Sex and Academic Performance

Academic Performance Index	Sex	Marital Status				Total	
		Single		Married			
		Don't Expect to Be Married Before Fall, 1961	Expect to Be Married Before Fall, 1961	No Children	One or More or Expecting	Per cent	N
Top Fifth and Above Average	Male	62	10	10	18	100	978
	Female	66	17	6	10	99	836
Bottom Half	Male	57	11	9	22	99	1,008
	Female	66	18	8	8	100	496

N   3,318
NA or Ex-Married   27
NA. API   52
                          ―――――
Total N   3,397

(Table 3.12 continued)

Table 3.12. Continued

b. Martial Status and Plans Index, Controlling for Sex and Academic Performance

Sex	Academic Performance	Plans	Marital Status			
			Single		Married	
			Don't Expect to be Married Before Fall, 1961	Expect to Be Married Before Fall, 1961	No Children	One or More or Expecting
Male	Top Fifth and Above Average	Next Year	56	45	55	38
		Later	33	40	32	47
		Never	11	14	13	15
		Total N =	100% 582	99% 99	100% 88	100% 166
	Bottom Half	Next Year	22	17	27	24
		Later	49	51	42	46
		Never	29	31	31	30
		Total N =	100% 550	99% 109	100% 84	100% 216
Female	Top Fifth and Above Average	Next Year	36	15	23	16
		Later	45	48	44	57
		Never	19	38	33	28
		Total N =	100% 532	101% 143	100% 48	101% 83
	Bottom Half	Next Year	18	6	8	12
		Later	54	47	58	53
		Never	28	47	35	35
		Total N =	100% 314	100% 85	101% 40	100% 40

N 3,179
NA or Ex-Married 26
NA. API 49
NA. Plans 143
Total N 3,397

ing to be married before the fall of 1961 or those married with no children expected to go on. Among men with children, however, the figure dropped to 38 per cent (a figure nonetheless higher than that for single low API men). Since there was no difference by family status among those who were never going on, we can conclude that for high API men being a father led to postponement of graduate studies, but marriage *per se* had little effect. Among low API men, there were no differences in plans regardless of family situation. Since high API fathers constituted only 9 per cent of the men, family responsibilities did not appear to be a major factor affecting rates of graduate study. However, it would have been expected that as the first years after college changed the status of bachelors and husbands without children, families played a major part in determining whether members of the "Later" group actually began their studies.

The impact of marriage was different among the women. Married women, whether they had children or not, were less likely to anticipate graduate school. Of the high API women, for example, 36 per cent of those who were single and did not expect to be married before the fall were planning to go on immediately, compared with 15 per cent of the engaged girls, 23 per cent of the married women with no children, and 16 per cent of the mothers. Among those who were "attached," however, the mothers, if anything, had higher educational aspirations than the brides! Thirty-eight per cent of the engaged high API women said they would never go on to school compared with 28 per cent of the mothers. Does this mean that women increase their interest in graduate training after the honeymoon is over? More probably it means that the married women with children in our sample were quite unrepresentative. They undoubtedly had a greater motivation for higher education or they wouldn't have been able to overcome the difficulties of completing undergraduate work while rearing a family.

Do these relationships explain the sex difference in plans? When we compare men and women in the same family categories and API groups, we see that in each case men were more likely to anticipate graduate work. It is not surprising that married men had higher rates than married women, but the fact that of the high API students who expected to be single in the fall of 1961, 56 per cent of the men and 36 per cent of the women planned to go on immediately is a little more surprising. Perhaps the *anticipation* of a future family diverted the interest of these young women, but the sex difference in plans was independent of the current marriage plans or marital situations of these young people.

Let us now examine the simultaneous relationships between sex, API, career, and the Plans Index. Table 3.13 gives the per cent who expected to go on in the fall of 1961 by sex, API, and a detailed occupational breakdown. Clearly, the sex and API differences were not artifactual. In every comparison where there are 50 or more cases per cell (except for social work where top fifth and above average API do not differ much), plans for the three API categories exhibit a steady progression. Taking the men in physics as an example, we see that 90 per cent of those in the top fifth, 63 per cent of the above average, and 42 per cent of those in the bottom half planned to go on immediately. Similarly, in every single comparison where there are 50 or more cases, men were more likely to anticipate graduate study within an API and career grouping. Even where there is little sex difference in career choice, as among social scientists in the top fifth, for example, 76 per cent of the men and 58 per cent of the women anticipated immediate advanced study.

The sex and API differences were so strong within each occupational preference that one wonders whether the occupational differences might be spurious and whether the plans rates for various fields can rather be explained by their sex and API composition. This does not seem to be the case. When the actual per cent who expected to go on in each field the next year is correlated with the per cent which would be expected if each field were made up of equal proportions of above average and bottom half API men (the only two groups in Table 3.13 with sufficient cases in each occupational preference), the adjusted rates show a striking correlation with the "raw" figures.

Our general conclusion is that sex, academic performance, and career choice contribute independently toward the predic-

Table 3.13. Anticipated Future Career, Sex, Academic Performance, and Plans Index (Per cent Expecting to Enter Graduate or Professional School Next Year)

Career	Academic Performance Index					
	Male			Female		
	Top Fifth	Above Average	Bottom Half	Top Fifth	Above Average	Bottom Half
Medicine	98 (551)	92 (574)	74 (221)	— (34)	44 (52)	— (34)
Law	86 (490)	80 (696)	56 (704)	— (25)	73 (56)	— (21)
Biological Sciences	92 (90)	72 (156)	49 (298)	47 (148)	40 (192)	25 (146)
Physics	90 (273)	63 (161)	42 (155)	— (33)	— (11)	— (2)
Other Physical Sciences	86 (67)	55 (129)	24 (131)	— (19)	— (25)	— (4)
Chemistry	81 (170)	69 (238)	40 (292)	49 (76)	28 (105)	10 (69)
Social Sciences	76 (341)	64 (497)	39 (512)	58 (260)	35 (310)	28 (144)
Humanities	80 (492)	36 (494)	33 (499)	56 (697)	35 (715)	20 (410)
Mathematics	86 (159)	57 (180)	19 (230)	37 (122)	13 (86)	— (42)
Other Professions	72 (323)	53 (623)	50 (927)	36 (315)	23 (484)	18 (531)
Engineering	63 (827)	35 (1,491)	17 (1,979)	— (6)	— (20)	— (19)
Education	52 (434)	41 (1,602)	25 (3,002)	30 (1,950)	23 (4,901)	16 (4,537)
Other Health Professions	— (49)	52 (181)	42 (403)	21 (263)	19 (662)	15 (508)
Social Work	— (16)	77 (53)	33 (139)	30 (131)	32 (290)	12 (321)
Agriculture and Related	38 (72)	33 (217)	12 (442)	— (3)	— (2)	— (1)
Business and Administration	36 (850)	23 (2,559)	10 (4,704)	17 (239)	13 (497)	13 (563)

N 49,814
Respondent circled "Job which has no near equivalent on this list" 1,434
Does not expect to work after graduation 862
N.A. Plans 2,428
N.A. API 830
N.A. Career Field 1,296
Total Weighted N 56,664

tion of senior plans for advanced study. Their joint effects are shown in Table 3.14, which also classifies those not going on by the reasons reported, so that the type of reason associated with these characteristics can be examined. Since Table 3.14 contains a considerable amount of information, it will help to break it down.

First, let us look at the per cent who expected to go on to graduate study in the fall of 1961.

	Per cent Expecting Advanced Study Next Year			
	API			
Career	Low		High	
	Women	Men	Women	Men
Law, Medicine	42 (55)	69 (917)	70 (167)	89 (2,304)
Arts and Sciences	22 (770)	37 (1,986)	45 (2,723)	73 (3,373)
All Other	16 (6,452)	20 (11,566)	25 (9,700)	40 (9,301)

Considering law and medicine as having the highest rates of students going on the next year[4], arts and science fields as next, and all other fields low in anticipated graduate enrollment, we see a range from 16 per cent to 89 per cent in the "Next Year" category as we move from low API women in fields of low enrollment to high API men in the major professions.

We can consider as less motivated any student not going on immediately who circled one or more of the items in the low interest cluster or who circled "I want to get practical experience first." How many students in these categories gave a motivational explanation?

There were strong sex, API, and career differences in motivation. Women, students lower in API, and students in the fields where graduate work is of less strategic significance were more likely not to go on immediately and to cite a motivational reason (of course, many gave other reasons, too). Among high API men aiming for careers in law or medicine, 3 per cent fell into this

[4]The career differences would be even greater if certain small "High Go" fields such as dentistry or theology were added.

	Per cent Not Going Next Year Who Gave a Motivational Reason			
Career	A P I			
	Low		High	
	Women	Men	Women	Men
Law, Medicine	38	7	11	3
Arts and Sciences	59	31	43	14
All Other	70	51	62	41

N's are the same as in the preceding table.

category, while among low API women in the "Low Go" fields, 70 per cent were so classified.

A rough test of whether motivational differences "explain" the observed differences by field, sex, and API can be made by dividing the students into three groups: a) Those who planned to go on next year, b) those who cited a motivational reason for going later or not at all, and c) those who said they were going later or not at all and did not cite a motivational reason, thus, in all probability facing external obstacles. When these figures are plotted on triangular coordinate graph paper, we can determine which factors vary with which type of plans (Charts 3.1, 3.2, 3.3).

The career differences appear to be almost entirely due to differences in motivation. In Chart 3.1, the per cent headed for graduate study the next fall and the per cent "Not motivated" vary regularly from law and medicine to arts and sciences to other fields within each sex and API group. There are almost no systematic career differences in "External obstacles," defined here as those students who did not plan to go on immediately but did not cite a motivational reason. The finding is obvious, in a sense, and tends to corroborate our previous interpretations of career differences in plans, but the effect is worth comment. For instance, since there is much less stipend aid available for students in law and medicine than for those in arts and sciences (as will be shown later), one might think that lawyers and doctors might be higher on external obstacles, which are often financial. Or since arts and science graduate schools are probably more selective than "other fields," one might expect that the arts and science group would be higher on "External obstacles" than the

Table 3.14. Sex, API, and Career Type by Plans for Advanced Study and Reasons for not Going On for Advanced Study (All Variables)

Future Career	API	Sex	Plans				Total	
			Next Year	Later or Never			Per cent	N
				Motivational Reason*	Financial Obstacles*			
					Yes	No		
Law or Medicine	High	Male	89	3	4	4	100	2,304
		Female	70	11	16	4	101	167
	Low	Male	69	7	10	14	100	917
		Female	42	38	7	13	100	55
Arts and Sciences	High	Male	73	14	8	5	100	3,373
		Female	45	43	11	1	100	2,723
	Low	Male	37	31	22	10	100	1,986
		Female	22	59	13	7	101	770
Other	High	Male	40	41	13	7	101	9,301
		Female	25	62	12	1	100	9,700
	Low	Male	20	51	17	12	100	11,566
		Female	16	70	11	3	100	6,452

N	49,314
N.A. API	724
N.A. Plans	2,428
N.A. Career Type	3,538
N.A. Reasons Not Going	571
N.A. One or More	89
Total Weighted N	56,664

students in "other" careers. Regardless of these possibilities, it appears that differences in motivation were the major differences between the broad groups of careers.

Chart 3.2 suggests that, as for career fields, the major factor in the sex difference was motivation. Regardless of API and career

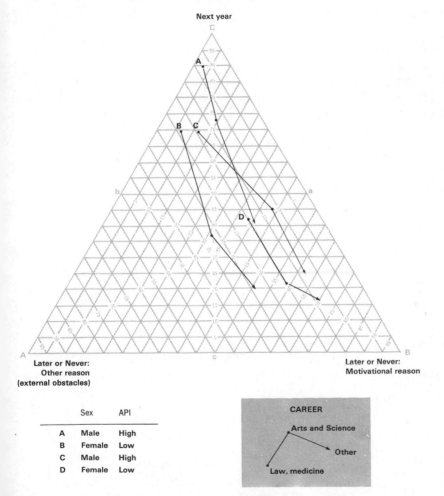

Next year

Later or Never:
Other reason
(external obstacles)

Later or Never:
Motivational reason

	Sex	API
A	Male	High
B	Female	Low
C	Male	High
D	Female	Low

CAREER

Arts and Science

Other

Law, medicine

Chart 3.1. Data in Table 3.14 Graphed to Show Effect of Career Type

type, women were much more likely to be in the group character-ized by lower motivation, while sex differences in "External obstacles" were not consistent.

The API differences (Chart 3.3) were also largely motivational. Except for males aiming at law and medicine, the students of

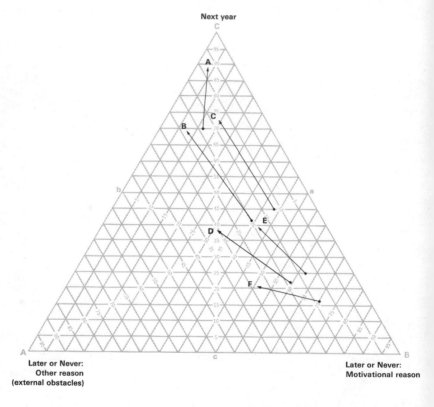

Group	Occupation	API
A	Law, medicine	High
B	Law, medicine	Low
C	Arts and sciences	High
D	Arts and sciences	Low
E	Other	High
F	Other	Low

Chart 3.2. Data in Table 3.14 Graphed to Show the Effect of Sex

lesser academic performance had a distinctly greater percentage citing low motivation and no greater percentage attributing their decision to external obstacles. Among the small group of men who planned careers in law and medicine, however, lower API went with perceived external obstacles, not motivation. These

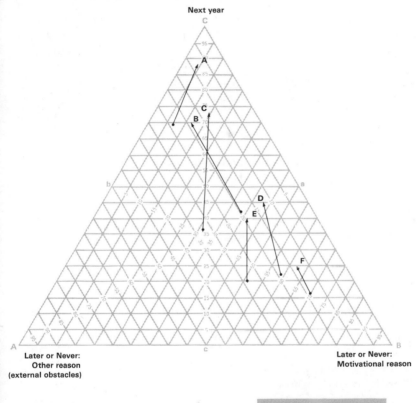

Next year

Later or Never:
Other reason
(external obstacles)

Later or Never:
Motivational reason

Group	Field	Sex
A	Law, medicine	Male
B	Law, medicine	Female
C	Arts and sciences	Male
D	Arts and sciences	Female
E	Other	Male
F	Other	Female

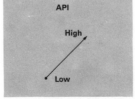

API

High

Low

Chart 3.3. Data in Table 3.14 Graphed to Show the Effect of API

findings help explain the discrepancy between the subjective reasons and the objective data on API. The student whose academic capacities were less outstanding apparently did not typically define this as a personal limitation, but rather defined the situation in such a way that graduate study appeared less attractive.

Because the category of external obstacles comprises obstacles other than financial ones, it is possible that the analysis above has concealed relationships between sex, API, career type, and financial obstacles. However, no consistent differences turn up when this reason is tabulated separately. The following data from Table 3.14 give the per cent of students who a) were not going on immediately, b) did not cite a motivational reason, and c) did give financial obstacles as their explanation.

Per cent Not Going the Next Year and Who Cited Only Financial Obstacles as Reason

Career	API			
	Low		High	
	Women	Men	Women	Men
Law, Medicine	7	10	16	4
Arts and Sciences	13	22	11	8
All Other	3	17	12	13

N's are the same as in the preceding table.

The percentages are not identical and fluctuate from three to twenty-two, but no discernible pattern emerges that enables us to say that perceived financial obstacles are related to sex, API, or career type. And in the strategic groups of high API men studying arts and sciences, law, and medicine, few students cited this reason. Many more, of course, circled "Financial Obstacles" in the questionnaire, but among high API men only 8 per cent in arts and sciences and 4 per cent in law and medicine fell into the group who were not going on immediately, giving financial but not motivational reasons for their decision.

SUMMARY

1. There is a striking API difference in plans for "Next Year." Regardless of sex, career field, or marital status, the academically superior are much more likely to plan immediate study. When the differences are examined in terms of the data on reasons, it appears that the lower API student sees his decision as stemming from lower motivation, not necessarily from perceived obstacles to advanced study.

2. Regardless of career field, API, or marital status, women are much less likely to plan immediate graduate study. Even among girls with no immediate marital plans, the difference is considerable. Examination of the reasons data suggests that the sex difference is primarily due to differences in motivation, not to perceived financial or other external obstacles.

3. Marital and family status play some role, but their effects are not consistent. The small group of high API married men with children do have a tendency for postponement, but among lower API men there is no difference, and among women the difference comes from marriage *per se*, not from the presence of children.

4. Within a sex and API group, career field continues to make for strong differences in plans. Thus, among high API men, 89 per cent of those going into law and medicine anticipated immediate study in comparison with 73 per cent of those going into arts and sciences and 40 per cent of those in other fields. It should be noted, nevertheless, that high API men in other occupations have about the same per cent anticipating immediate study as low API women in law and medicine, the variation by sex and API within occupations being considerable.

Now we have a more rounded view of the crucial issue of "talent loss." While the fact remains that the over-all rates of postponement, particularly in the strategic arts and science fields, are unsettling, the figures are less grim when sex and API are taken into consideration. Without appearing to be anti-feminist or to endorse intellectual elitism, we can reasonably state that men in the top fifth on API constitute the most strategic group. By re-percentaging data in Table 3.13, we derive the following figures for the per cent of high API men in selected fields who expected to begin advanced study in the fall of 1961:

	Per cent	N
Medicine	98	551
Biological Sciences	92	90
Physical Sciences	86	510
Humanities	80	492
Social Sciences	76	341

The fact that one out of five top fifth men in the humanities and the social sciences was not going on immediately was not heartening, but the talent loss was small in medicine and the natural sciences. Viewed in percentages, the situation is not shocking.

OBJECTIVE CORRELATES: BACKGROUND CHARACTERISTICS

The factors considered so far — sex, API, and career preference — had an obvious direct connection with decisions to go on for advanced study. After all, the strategic significance of graduate work varies with anticipated lines of work, the significance of having a career at all varies with sex, and the higher motivation of the academically able is not puzzling. In turning to consideration of social background characteristics — race, SES, hometown, and religion — we come to an area where connections are less obvious and problems of social policy begin to emerge. It is therefore useful to begin with a disclaimer. We shall see in this section that social factors did affect plans for postgraduate study, independent of the control variables of sex, API, and career type. Yet these differences were limited in scope. For instance, our conclusion will be that while SES did affect plans, the SES effect is much smaller than the API difference. In contrast, a large number of research studies on the college plans of high school students show that SES and IQ contribute about equally to anticipations of college attendance. While we shall show differences that move in directions similar to previous research on earlier educational levels, it is important to remember that the strength of the effects is generally less.

This diminution apparently continues with each step up the educational ladder. In NORC's survey of arts and science graduate students already enrolled,[5] background factors seemingly

[5]James A. Davis, *et. al., op. cit.*

made very little difference to career plans and outcomes. The trend is not by any means inexplicable. The lower class or small town or minority group student who survives the attrition process and graduates from college is undoubtedly quite unrepresentative of his subgroup to begin with; he has been exposed to a relatively cosmopolitan upper—status environment for some time, and, in most cases, he has been living away from his early milieu (23 per cent of the total sample lived with their parents during their senior year, 65 per cent went to a school beyond "commuting distance" of their hometown—RSS). Thus, compared with younger and older people, the graduating senior may be seen as being to some extent free from the powerful pressures of class, community, and subculture. He has been liberated from his early home environment and has not yet established his adult niche. Thus, for these young people, perhaps more than for any other group in the nation, the effects of class and subculture are diminished. That they appear at all is a wry tribute to the influence social groupings have on individual decisions.

Race

Although, compared with whites, a greater proportion of the small number of students of Oriental extraction said they were continuing their studies immediately (42 per cent as compared with 32 per cent), Negro students appeared at a slight disadvantage (Table 3.15). Twenty-eight per cent of them were classified as "Next Year." This difference is, in itself, trivial, but since only 4 per cent of the Negroes, in contrast with 24 per cent of the whites, said they were never going on, a high proportion of Negro students were postponing their studies. Thus, of those going on the next year or later, 58 per cent of the whites and 70 per cent of the Negroes chose "Later." The small difference in "Next Year" appears as a sharp disadvantage for Negro seniors when evaluated in terms of the total number who anticipate graduate study.

Our procedure has been to compare Negroes with Protestant, lower SES, smaller hometown whites as well as with white students in general, because Negroes tend to be Protestant, lower in SES, and from smaller cities. In Table 3.16a we see plans and reasons tabulated for Negroes, whites in general, and white

Protestants who were low SES and from smaller cities. The results support the inference that Negroes have a relatively high interest in advanced study but considerable obstacles to immediate enrollment.

a. When compared with whites in general, Negroes were a little less likely to anticipate immediate study, but when matched with comparable whites, *more* Negroes were going on next year (29 per cent v. 23 per cent).

b. Negroes were considerably *less* likely to report low motivation (31 per cent) when compared with either group of whites, in both of which about one-half reported low motivation.

c. Negroes were considerably *more* likely to report external financial obstacles (34 per cent) when compared both with whites in general (12 per cent) and with Protestant low SES, smaller-city whites (20 per cent).

d. There was no difference by race in the per cent reporting non-financial external obstacles.

Because the Negro students are more often female and less often high on API, these factors, as well as career type, should be controlled. This is done in Table 3.16. No tabulation is given for some groups in the arts and science careers since there were too few Negro women or high API Negro men, nor were there enough Negro cases to tabulate law and medicine. In the remain-

Table 3.15. Race and Plans Index, Controlling for Sex and Academic Performance Index

Race	Plans Index			Total	
	Next Year	Later	Never	Per cent	N
Oriental	42.0	37.0	20.8	99.8	927
White	32.4	43.9	23.5	99.8	50,295
Negro	28.3	67.1	4.4	99.8	1,622
Other	18.9	58.3	22.6	99.8	384

N	53,228
NA Race	1,008
NA Plans	2,428
Total Weighted N	56,664

ⴰble 3.16. Race, Plans, and Reasons for not Going On Next Year

a. Controlling Background Characteristics

Index of Background Characteristics	Plans				Total	
	Next Year	Later or Never				
		Motivational Reasons	Financial Obstacles		Per cent	N
			Yes	No		
White	32	49	12	6	99	45,582
Negro	29	31	34	6	100	1,609
Protestant, low SES, smaller-city whites only	23	51	20	6	100	9,916

N	47,191
NA Background	6,474
NA Plans	2,428
NA Reasons Not Going	571
Total Weighted N	56,664

b. Controlling Career Field, Sex, and API*

Career	Sex	API	Race	Plans				Total	
				Next Year	Later or Never				
					Motivational Reasons	Financial Obstacles		Per cent	N
						Yes	No		
ⴰts d iences	Male	Low	All whites	37	32	21	10	100	1,636
			Negroes	40	7	34	19	100	83
			Comparable whites‡	22	36	30	12	100	476
	Male	High	All whites	40	41	12	7	100	8,087
			Negroes	39	19	38	4	100	170
			Comparable whites‡	33	43	18	6	100	1,816
ⴰer		Low	All whites	20	52	16	12	100	9,997
			Negroes	28	28	33	12	101	304
			Comparable whites‡	16	52	22	10	100	2,831
	Female	High	All whites	23	65	11	1	100	8,325
			Negroes	23	31	44	2	100	296
			Comparable whites‡	16	63	19	1	99	1,555
		Low	All whites	14	73	10	2	99	5,137
			Negroes	23	49	24	3	99	378
			Comparable whites‡	8	74	17	1	100	1,286

N	34,413
Excluded:	
Law and Medicine	3,111
Women in Arts and Sciences	3,008
High API men in Arts and Sciences	2,954
NA, API	692
NA, Career Field	3,013
NA, Background	6,474
NA, Plans	2,428
NA, Reasons Not Going	571
Total Weighted N	56,664

ⴰw and medicine, women in arts and sciences, and high API men in arts and sciences have been excluded because the
ⴰed total of Negro cases in each of these categories is less than 50.
ⴰw SES and smaller hometown on Index of Background Characteristics

ing groups the trends noted above remained when sex, API, and career field were controlled.

a. Negroes were as likely to go on immediately as whites in general and were more so than Protestant, low SES, smaller-hometown whites.

b. Negroes were considerably less likely to be low on motivation, the percentage *differences* running 20 or more in each comparison with either white control group.

c. Negroes were distinctly more likely to report financial obstacles when compared with all whites and somewhat more likely to do so when compared with Protestant, low SES, smaller-city whites.

d. There were no important differences in the proportion reporting themselves as blocked by non-financial external obstacles.

These materials suggest that the plans distribution for Negroes is a result of contradictory forces. On the one hand, the Negroes generally were strongly motivated for graduate study, particularly when matched with whites of similar religion, sex, API, career type, SES, and hometown. On the other hand, the Negro student was much more likely to look upon finances as a bar to immediate study, even when he was matched with low SES whites. (The Negro students probably came from families lower in SES than our group of low SES whites, so these findings do not demonstrate that there is a racial financial bar in addition to the SES one, but they do tell us that Negroes as a whole see their financial obstacles as worse than whites in the bottom half in SES.) Moreover, he suffered from the greater external obstacles common to lower SES, smaller-city students. The outcome of all of this is that Negro students, when compared with whites similar in other characteristics, *were more likely to anticipate immediate advanced study than disadvantaged whites and just about as likely as whites in general.* At the same time, it is clear that high motivation produced the favorable outcomes, for considering only students motivated to go on, the Negroes were much less likely to anticipate going "Next Year" than were whites comparable in religion, sex, API, SES, hometown, and career type.

SES and Hometown Among Whites
Turning now to the white students in the Index of Background

Characteristics, we shall examine the effects of the socio-economic status of the parental family and the size of the hometown. Each had an effect on plans for advanced study and, because of their strong statistical association, it is necessary to consider them simultaneously.

Both in terms of its components and as a global index, socio-economic status is positively related to plans to attend graduate school immediately after graduation. In terms of income (Table 3.17a), those who were going on the next year ranged from 29 per cent of those reporting parental incomes of less than $5,000 to 40 per cent of those reporting $20,000 or more. For father's occupation (Table 3.17b) the range was from 22 per cent for farmer fathers to 38 per cent for professional fathers. Twenty-nine per cent of those whose fathers had had an eighth-grade education or less were going on the next year in contrast with 44 per cent of those whose fathers had gone on to graduate school (Table 3.17c).

It is interesting to note too that the per cent of those never going on also increased with income. The children of proprietors were higher on "Never" than the children of any other group. Considering the father's education, we see that the per cent never going on increased up to the bachelor's degree and then dropped

Table 3.17.   Plans Index and Socio-Economic Status

a. Parental Income and Plans

Reported Annual Income of Parental Family	Next Year	Later	Never	Total	
				Per cent	N
Less than $5,000	28.7	52.4	18.9	100.0	9,506
$5,000–$7,499	31.4	48.0	20.5	99.9	12,954
$7,500–$9,999	33.0	45.6	21.4	100.0	8,384
$10,000–$14,999	35.8	40.8	23.4	100.0	7,500
$15,000–$19,999	35.6	37.7	26.6	99.9	3,089
$20,000 and over	40.4	31.1	28.5	100.0	5,004

N	46,437
Don't Know Income	6,082
NA on Income	1,717
NA on Plans	2,428
Total Weighted N	56,664

(Table 3.17 continued)

Table 3.17. *Continued*

b. Occupation of Father and Plans

Occupation of Father	Next Year	Later	Never	Total Per cent	Total N
Professional	38.5	39.0	22.3	99.8	11,929
Proprietor/Manager	33.1	39.9	26.7	99.7	12,239
Sales	31.4	43.9	24.5	99.8	3,257
Clerical	33.2	46.3	20.3	99.8	1,870
Skilled	31.3	48.3	20.4	99.8	8,292
Semi-skilled	28.7	53.5	17.6	99.8	3,664
Service	31.6	49.0	19.2	99.8	1,528
Unskilled	27.5	51.4	20.8	99.7	1,671
Farmer	21.8	51.8	26.3	99.9	3,840

N	48,290
NA Father's Occupation Only*	1,584
NA Plans Only	2,128
NA on Both	82
Total listing father as head of household	52,084
Excluded: Total listing mother as head of household	4,580
Total Weighted N	56,664

*Including respondents who indicated only that father was retired.

c. Father's Education and Plans

Father's Education	Plans Next Year	Plans Later	Plans Never	Total Per cent	Total N
8th grade or less	29	50	21	100	11,571
Part high school	31	48	20	99	8,480
High school graduate	30	46	24	100	11,043
Part college	33	43	24	100	7,858
Bachelor's degree	34	38	28	100	7,033
Graduate or professional degree	44	36	20	100	6,828

N	52,813
NA, Father's Education	1,423
NA, Plans	2,428
Total Weighted N	56,664

for those whose fathers had gone to graduate or professional school. This suggests a pocket of upper-class disinterest in advanced study which stems from the fact that the son of the owner often does not need a master's degree in business administration to rise in the corporate hierarchy. An examination of the partial data on parental occupation (Table 3.18) shows that the difference disappeared among women but remained among the men; sons of managers, proprietors, and salesmen were higher on "Never" than other sons, an indirect support of the interpretation. Not too much should be made of this eddy in the data, for even among bottom-half API men, two-thirds of the businessmen's sons planned graduate study, although the figure is lower than the three-fourths typical of most of the other occupational groups among men in the bottom half on API.

As a necessary converse of these two trends, lower SES origins are associated with higher proportions "Later." While 31 per cent of those with parental incomes of $20,000 or more report postponed plans, among those from families with incomes of less than $5,000 a year, the figure is 52 per cent. As in the case of the Negro students, the figures suggest higher interest in graduate school among those from lower status levels along with a lesser opportunity to implement this interest.

Most of these differences come from extremes on the measures; when the data are based on the simple division of the SES index into high and low, we see that 36 per cent of the high and 29 per cent of the low SES seniors anticipated immediate graduate study (Table 3.19). There was no zero order SES difference in motivation or non-financial external obstacles, but 8 per cent of the high SES students were in the financial obstacles category, while 17 per cent of the low SES students were. Thus, the zero order SES effects on plans for the next year appeared as financial, not motivational.

It is not obvious why size of the high school hometown should have affected graduates' plans for advanced study, but it did (Table 3.19). Examining the detailed distribution on hometown, we see that there was a general increase in those going on next year as hometown size increased (Table 3.20). Twenty-one per cent of those from rural surroundings were going on at once; of

Table 3.18 Occupation of Head of Parental Family (Father or Mother) and Plans, Controlling for Sex and API

API	Parental Occupation	Male Next Year	Male Later	Male Never	Male Total %	Male Total N	Female Next Year	Female Later	Female Never	Female Total %	Female Total N
Top Fifth	Professional	75.7	19.0	5.3	100.0	1,673	38.3	37.9	23.8	100.0	1,678
	Prop./Mgr.	66.9	21.9	11.2	100.0	1,372	36.4	44.1	19.5	100.0	1,121
	Sales	68.9	20.4	10.7	100.0	383	31.2	40.8	28.1	100.1	292
	Clerical	68.2	24.3	7.6	100.1	276	37.4	40.6	21.9	99.9	283
	Skilled	64.0	26.9	9.1	100.0	628	38.7	47.5	13.9	100.1	554
	Semi-skilled	64.4	28.1	7.6	100.1	331	43.9	42.9	13.2	100.0	189
	Service	71.1	26.7	2.2	100.0	180	28.3	60.4	11.3	100.0	106
	Unskilled	51.9	38.3	9.9	100.1	162	22.7	54.8	22.6	100.1	84
	Farmer	50.6	35.7	13.7	100.0	255	17.9	55.9	26.2	100.0	195
Above Average	Professional	53.7	34.5	11.7	99.9	2,262	27.3	44.0	28.8	100.1	2,575
	Prop./Mgr.	47.2	33.1	19.8	100.1	2,395	24.2	47.5	28.4	100.1	2,362
	Sales	44.7	41.1	14.2	100.0	674	22.1	52.9	25.0	100.0	560
	Clerical	46.4	41.9	11.7	100.0	597	22.9	56.9	20.1	99.9	418
	Skilled	41.5	45.1	13.5	100.1	1,720	25.7	54.4	19.9	100.0	1,191
	Semi-skilled	38.6	49.7	11.7	100.0	878	20.2	60.2	19.5	99.9	503
	Service	41.1	43.4	15.5	100.0	399	25.1	56.4	18.5	100.0	259
	Unskilled	37.0	51.6	11.3	99.9	432	24.3	62.7	13.1	100.1	260
	Farmer	36.1	47.2	16.8	100.1	702	11.6	57.6	30.7	99.9	687
Bottom Half	Professional	28.4	47.9	23.7	100.0	2,743	16.9	47.5	35.6	100.0	1,801
	Prop./Mgr.	23.9	42.9	33.1	99.9	3,531	15.4	46.3	38.3	100.0	1,716
	Sales	23.6	44.8	31.6	100.0	983	14.5	54.8	30.8	100.1	533
	Clerical	21.7	51.5	26.8	100.0	761	18.5	48.4	33.1	100.0	399
	Skilled	24.5	50.4	25.0	99.9	3,092	19.9	53.7	26.4	100.0	1,273
	Semi-skilled	22.2	54.8	23.0	100.0	1,392	14.4	68.3	17.3	100.0	624
	Service	22.3	54.4	23.3	100.0	566	17.2	50.6	32.2	100.0	267
	Unskilled	22.0	54.3	23.7	100.0	822	13.3	55.0	31.7	100.0	278
	Farmer	21.6	49.9	28.5	100.0	1,258	9.8	59.2	31.0	100.0	799

N 51,474
NA. Parental Occupation Only 1,980
NA. API Only 782
NA. Plans Only 2,240
NA. Two or More 188

Table 3.19. SES and Size of Hometown by Plans and Reasons for Not Going On for Advanced Study

Background Variable	Plans				Total	
	Next Year	Later or Never			%	N
		Motivational Reasons	Financial Obstacles			
			Yes	No		
SES:						
High	36	49	8	6	99	24,605
Low	29	48	17	6	100	20,977
High - Low	+ 7	+ 1	– 9	0		
Hometown:						
Larger	39	46	10	6	101	21,611
Smaller	28	52	15	6	101	23,971
Larger - Smaller	+11	– 6	– 5	0		

N	45,582
N.A., Background and Negro	8,083
N.A., Plans	2,428
N.A., Reasons Not Going	571
Total Weighted N	56,664

Table 3.20. Size of Hometown and Plans Index (Representative Sub-sample)

Plans	Location Within Metropolitan Area	Size of Metropolitan Area				
		2 Million or More	500,000–1,999,999	100,000–499,999	Less than 100,000	Rural
Per cent "Next Year"	Central City	50 (290)	36 (161)	32 (236)	27 (697)	—
	Suburb	41 (314)	37 (279)	34 (236)	30 (275)	—
	Rural	—	—	—	—	21 (678)
	Total	45 (604)	37 (440)	33 (472)	27 (972)	21 (678)
Per cent "Later"	Central City	38 (290)	46 (161)	40 (236)	48 (697)	—
	Suburb	39 (314)	38 (279)	40 (236)	47 (275)	—
	Rural	—	—	—	—	53 (678)
	Total	39 (604)	41 (440)	40 (472)	48 (972)	53 (678)
Per cent "Never"	Central City	12 (290)	18 (161)	28 (236)	25 (697)	—
	Suburb	20 (314)	25 (279)	26 (236)	23 (275)	—
	Rural	—	—	—	—	26 (678)
	Total	16 (604)	22 (440)	27 (472)	25 (972)	26 (678)

N   3,166
NA Hometown   90
NA Plans   141
Total N   3,397

those from cities of two million or more, 45 per cent had such plans. Within any given size group, however, there was no consistent difference between those from the central cities and those from the suburbs. It appears that the student's immediate neighborhood did not produce the difference, but rather the degree of metropolitanism of his general setting.

It has long been known that there are fairly sharp regional differences in educational attainment. Because the regions with greater rates of school attainment are generally more urban, the possibility arises that the hometown difference was a spurious function of regional effects. The evidence is not clear, but this does not seem to be the case. The questionnaire did not ask the student to indicate his hometown region, but the sample can be classified by the regions of the undergraduate institutions. Because 78 per cent of the sample reported that their school was in the same state or within four hours' drive of their hometown (RSS), the correlation between region of hometown and region of undergraduate institution must be high. When plans are cross-tabulated by region and hometown (Table 3.21), it is seen that the two differences were independent. Within each region there was a

Table 3.21. Hometown by Region of Undergraduate Institution and Plans Index (Per cent "Next Year")

Hometown	Region of Undergraduate Institution			
	New England, Middle Atlantic	North Central	Mountain, Pacific	South, South Central
Larger	45 (679)	36 (456)	36 (209)	28 (172)
Smaller	29 (440)	27 (470)	26 (276)	18 (464)
N	1,107	926	485	636
Per cent Larger	60	49	43	27
Per cent "Next Year"	39	31	31	21

N	3,166
NA Plans Only	141
NA Hometown Only	88
NA Both	2
Total N	3,397

difference by hometown, and within a hometown group there was a consistent regional difference, for students from schools in the South were lower on plans to go on immediately, students from northeastern schools were higher, and those from north central and western schools were intermediate. At the extremes, 18 per cent of the smaller-city students from southern schools planned immediate advanced study in comparison with 45 per cent of the larger-city students from the Northeast.

Looking at the figures for larger and smaller hometowns (Table 3.19), we see that 39 per cent of those from larger cities were going on immediately as compared with 28 per cent of those from smaller cities. Since the 11 per cent difference combines a 6 per cent difference in motivation and a 5 per cent difference in external financial obstacles, it would appear that students from smaller towns were a little less motivated and somewhat more often thought they faced financial barriers.

When SES and hometown are cross-tabulated against plans and reasons, controlling for sex, API, and career type, a large number of cells is generated (Table 3.22). Even though there were too few women aiming for careers in law and medicine to justify tabulations, the table shows 20 possible comparisons for each characteristic. By and large, both SES and hometown affected plans, independent of sex, API, and career type. In 18 out of 20 comparisons, the student from a larger city more often said he would be going on the next year. The SES effect was much less consistent. The higher SES students were planning on study for the next year in only 13 out of 20 comparisons.

With tables of such complexity, it is often easier to interpret the findings by considering a "difference table" in which the entries are percentage differences for the various categories rather than the original percentage table (Tables 3.22b, 3.22c). The hometown effect, Table 3.22b, for example, tells us that among high SES, high API males aiming for arts and science careers, 80 per cent of those from larger cities were to be graduate students the next year, as were 77 per cent of otherwise similar students from smaller cities. Subtracting 77 from 80 we can say that the percentage difference for hometown in this group is +3, which is the entry for that cell in Table 3.22b. Because out-

Table 3.22. SES and Size of Hometown by Plans for Advanced Study and Reasons for not Going On for Advanced Study, Controlling Sex, API and Career Type (Per cent "Next Year")

c. SES, Hometown, Sex, API, Career Type, and Plans

Future Career	API	SES	Male Hometown Larger	Male Hometown Smaller	Female Hometown Larger	Female Hometown Smaller
Law Medicine	High	High	92 (1.038)	91 (529)	— (45)	— (31)
		Low	92 (255)	76 (248)	— (31)	— (25)
	Low	High	74 (316)	76 (207)	— (4)	— (22)
		Low	68 (135)	52 (157)	— (0)	— (8)
Arts and Sciences	High	High	80 (966)	77 (631)	47 (1.016)	37 (605)
		Low	71 (637)	62 (673)	47 (333)	50 (345)
	Low	High	53 (345)	39 (346)	24 (240)	13 (158)
		Low	41 (337)	25 (608)	30 (90)	19 (138)
Other	High	High	44 (2.264)	40 (1.782)	29 (2.710)	21 (2.471)
		Low	42 (1.706)	34 (2.335)	28 (1.141)	18 (2.003)
	Low	High	21 (2.155)	18 (2.139)	18 (1.214)	12 (1.372)
		Low	26 (2.049)	17 (3.654)	20 (861)	10 (1.690)

N	42.065
N A Career Field	2.860
N A API	595
N A Background or Negro	7.249
N A One or More	896
N A Plans	2.428
N A Reasons Not Going	571
Total Weighted N	56.664

(Table 3.22 continued)

Table 3.22. Continued

b. Difference Table: Hometown (Larger-Smaller)*

Career	SES	API	Male				Female			
				Plans				Plans		
			Next Year	Later or Never			Next Year	Later or Never		
				Motivational	Financial	Other		Motivational	Financial	Other
Law, Medicine	High	High	+ 1	0	− 2	− 1				
		Low	− 2	− 2	− 1	+ 5		Insufficient Cases		
	Low	High	+16	− 1	−14	− 1		To Tabulate		
		Low	+16	+ 2	− 6	−11				
Arts and Sciences	High	High	+ 3	− 1	− 1	− 1	+10	−10	− 2	+2
		Low	+14	− 4	−12	+ 2	+11	− 2	− 6	−2
	Low	High	+ 9	− 2	− 8	+ 1	− 3	− 3	+ 2	+4
		Low	+16	− 4	−13	0	+11	− 4	− 2	−5
Other	High	High	+ 4	− 1	0	− 2	+ 8	− 8	− 2	0
		Low	+ 3	− 4	+ 1	− 1	+ 6	− 6	0	−1
	Low	High	+ 8	− 4	− 3	− 1	+10	− 4	− 4	−1
		Low	+ 9	− 2	− 9	+ 1	+10	− 6	− 5	+1

*Cell entry = per cent for larger hometown minus per cent for smaller hometown. Rows do not always sum to zero because of rounding.

c. Difference Table: SES (High-Low)*

Career	Hometown	API	Male				Female			
			Plans				Plans			
			Next Year	Later or Never			Next Year	Later or Never		
				Motivational	Financial	Other		Motivational	Financial	Other
Law, Medicine	Larger	High	0	0	−2	+1	Insufficient Cases To Tabulate			
		Low	+6	−3	−12	+9				
	Smaller	High	+15	−1	−14	+1				
		Low	+24	+1	−17	−7				
Arts and Sciences	Larger	High	+9	−4	−4	0	0	+7	−3	−2
		Low	+12	−2	−10	+1	−6	+2	+1	+4
	Smaller	High	+15	−5	−11	+2	−13	+12	+1	0
		Low	+14	−4	−11	−1	−6	0	+5	+1
Other	Larger	High	+2	+3	−7	+3	+1	+2	−5	+1
		Low	−5	+5	−2	+3	−2	+4	−3	0
	Smaller	High	+6	0	−10	+4	+3	+6	−8	0
		Low	+1	+6	−12	+5	+2	+4	−8	+2

*Cell entry = per cent for high SES minus per cent for low SES. Rows do not always add to zero because of rounding.

comes are considered — 1) Going on the next year, 2) Not going
on and citing a motivational reason, 3) Not going on, not citing a
motivational reason but citing financial obstacles, and 4) Not going on and not citing motivational or financial reasons — the differences for each of these four outcomes should, except for rounding, sum to zero (if a certain group was more likely to have a
given outcome, then they might have been that much less likely
to have other outcomes). In a sense, we can read off in the three
reasons columns the explanation for the difference in the "Next
Year" column. Consider, as an example, the entries in Table
3.22b for hometown differences among low SES, high API men
in law and medicine. The figures are below:

Next Year	*Motivational*	*Financial*	*Other*	*Total*
	−1	−14	−1	
+16		−16		0

   The interpretation is: Among this group, the students from
larger cities were more likely to have plans for the next year,
their percentage advantage being 16 per cent. It is seen, however,
that for external financial obstacles the entry is −14 and for the
other two the entries are −1. If the hometown difference in finances is removed (if, for example, the surplus of those with
financial obstacles in low SES as compared with high SES were
shifted to "Next Year"), the hometown difference in "Next
Year" would drop from 14 to 2. In this sense, we can say that
financial factors are the major part of the hometown difference
within this group.

   With these ideas in mind, let us scan Table 3.22b. As we stated
previously, all but two of the "Next Year" differences were positive — except for high API, low SES women in arts and sciences
and low API, high SES men in law and medicine, students from
larger cities were more likely to plan immediate advanced study.
Running down the motivational column, we see negative entries
in 18 out of 20 comparisons, and the financial column shows
negative relationships in 16 out of 20 comparisons. The final
column, which is indicative of external, non-financial obstacles,
has no consistent pattern.

We draw the following conclusion:

Controlling for sex, API, SES, and career type, the student from a smaller town was less likely to anticipate immediate graduate or professional study because of both lower motivation and perceived external financial barriers.

A similar analysis of SES yields less clear-cut results, since the SES effects were less consistent. Among women, to begin with, positive and negative signs appear equally in each column. Hence, SES apparently had no consistent effect on women's plans for advanced study. Among men, the entries for "Next Year" are positive in 10 out of 12 comparisons. Hence, for males but not females, high SES was associated with plans for immediate study, independent of API, career, and hometown.

Turning to the reasons columns of Table 3.22c, generally negative entries appear for financial reasons; all 12 entries were negative for men, five out of eight were negative among the women. It is difficult to draw a conclusion about motivation. Among women higher SES apparently goes with lower motivation, since all the entries for women's comparisons were positive. Among men, the signs scatter. It will be shown in the next section, however, that when religion is also controlled, the over-all net effect of SES on motivation was negative.

Because the findings on SES are important from the viewpoint of social policy, calculations were made of the relationship between SES and plans in a detailed occupational breakdown, in order to determine whether some careers showed greater or lesser SES barriers to immediate study (Table 3.23). As expected, the results among women were inconsistent, but among men there was only one exception among the SES groups with 50 or more weighted cases. The single exception was high API men in medicine where 100 per cent of the 111 low SES cases and 96 per cent of the 415 high SES cases planned immediate study. It is possible that the percentage differences are higher in social sciences than in other careers, but no other patterns of differential effect appear. The indirect suggestion of these negative findings is that the SES effect had little to do with stipends, for stipend availability ranges widely with career fields, while SES differences do not.

SES had no consistent effect among women, but among male students higher SES was generally associated with immediate advanced study, lower SES was associated with perceived financial obstacles, and there was no consistent SES difference in motivational reasons.

The results for SES have an obvious interpretation—the student from a less affluent background probably had less in savings, greater debts, and less expectation of help from home; therefore he saw greater financial obstacles. Why this should not have applied to women also is not clear.

The results for hometown, actually the more powerful predictor, are less obvious. The "financial obstacles" difference by city size makes some sense if we assume that a considerable proportion of the students expected to return home. The smaller the city, the less likely there is to be a graduate school that a student could attend while working and living at home. Students from smaller communities who want to go on for advanced study more often must move and seek out new employment, a kind of finan-

---

Table 3.23. SES and Plans Index, Controlling for Graduate Field, Sex, and API

a. Q Correlations Between "High SES" and "Going Next Year"

| Graduate Field | Per cent High SES | Male | | | Female | | |
| | | API | | | API | | |
		Top Fifth	Above Average	Bottom Half	Top Fifth	Above Average	Bottom Half
Law	70.2	+ .33	+.30	+.34	−.24	−.65	+ .11
Medicine	69.7	−1.00	+.05	+.19	−.80	+.61	+1.00
Humanities	60.1	+ .15	+.21	+.14	+.06	+.03	− .06
Social Sciences	57.8	+ .38	+.26	+.38	−.24	−.09	− .19
Social Work	54.8	*	−.47	−.44	+.23	+.35	+ .01
Business	54.2	+ .17	+.18	+.11	+.88	+.45	+ .31
Other Health	49.2	+ .30	+.48	+.37	−.02	+.35	+ .44
Biological Sciences	47.2	+ .08	+.22	+.39	+.02	−.13	+ .59
Physical Sciences	47.2	+ .26	+.18	+.11	−.18	.00	+ .56
Engineering	45.6	+ .32	+.18	+.01	*	*	*
Other Professions	45.5	− .30	+.33	−.19	+.18	−.01	+ .59
Education	43.2	+ .34	+.09	.00	+.27	+.14	+ .03

*Number of cases insufficient to support correlation.

Table 3.23. *Continued*

b. Per Cent Going Next Year

Graduate Field	SES	Male API			Female API		
		Top Fifth	Above Average	Bottom Half	Top Fifth	Above Average	Bottom Half
Law	High	85.5 (427)	77.4 (558)	61.4 (562)	— (20)	— (39)	— (14)
	Low	74.7 (91)	64.7 (224)	43.6 (346)	— (4)	— (11)	— (8)
Medicine	High	96.4 (415)	92.2 (359)	70.4 (125)	— (17)	— (27)	— (20)
	Low	100.0 (111)	91.5 (176)	61.9 (63)	— (23)	— (30)	— (8)
Humanities	High	77.8 (361)	57.7 (362)	36.7 (264)	56.2 (698)	37.0 (692)	26.1 (349)
	Low	72.3 (224)	47.3 (347)	30.5 (387)	53.1 (258)	35.5 (330)	28.4 (243)
Social Sciences	High	81.1 (244)	62.3 (321)	42.4 (278)	46.9 (213)	40.4 (213)	23.5 (98)
	Low	65.7 (140)	49.3 (221)	25.1 (331)	58.9 (95)	44.6 (130)	31.0 (71)
Social Work	High	— (4)	— (14)	— (35)	33.8 (65)	44.4 (169)	14.3 (91)
	Low	— (9)	— (33)	47.2 (53)	— (33)	27.9 (68)	14.0 (107)
Business	High	52.3 (308)	38.2 (798)	21.6 (1,011)	— (49)	38.7 (93)	44.6 (65)
	Low	44.0 (207)	29.9 (675)	18.1 (952)	— (16)	— (36)	30.0 (70)
Other Health	High	— (17)	85.2 (54)	77.0 (126)	32.8 (61)	37.9 (182)	57.1 (77)
	Low	— (11)	66.7 (66)	60.7 (122)	33.9 (62)	22.9 (153)	34.3 (108)
Biological Sciences	High	— (45)	74.4 (125)	64.0 (172)	53.3 (122)	42.6 (136)	44.6 (65)
	Low	82.1 (56)	64.8 (125)	43.5 (193)	— (44)	49.4 (79)	17.0 (88)
Physical Sciences	High	88.1 (388)	65.9 (343)	36.3 (314)	51.4 (140)	39.8 (93)	— (40)
	Low	81.5 (286)	57.5 (412)	31.2 (497)	60.5 (76)	39.8 (128)	11.9 (59)
Engineering	High	78.1 (384)	49.2 (472)	27.3 (461)	— (1)	— (4)	— (4)
	Low	67.8 (326)	40.3 (596)	27.0 (641)	— (2)	— (9)	— (1)
Other Professions	High	68.6 (169)	71.4 (301)	43.6 (397)	59.6 (104)	32.8 (189)	34.8 (158)
	Low	82.3 (142)	55.6 (365)	53.0 (628)	50.5 (93)	33.1 (145)	12.2 (197)
Education	High	63.4 (131)	43.9 (381)	27.1 (627)	39.8 (763)	29.7 (1,669)	22.4 (1,147)
	Low	45.8 (168)	41.6 (817)	26.9 (1,675)	26.2 (462)	24.3 (1,446)	21.5 (1,598)

N	37,247
NA API Only	526
NA Graduate Field Only	1,954
NA SES Only	1,913
NA Two or More	213
Excluded:	
Not Going to Graduate School	12,383
NA Plans	2,428
Total Weighted N	56,664

cial barrier. The motivational difference by city size is a little more puzzling. Perhaps the explanation is to be found in the kinds of colleges attended by small-town students. Perhaps they knew fewer people who went to graduate school, or perhaps the greater sophistication that seems to characterize the students from large cities explains the difference.

Wishing to remain conservative, we stress that the effects of hometown and SES are much less striking for postgraduate study than they are for the decision to attend college. At the same time, the differences are not negligible, particularly when the two characteristics are treated together. Of the high API men aiming for arts and science careers — the particularly strategic and problematical group who have received special attention throughout — 80 per cent from high SES, larger city origins anticipated immediate graduate study, in contrast with 62 per cent of those from smaller cities and low SES families (Table 3.22a).

Religion

The relationship between religion and plans for advanced study is of considerable interest because of the number of writers and researchers who have claimed that the "Protestant Ethic" or "Jews' high evaluation of learning" affect career and educational choices.

Ordering plans for advanced study by religion yields a distinct zero order difference (Table 3.24). Forty-five per cent of the Jews, 37 per cent of the Catholics, and 26 per cent of the Protestants reported plans for study in the fall of 1961 (RSS). The high rates for Jews are consistent with other research; the higher

Table 3.24. Religious Preference and Plans Index (Representative Sub-sample)

Current Religious Preference	Plans			Total	
	Next Year	Later	Never	Per cent	N
Jewish	45	38	17	100	219
None	44	42	14	100	349
Other	40	44	17	101	126
Catholic	37	39	24	100	787
Protestant	26	48	26	100	1,686

N	3,167
NA on Religion	87
NA on Plans	143
Total N	3,397

rate for Catholics over Protestants does not square as neatly with current stereotypes.[6]

An examination of the relationships between original religion, rather than current religion, and plans and reasons gives similar results (Table 3.25a). Compared with Catholics, Jews showed an 18 per cent advantage in immediate plans, an 11 per cent deficit in low motivation, a 5 per cent deficit in financial obstacles, and a 2 per cent deficit in other external obstacles. Compared with white Protestants, Catholics showed a 6 per cent advantage in "Next Year," most of which came from a 6 per cent deficit in motivation.

Since religion is closely interrelated with API, career choice, SES, and hometown, it is necessary to control all of these variables to tease out any genuine "religious" differences, thus isolating them from differences that appear because of social factors associated with religion. The result is a percentage table with 480 cells, which will not be presented. In order to examine the religious data, it will be more useful to consider a series of difference tables in which religious *differences* in plans and reasons are shown for various sex, API, career, SES, and hometown groups.

Table 3.25b gives the Jewish-Catholic differences for all cells in the master table where there was a weighted total of 50 or more in each religious origin group.[7] Our conclusions are:

a. The Jewish-Catholic difference in plans was not a spurious effect of API, career type, SES, sex, or hometown. In 16 out of 19 possible comparisons, Jews were higher on "Next Year," when the other factors were controlled simultaneously.

b. Both motivation and perceived financial obstacles were related

[6]As noted previously, Andrew Greeley of NORC conducted an extensive analysis of religious differences. His more detailed tabulations supported the general line of conclusions here.

[7]We have used the conservative number of 50 as a minimum cell size for data based on TWS tabulations, because the clustering of the sample and the weighting of cards means that the "true" N's are considerably smaller than the N's in the tables. For RSS data, where there are no duplicated cases, we have set ten as a minimum, although cells with ten cases are not highly reliable.

Table 3.25. Original Religion, Plans for Advanced Study, and Reasons for Not Going on for Advanced Study

a. All Variables

Religion	Plans				Total	
	Next Year	Later or Never			Per cent	N
		Motivational Reasons	Financial Obstacles			
			Yes	No		
Jewish	53	35	7	5	100	4,026
Catholic	35	46	12	7	100	12,514
Protestant	29	52	13	6	100	29,042
Difference						
Jewish—Catholic	+18	−11	−5	−2	0	
Catholic—Protestant	+6	−6	−1	+1	0	
Jewish—Protestant	+24	−17	−6	−1	0	

N 45,582
N A Background and Negro 8,083
N A Plans 2,428
N A Reasons Not Going 571

Total Weighted N 56,664

Table 3.25. *Continued*

b. Difference Table: (Jewish minus Catholic)

Career	API	Male				Female			
		Hometown				Hometown			
		Larger		Smaller		Larger		Smaller	
		SES		SES		SES		SES	
		High	Low	High	Low	High	Low	High	Low
I) Next Year									
Medicine, Law	High	+ 6	+ 1	− 1	*	Insufficient Cases To Tabulate			
	Low	+23	*	*	*				
Arts and Sciences	High	+ 8	+14	*	*	− 8	+37	*	*
	Low	*	+36	*	*	*	*	*	*
Other	High	+ 9	+11	*	*	0	+16	+10	*
	Low	+10	+18	+ 4	*	+12	+12	*	*
II) Motivational Reasons									
Medicine, Law	High	− 1	0	+ 1	*	Insufficient Cases To Tabulate			
	Low	+ 1	*	*	*				
Arts and Sciences	High	− 2	− 8	*	*	+ 7	−28	*	*
	Low	*	−11	*	*	*	*	*	*
Other	High	+ 1	− 5	*	*	− 2	−13	−20	*
	Low	− 3	−10	+ 6	*	−15	− 1	*	*
III) Financial Obstacles									
Medicine, Law	High	0	− 3	+ 3	*	Insufficient Cases To Tabulate			
	Low	− 5	*	*	*				
Arts and Sciences	High	− 2	− 5	*	*	+ 1	−17	*	*
	Low	*	−12	*	*	*	*	*	*
Other	High	− 5	− 7	*	*	+ 4	− 3	+ 9	*
	Low	− 7	− 8	− 1	*	+ 5	− 8	*	*

*Insufficient cases to tabulate.

(Table 3.25 continued)

to the difference—Jews were less likely to be lower in motivation in 13 out of 19 comparisons, less likely to claim financial obstacles in 13 out of 19 comparisons. Neither type of reason was entirely consistent and both appeared about as strong, so the difference cannot be attributed either to motivation or finances alone.

c. The same conclusions applied with even greater consistency when Jews were compared with Protestants (Table 3.25d). Here Jews were higher on "Next Year" in 18 out of a possible 19 comparisons, lower on low motivation in 14, and lower on financial obstacles in 13.

However, when the Protestant-Catholic difference was analyzed (Table 3.25c), it thinned out. Of 36 possible comparisons, there was a Catholic advantage in "Next Year" for 25 compari-

Table 3.25. *Continued*

c. Difference Table: (Catholic minus Protestant)

Career	API	Male				Female			
		Larger		Smaller		Larger		Smaller	
		SES		SES		SES		SES	
		High	Low	High	Low	High	Low	High	Low
I) Next Year									
Medicine, Law	High	0	+ 1	+ 5	−17	Insufficient Cases To Tabulate			
	Low	−13	*	+ 9	+15				
Arts and Sciences	High	− 3	+ 4	− 3	+ 5	+ 3	− 7	+17	+17
	Low	− 4	0	+15	+13	− 1	*	*	*
Other	High	+ 3	−10	+ 1	+ 6	+14	+ 2	+ 1	+ 7
	Low	+ 5	− 7	+ 2	+ 1	+ 8	+ 6	+ 7	+ 9
II) Motivational Reasons									
Medicine, Law	High	− 1	+ 1	− 3	+ 6	Insufficient Cases To Tabulate			
	Low	− 2	*	+ 2	+ 3				
Arts and Sciences	High	+ 5	+ 1	− 9	+ 2	− 4	− 1	− 4	−11
	Low	−13	+10	− 7	− 7	− 4	*	*	*
Other	High	− 7	+ 9	− 4	− 5	−15	− 5	+ 4	+ 4
	Low	− 9	+ 4	− 5	− 5	−12	−14	− 2	− 3
III) Financial Obstacles									
Medicine, Law	High	+ 1	− 3	+ 1	+10	Insufficient Cases To Tabulate			
	Low	+ 4	*	− 6	− 7				
Arts and Sciences	High	− 2	− 2	+ 5	− 6	0	+14	−12	− 6
	Low	+13	−19	−16	+ 3	+ 3	*	*	*
Other	High	+ 1	+ 1	+ 3	− 2	0	+ 3	− 5	−10
	Low	+ 1	0	− 2	+ 4	+ 4	+ 8	− 2	− 9

sons, a Protestant advantage for nine comparisons, and no difference in two comparisons. There was a possible relationship with sex, for the Catholic-Protestant difference obtained in 11 out of 13 comparisons for women, but in only 14 out of 23 comparisons among men.

The methodology of evaluating complex percentage tables is not well developed — partly, of course, because so few chances arise to work with tables with sufficient cases in several hundred cells — and it is hard to draw conclusions on narrowly statistical grounds. It is unrealistic to require that a difference obtain in every single comparison in such tables, for as the number of comparisons increases, the *size of difference* is subject to random fluctuation, and sometimes there is no observable difference, just

Table 3.25. *Continued*

d. Difference Table: (Jewish minus Protestant)

Career	API	Sex							
		Male				Female			
		Hometown				Hometown			
		Larger		Smaller		Larger		Smaller	
		SES		SES		SES		SES	
		High	Low	High	Low	High	Low	High	Low
		I) Next Year							
Medicine, Law	High	+ 6	+ 2	+ 4	*	Insufficient Cases To Tabulate			
	Low	+10	*	*	*				
Arts and Sciences	High	+ 5	+18	*	*	− 5	+30	*	*
	Low	*	+36	*	*	*	*	*	*
Other	High	+12	+ 1	*	*	+14	+18	+11	*
	Low	+15	+11	+ 5	*	+20	+18	*	*
		II) Motivational Reasons							
Medicine, Law	High	− 2	+ 1	− 2	*	Insufficient Cases To Tabulate			
	Low	− 1	*	*	*				
Arts and Sciences	High	+ 3	− 7	*	*	+ 3	−29	*	*
	Low	*	− 1	*	*	*	*	*	*
Other	High	− 6	+ 4	*	*	−17	−18	−16	*
	Low	−12	− 6	+ 1	*	−27	−15	*	*
		III) Financial Obstacles							
Medicine, Law	High	+ 1	− 6	+ 4	*	Insufficient Cases To Tabulate			
	Low	− 1	*	*	*				
Arts and Sciences	High	− 4	− 7	*	*	+ 1	− 3	*	*
	Low	*	− 3	*	*	*	*	*	*
Other	High	− 4	− 6	*	*	− 4	0	+ 4	*
	Low	− 6	− 8	−3	*	+ 9	− 2	*	*

as an occasional Republican is sampled in deep South precincts. In addition, the case bases vary considerably.

The technique of "weighted net percentage differences"[8] has been used to avoid some of these problems. The results are as follows:

[8] In order to arrive at an over-all figure, one may average all the percentage differences in the table. However, because of item frequencies and intercorrelations, the various percentage differences will be based on different numbers of cases. In order to give more weight to differences that are characteristic of larger groups of students and to avoid giving undue weight to unreliable differences based on small numbers, the percentage differences were weighted by the case base involved and no percentage was included where either of the two groups was based on less than 50 cases (TWS). The procedure was as follows: a) Each difference was multiplied by the total number of cases in the two comparison cells, b) the resultant figures were summed algebraically (i.e., positive differences were added, negative ones subtracted), and c) the total was divided by the total number of cases in the comparisons. We will term the resultant figure the weighted net percentage difference.

a. Jewish minus Catholic Percentage Difference			
	Next Year	Motivational	Financial Obstacles
Zero Order	18	−11	−5
Net Weighted	10	− 5	−6
b. Catholic minus Protestant			
Zero Order	6	− 6	−1
Net Weighted	3	− 3	−1

Although both differences in "Next Year" were reduced when other factors were controlled, implying that roughly half of the religious differences in "Next Year" stemmed from religious differences in career, sex, API, SES, and hometown, the Jewish-Catholic difference was still 10 per cent while the Catholic-Protestant difference was 3 per cent.

Courses in statistics accustom us to thinking of differences in "either-or" terms. In this situation, however, the variation was one of degree. The Jewish advantage in "Plans" was a relatively strong one, turning up in most of the comparisons and producing a net weighted difference of 10. The Catholic-Protestant difference cannot be said to be spurious, for it did appear in a majority of the comparisons and produced a net weighted difference of three. The Catholic-Protestant difference, however, was so small it cannot be considered a major factor.

SUMMARY:

a. Both for the total sample and in comparison with Protestant and Catholic whites matched in career type, sex, SES, hometown, and API, the Jewish students are more likely to plan immediate advanced study and less likely to cite motivational or financial reasons for not going on. A considerable proportion of their zero order difference, however, stems from the fact that Jews are high on API, high on SES, from larger cities, and overchoose occupations with high rates of intention for immediate graduate study.

b. For the total sample, Catholics are more likely to plan immediate advanced study than Protestants, but when other predictors are controlled, the difference diminishes considerably. If anything, Catholics have "greater aspirations" than Protestants, but the difference is slight.

In different ways and to different degrees students who differed in sex, academic performance, SES, race, hometown, and religion varied in their plans for postgraduate study, even though they may have intended to enter careers in which it is equally advantageous to pursue postgraduate work. Having considered how each of these factors made an independent contribution to plans and reasons for going on to graduate school, we can now analyze their simultaneous effect.

It is simplest to summarize with weighted net percentages. Listed below are the results for differences in the per cent of students who planned to begin study the next year.

	Weighted Net Percentage Difference in "Next Year"		
Item	Comparison	Zero Order	Weighted Net
API	High minus low	+20	+18
Sex	Male minus female	+15	+14
Race	Negro minus low SES, smaller city, Protestant whites	− 3	+11
Religion	Jewish minus Catholic	+18	+10
Hometown	Larger minus smaller	+11	+ 6
Religion	Catholic minus Protestant	+ 6	+ 3
SES	High minus low	+ 7	+ 2

Sex and API made the strongest differences, considerably outweighing the effects of the social characteristics. Race, hometown, and the fact of being Jewish were the stronger of the social factors, while SES and Catholic-Protestant differences had lesser net effects. Interestingly enough, the race difference reverses in the net figures. Although in general Negroes were less likely to expect to go on immediately, rates for them were considerably higher than for the low-attending Protestant, low SES, small-town whites — social characteristics of Negroes apparently provided a considerable impediment to their plans.

Turning now to motivation, we shall consider differences in the percentages of those who said they were never going on or were going on later and those who circled "Want to get practical experience first" or one of the low interest items:

	Weighted Net Percentage Differences in Motivation		
Item	Comparison	Zero Order	Weighted Net
Race	Negro minus Protestant, low SES, smaller-city whites	−18	−26
Sex	Male minus female	−24	−22
API	High minus low	−11	−10
Religion	Jewish minus Catholic	−11	− 5
Religion	Catholic minus Protestant	− 6	− 3
SES	High minus low	+ 1	+ 3
Hometown	Larger minus smaller	− 6	− 2

The race difference — the strongest in the set — and those of sex and API were the only three factors whose net differences amounted to 10 per cent or more. The fact that Negroes especially, and Jews, Catholics, and low SES students to some extent were higher on motivation suggests one of the problems of recruitment to graduate study. By and large, the strongest motivation is among the upwardly mobile and the minority group members who perhaps see in the certification of advanced study routes to success and protection against discrimination. Yet, at the same time, the minority student is often less able to implement his desires because of such handicaps as lower academic performance or lower SES. Jews and Negroes provide an interesting contrast from this point of view. Both have very high motivation for graduate school, but the Jews are able to implement their motivations with very high rates of anticipated immediate study because they also have high API, high SES, and urban backgrounds on their side. The Negro student, whose motivation is, if anything, even higher than the Jew's, has all these same factors working against him and his zero order rates are lower than for whites.

Below is a breakdown of those whose plans were for "Later" or "Never" and who did not mention any of the motivational items but circled "Financial Obstacles":

Weighted Net Percentage Differences in Financial Obstacles

Item	Comparison	Zero Order	Weighted Net
Race	Negro minus white, Protestant, low SES, smaller city	+22	+15
SES	High minus low	− 9	− 6
Religion	Jewish minus Catholic	− 5	− 6
Sex	Male minus female	− 9	− 3
Hometown	Larger minus smaller	− 5	− 2
API	High minus low	− 4	− 1
Religion	Catholic minus Protestant	− 1	− 1

Except for the race difference of 15, all the weighted net differences were small, even SES making only a 6 per cent difference. With the advantage of hindsight, however, these results appear reasonable. After all, for a single young person it would be unusual if existing financial burdens really prohibited advanced study. At the worst, one could borrow money and, except in law and medicine, the majority of graduate students in the United States work their way through. Thus, the financial obstacles to undertaking graduate study are not like financial obstacles to owning a Rolls Royce, but rather are financial and motivational reasons combined; the students who claimed financial obstacles really "meant" to say, "The financial costs are not actually prohibitive, but they are so high that graduate study is not worth that much to me right now." Thus, the fact that Jews reported fewer financial obstacles than Catholics when matched on SES and city size suggests, not that they had mysterious sources of money, but that they considered graduate study a greater bargain than did the Catholics.

We have not been able to include the small group of high API men with children in these tabulations, but had this been possible, our *guess* is that it would have turned out that these young men faced genuine and difficult financial obstacles. For the remainder of students, however, our guess is that *purely* financial problems were rare and that it is more realistic to think of plans as a function of the ratio between motivation and financial resources rather than a function of one or the other.

Reviewing the same figures from a different perspective, we can see the differential effects of each variable:

Weighted Net Differences by Characteristics
(Difference for Other External Obstacles Estimated by Subtraction)

1. API (High minus low)

Next Year	+18
Motivational	−10
Other External	− 7
Financial	− 1

2. Sex (Male minus female)

Next Year	+15
Motivational	−22
Other External	+ 4
Financial	+ 3

3. Race (Negro minus white, Protestant,
   low SES, smaller city)

Next Year	+11
Motivational	−26
Financial	+15
Other External	0

4. Religion (Jewish minus Catholic)

Next Year	+10
Financial	− 6
Motivational	− 5
Other External	+ 1

5. Hometown (Larger minus smaller)

Next Year	+ 6
Financial	− 2
Motivational	− 2
Other External	− 2

6. Religion (Catholic minus Protestant)

Next Year	+ 3
Motivational	− 3
Financial	− 1
Other External	+ 1

7. SES (High minus low)

Next Year	+ 2
Financial	− 6
Motivational	+ 3
Other External	− 1

Actually, no calcu'ations were made of the net effects for "Other External Obstacles," but since net weighted differences must sum to zero, they can be estimated by subtraction. Having done this, we can draw the following conclusions about our items, beginning with the one producing the most difference and moving on to the less powerful ones:

1. API showed its effects mostly on motivation and external obstacles (perceived low grades?); the API difference in financial obstacles was very small, despite sharp API differences in stipend awards.

2. The sex difference was primarily motivational, although men did see greater financial and external (military?) obstacles than did women.

3. The race difference, as we have seen, was associated both with greater motivation and with greater financial obstacles for Negroes.

4. Religion and hometown effects came equally from small motivational and small financial obstacle differences.

5. The slight SES difference is a diluted form of the race difference, the low-status students being higher in motivation, but also more likely to report financial obstacles. Previous evidence suggests that this was more true of women than of men.

A different, but perhaps equally useful, way of reviewing the combined effects of these factors is by means of prediction tables in which percentages with various plans and reasons are tabulated for particular subgroups. We shall examine tables for law and medicine and for arts and sciences.

Table 3.26 is the prediction table for law and medicine. Because their differences were small, hometown and SES were combined into a summary index. The "Highs" are high SES students from larger cities, the "Lows" are low SES students from smaller cities, and the larger-city, low SES and smaller-city, high-SES groups were combined and made the intermediate group on the Index. As the Protestant-Catholic differences were slight and inconsistent among men, the religious comparison was limited to Jews and Christians. Women were grouped by API only.

Among those entering the major professions, plans for going on the next year were high regardless of the subgroup, but personal characteristics produced definite differences. At the extremes, 96 per cent of the high API, high SES, larger-city Jewish men anticipated immediate study, while 75 per cent of the low SES, smaller-city, high API Protestants and Catholics and 52 per cent

Table 3.26. Plans for Advanced Study and Reasons for not Going On for Advanced Study Among Students Naming Law and Medicine as Future Career

a. Per cent Next Year

API	SES	Hometown	Men			All Women
			Negro	White Protestant–Catholic	White Jewish	
High	High	Larger		90 (676)	96 (362)	70 (167)
		Smaller		90 (642)	93 (142)	
	Low	Other	— (32)	75 (244)	– (4)	
Low	High	Larger		68 (227)	87 (89)	42 (55)
		Smaller		72 (311)	– (31)	
	Low	Other	— (23)	52 (153)	– (4)	

b. Per cent Motivational Reasons

API	SES	Hometown	Men			All Women
			Negro	White Protestant–Catholic	White Jewish	
High	High	Larger		4 (676)	2 (362)	11 (167)
		Smaller		3 (642)	3 (142)	
	Low	Other	— (32)	4 (244)	– (4)	
Low	High	Larger		4 (227)	4 (89)	38 (55)
		Smaller		7 (311)	– (31)	
	Low	Other	— (23)	5 (153)	– (4)	

c. Per cent Financial Reasons

API	SES	Hometown	Men			All Women
			Negro	White Protestant—Catholic	Jewish	
High	High	Larger		0 (676)	1 (362)	16 (167)
		Other		2 (642)	2 (142)	
		Smaller	— (32)	16 (244)	— (4)	
Low	Low	Larger		6 (227)	2 (89)	7 (55)
		Other		9 (311)	— (31)	
		Smaller	— (23)	24 (153)	— (4)	

	N
N	3,162
Excluded Arts and Sciences and Other	39,014
NA Career Field	2,860
NA API	595
NA Background	7,138
NA One or More	896
NA Plans	2,428
NA Reasons Not Going	571
Total Weighted N	56,664

of the low API, low SES, smaller-city Protestants and Catholics did so. As was expected, the percentages for motivation were very small, and there were no important trends. Big differences showed up in financial obstacles, which are associated with API and the city-SES index. Less than 1 per cent of the high API, high SES, big-city men students gave this explanation, in contrast with 16 per cent of the high API, low SES, small-city Christians, and 24 per cent of the low API, low SES, small-city Christians.

Because recruits to law and medicine were concentrated in the groups whose rates for planning to study the next year were high, there was very little postponement. However, of the minority of better students recruited from low SES, smaller-city families, one-quarter were not going on immediately and 16 per cent cited financial obstacles, not motivation, as their reason.

The small number of women aspiring to studies in law and medicine, within an API grouping, showed lower rates for "Next Year" than *any* kind of man and higher rates for motivation; roughly the same per cent cited financial obstacles. Even in these fields characterized by high motivation for advanced study, the women showed less interest in going on immediately.

Table 3.27 predicts plans and reasons for students anticipating careers in the arts and sciences. The results generally substantiated for the arts and sciences the patterns discussed above.

a. Those going on the next year ranged from 84 per cent of the high API, Jewish men from larger cities and higher SES families to 19 per cent of the low API, Christian, low SES, smaller-hometown women.

b. Among Christian men, the SES-city index produced a range in "Next Year" from 61 to 78 per cent for high API and 25 to 50 for low API; among women and Jews of either sex, this variable made little difference. If anything, low SES, big-city Jews had higher rates for "Next Year" than did high SES Jews.

c. The sex difference was quite strong. Even of the high API women in the highest category of SES-hometown, only about one-half planned to go on immediately.

d. The only group with sufficient cases of Negroes to tabulate, showed the expected difference. Forty per cent of the low API, Negro men were

TABLE 3.27. Plans for Advanced Study and Reasons for Not Going On for Advanced Study Among Students Naming an Arts and Science Field as a Future Career

a. Per cent Next Year

API	SES	Hometown	Female Protestant and Catholic	Female Jewish	Female Negro	Male Protestant and Catholic	Male Jewish	Male Negro
High	High	Larger	49 (873)	42 (143)	→	78 (744)	84 (222)	→
		Other	38 (832)	59 (106)		72 (1,137)	85 (131)	
	Low	Smaller	50 (339)	– (6)	– (48)	61 (663)	– (10)	– (47)
Low	High	Larger	20 (213)	– (27)	→	50 (297)	– (48)	→
		Other	18 (219)	– (29)		38 (626)	70 (57)	
	Low	Smaller	19 (135)	– (3)	– (35)	25 (606)	– (2)	40 (83)

b. Per cent Motivational Reasons

API	SES	Hometown	Female Protestant and Catholic	Female Jewish	Female Negro	Male Protestant and Catholic	Male Jewish	Male Negro
High	High	Larger	41 (873)	46 (143)	→	12 (744)	13 (222)	→
		Other	49 (832)	27 (136)		15 (1,137)	9 (131)	
	Low	Smaller	39 (339)	– (6)	– (48)	18 (663)	– (10)	– (47)
Low	High	Larger	63 (213)	– (27)	→	28 (297)	– (48)	→
		Other	62 (219)	– (29)		32 (626)	23 (57)	
	Low	Smaller	61 (135)	– (3)	– (35)	34 (606)	– (2)	7 (83)

(Table 3.27 continued)

Table 3.27. Continued

c. Per cent Financial Reasons

API	SES	Hometown	Female			Male		
			Protestant and Catholic	Jewish	Negro	Protestant and Catholic	Jewish	Negro
High	High	Larger	9 (873)	10 (143)	→	4 (744)	1 (222)	→
		Other	12 (832)	7 (106)		7 (1,137)	2 (131)	
	Low	Smaller	11 (339)	— (6)	— (48)	17 (663)	— (10)	— (47)
Low	High	Larger	11 (213)	— (27)	→	9 (297)	— (48)	→
		Other	13 (219)	— (29)		20 (626)	2 (57)	
	Low	Smaller	12 (135)	— (3)	— (35)	31 (606)	— (2)	34 (83)

N	7,681
Excluded: Law and Medicine and Other	34,597
NA Career Field	2,860
NA API	595
NA Background	7,036
NA One or More	896
NA Plans	2,428
NA Reasons Not Going	571
Total Weighted N	56,664

going on immediately in comparison with 25 per cent of the low API, low SES, smaller-city, Christian, white males.

e. Among men, low API and low scores on the SES-city index were associated with lessened motivation. Twelve per cent of the high API, high SES, larger-city men reported motivational reasons as compared to 34 per cent of the low API, low SES, amaller-city men. (These comparisons were based on Christians, since there were too few small-town Jews for tabulations.)

f. Christians were more likely than Jews to be low in motivation.

g. Among women, motivation was associated with API but not with SES, city, or religion; low motivation was frequent. This reason was given by over one-third of the high API girls and by over 60 per cent of the low API women.

h. Financial obstacles among men were associated mostly with the SES-city index, with a range of from 4 to 17 per cent for high API Christians, to 9 to 31 per cent for low API Christians.

i. Jews cited financial obstacles less often than Christians.

j. About 10 to 12 per cent of each category of women cited financial reasons, thus creating no clear-cut associations.

k. Among high API men, financial obstacles were rare, being cited by less than 10 per cent of each group except among the low SES Christians from smaller cities. However, 17 per cent of that group fell into this classification.

Low API students and women had low rates for "Next Year." Yet it is debatable whether the national interest would be served by pumping into immediate graduate study students from the reservoir of the bottom half of the national graduating class or whether the delay or abandonment of the graduate plans of women is scandalous in any society that looks upon the family as a major social institution. That leaves high API men as the group for which there may be justifiable concern.

Let us examine this group in isolation, beginning with a repercentaging of data from Table 3.27. Negroes are arbitrarily assigned to the low SES, smaller-city category, as usual. (See next page.)

Chart 3.4 distributes these cases in graph form into three groups: I) "Next Year," II) "Motivational," III) "External Obstacles," as defined by our Plans-Reasons Index.

The resulting graph, resembling an archery bow, is essentially

		Percentage Distribution of High API Men			
SES	Hometown	Whites		Negroes	Total Per cent
		Christians	Jews		
High Larger		25	8	0	33
Other		38	4	0	42
Low Smaller		22	0	2	24
Total Per cent		85	12	2	99

N = 2,954

a line running from 100 per cent "Next Year" toward 100 per cent "External Obstacles," although in the center it is pulled a little toward the "Motivational" pole. *Among high API males, therefore, most of the social differences are associated with perceived obstacles, not with differences in motivation for advanced study.*

Moving along the SES-city scale of Christian whites, we see a 17 per cent variation in plans for immediate study. Most of this comes from perceived external obstacles which vary from 10 per cent in the top group to 21 per cent in the bottom. Motivation does decrease a little with the index, the per cent with low motivational reasons rising from 12 to 18.

The figures for the two Jewish groups are pulled well toward "Next Year" in comparison with Christians matched in SES-city, with the result that the group with the highest rates of all were Jews from the *middle* of the SES-city index; their rates for "Next Year" were 1 per cent higher than the high SES Jews. Although this apparently stems from fewer external obstacles for Jews, we think it should really be attributed to motivation. At the opposite pole, the rates for Negroes are depressed and their rates for external obstacles are raised when compared with low SES, smaller-city Christians.

We draw three general conclusions about plans for advanced study in arts and sciences.

1. The fact that almost 85 per cent of the high API Jews plan immediate study, regardless of SES (variations on the SES-city index

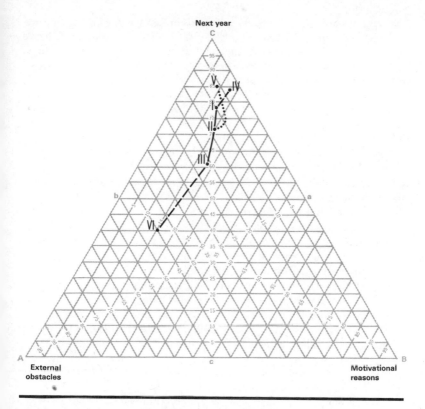

(Data on Negroes Added)

Group	SES	Hometown	Religion	Race	N
I	High	Larger	Protestant, Catholic	White	744
II		Other	Protestant, Catholic	White	1,137
III	Low	Smaller	Protestant, Catholic	White	663
IV	High	Larger	Jewish	White	222
V		Other	Jewish	White	131
VI			—	Negro	47

Excluded: Low SES, smaller
hometown Jewish   10
Total High A.P.I. Males   2,954

Chart 3.4. Table 3.27 in Graphed Form (High API Men Only)

among Jews are almost entirely variations in SES), sets a kind of "norm" that can serve in evaluating other groups, for we can interpret this figure as the rate for immediate advanced study to be expected of a qualified highly-motivated group, living where schools are available. The remaining 15 per cent is probably pretty much irreducible.

2. Among the 87 per cent of the high API males who are not Jewish, rates for immediate study vary from 40 to 78 per cent; all are well below the Jewish rates. This suggests that there is considerable room for improvement in the recruitment to graduate school of high performers from social groups whose motivation and location work against them. In particular, the 61 per cent attendance expectations of the low SES, smaller-city students (who constitute 22 per cent of the high API arts and science men) are disturbing.

3. The fact that the greater part of the variation is in "External Obstacles," not in "Motivation" needs stress — and a little reinterpretation. The low rates for motivational reasons are important, in that they indicate that the great bulk of these students accepted the desirability of advanced study; the problem is not one of "selling" graduate school to them. At the same time, there could well be a motivational component to the "External Obstacles" group. If it were somehow possible to "sell" even harder the advantages of graduate school, many could undoubtedly triumph over the obstacles. There would undoubtedly remain a hard core of genuine financial problems among young fathers, students who are living where there is no graduate school, and students who have incurred debts during college. Financial aid programs could perhaps be developed and expanded to meet their needs.

Our personal belief — one that goes beyond the data — is that students are not well informed on the "facts of life" regarding graduate school, the economic costs of postponement, the availability of stipends, and the availability of schools. If a systematic attempt were made to counsel, during their junior year in college, all high API men with arts and science majors or career preferences, considerable improvement in these rates might result. America's colleges and universities are continually blamed for not taking on this task or that, but the writer's feeling is that if counseling for postgraduate study were as effective as high school counseling for college attendance — an imperative in the light of the facts that the bright college senior is more likely to go to graduate school than is the bright high school senior to go to college and that the now likely postponement of the beginning of his studies appears to constitute a social problem — conspicuous improvement could be made on the now shaky bridge that connects college and graduate school.

4

The Future Graduate Student

In Chapter 3 plans for graduate study were analyzed considering only very broad groupings of career fields. Thus, the treatment of the Plans Index ignored differences between chemists and historians, as well as differences between chemists and physicists. Such a crude classification was justified by the fact that, compared with other fields, all the fields within the broad groups have quite similar distributions on the Plans Index.

In this final chapter we will move in for a finer focus on specific fields of study. Because of the high rates of anticipated graduate work and the strong association between graduate field and career field, a number of the results may be anticipated immediately. It would be amazing to find much difference between the students planning to *study* medicine and the previous findings on students planning *careers* in medicine. For other fields, however, the situation is not so obvious. While education is a woman's field, men are much more likely to anticipate graduate study. And so are the graduate students[1] in education predominantly men or predominantly women? In addition we shall be able to examine a finer breakdown of fields — the arts and science grouping are classified into 23 fields rather than four divisions, and nursing, social work, and health professions other than medicine or nursing are broken out from the group previously called "Other Professions."

[1] For literary convenience we shall speak of all students falling into "Next Year" or "Later" on the Plans Index as graduate students, although a number will undoubtedly fall by the wayside.

141

A price will be paid for this additional detail, for the numerous small groupings make complex statistical controls cumbersome, and it will be impossible in most instances to report "partial" relationships. However, the gain in detail may offset the loss in understanding of complex causal relationships.

The classification of fields used in this chapter, along with the weighted total cases, is shown in Table 4.1.

Students who anticipated advanced study in these 33 fields will be compared on a number of items. Three general groups of characteristics will be reported—personal characteristics, academic plans, and career plans.

PERSONAL CHARACTERISTICS

We shall compare graduate students by the following measures: API, sex, SES, hometown, religion, and occupational values ("People," "Original," "Money"), as well as by self-ratings of conventionality and political ideology.

The questionnaire asked each student to place himself on a continuum stretching from "Conventional in opinions and values" to "Unconventional in opinions and values." While we do not claim that this crude measure approximates the more precise instruments used in personality research, we included the question because of the large number of personality studies on "authoritarianism," "creativity," "open-mindedness," and so on that suggest that there are important differences between people who are conventional and unconventional in their opinions and values.

No validity data are available on this item, but some of its flavor may be inferred from its association with items in the self-rating adjective check-list questions. The following self-descriptions were associated with this question at a Q value of .15 or more (RSS). The 45 per cent of students who defined themselves as *less* conventional ("Fairly Unconventional," "Very Unconventional," "Neither") were more likely to describe themselves as rebellious, intellectual, impetuous, dominant, lazy, sophisticated, high-strung, moody, forceful, idealistic, talkative, witty, and cultured. The 55 per cent of students who defined themselves as very or fairly conventional were more likely to describe themselves as cooperative, happy, and reserved.

ıble 4.1. Classification of Graduate Fields (Among Students Who are ᴎext Year" or "Later" on Plans)

Group	Field	N
	Education	11,691
	Business	4,561
	(Accounting, Advertising, Public Relations, Secretarial Science, Industrial or Personnel Psychology, All Other Business and Commercial Fields)	
	Engineering	3,060
	Law	2,456
	Medicine	1,440
Professional	Social Work, Group Work	724
	Other Health	669
	(Dentistry, Optometry, Pharmacy, Physical Therapy, Veterinary Medicine, Medical Technology, Dental Hygiene, Other Health Fields)	
	Nursing	438
	Other	3,038
	(Military Science, Public Administration, Agriculture, Forestry, Fish and Wild Life, Architecture, City Planning, Home Economics, Journalism, Library Science, Theology, Religion, Other Professions)	
	Mathematics and Statistics	902
	Chemistry	864
	Physics	727
Physical Sciences	Earth Sciences	272
	(Geology, Geography, Geophysics)	
	Other	158
	(Astronomy, Astrophysics, Oceanography, Metallurgy, Meteorology, Physical Science, General and Other)	
	Biology	363
	Biochemistry	188
	Zoology	158
Biological Sciences	Microbiology	132
	Botany	106
	Physiology	98
	Other	290
	(Anatomy, Biophysics, Entomology, Genetics, Pathology, Pharmacology, Other)	
	Political Science, International Relations	690
	Economics	470
	Sociology	379
	Clinical Psychology	375
Social Sciences	Other Psychology	285
	(Social Psychology, Experimental and General, Other)	
	Other	288
	(Anthropology, Archeology, Area and Regional Studies, Social Science, General and Other)	
	Fine and Applied Arts	1,429
	(Art, Music, Speech, Drama, etc.)	
Humanities	English, Creative Writing	1,201
	History	1,142
	Classical and Modern Languages	726
	Philosophy	205
	General and Other	201

N	39,726
NA, Graduate Field	2,127
Excluded from this Table:	
Not Going to Graduate School	12,383
NA, Plans	2,428
Total Weighted N	56,664

The question on political ideology divided the students into those claiming to be fairly or very "Politically Liberal" and those claiming to be fairly or very "Politically Conservative" or "Neither." The question was included, not because of its association with any known research, but because of its intrinsic interest, indicating as it did the social perspectives of young people oriented toward different fields.

API / JD SEX

How did the future graduate students of varying degrees of academic ability distribute themselves among the different fields of study? The measure used in this research, the Academic Performance Index, is fairly crude, being simply the student's reported cumulative grade point average weighted by the quality of his institution. Yet API has demonstrated that it is predictive of certain career choices and highly predictive of plans for postgraduate study.

Table 4.2 gives the distribution by anticipated graduate field. There was considerable variation; for example, 44 per cent of those in English were in the top fifth of their classes as contrasted with 7 per cent of those in the health professions other than medicine and nursing.

Table 4.2b gives the distribution of top fifth API, grouping the fields according to division. Although the arts and science fields, generally speaking, surpassed the professional fields, the variation within divisions was considerable. In each column in Table 4.2b there were one or more fields that surpassed future graduate students as a whole and one or more fields that fell below graduating seniors as a group.

Within the professional fields, medicine, as expected, had the top position. Forty-two per cent of those choosing it were in the top fifth and it was the only professional field whose students surpassed the general level of future graduate students. Nursing, engineering, and law came next, being above seniors in general but below the total group of graduate students. At the other extreme, graduate students in health, business, education, social work, and other professions were less likely to come from the top fifth than were graduating seniors in general.

Within the science fields, too, there was considerable variation. Physicists, mathematicians, other physical scientists, and biochemists surpassed graduate students in general, physicists being particularly high; chemists, microbiologists, zoologists, physiologists, and other biological scientists surpassed the senior class in general, but fell below graduate students in general; and botanists, general biologists, and earth scientists fell into the bottom group.

In the social sciences and humanities, English, philosophy, languages, and political science students fell into the top group. Clinical psychology, other psychology, history, other social sciences, economics, and art fell in the middle group; other hu-

Table 4.2. Graduate Field by Academic Performance Index

a. Ranked by Per cent in the Top Fifth on API

Graduate Field	Academic Performance Index			Total	
	Top Fifth	Above Average	Bottom Half	Per cent	N
English	43.9	37.1	19.0	100.0	1,185
Physics	42.3	28.6	29.1	100.0	719
Medicine	42.1	42.4	15.5	100.0	1,422
Philosophy	40.7	40.7	18.6	100.0	204
Language	40.2	40.8	19.1	100.1	719
Political Science	36.9	41.3	21.8	100.0	680
Other Physical Sciences	34.2	45.0	20.8	100.0	149
Mathematics	33.2	35.3	31.5	100.0	895
Biochemistry	32.1	41.7	26.2	100.0	187
Clinical Psychology	29.9	31.5	38.5	99.9	371
History	28.8	35.9	35.3	100.0	1,134
Other Psychology	28.1	35.6	36.3	100.0	281
Nursing	27.6	47.7	24.8	100.1	428
Other Social Sciences	27.4	44.2	28.4	100.0	285
Economics	27.4	36.6	36.0	100.0	464
Microbiology	26.9	27.7	45.4	100.0	130
Chemistry	25.9	37.3	36.8	100.0	857
Fine Arts	25.3	39.9	34.8	100.0	1,398
Engineering	24.6	37.3	38.1	100.0	3,023
Zoology	24.4	36.5	39.1	100.0	156
Law	23.5	36.0	40.5	100.0	2,430
Other Biological Sciences	20.2	33.3	46.5	100.0	282
Physiology	19.6	29.3	51.1	100.0	92
Other Professions	17.8	34.4	47.9	100.1	2,990
Geology-Geography (Earth)	17.5	44.4	38.1	100.0	268
Botany	17.0	31.0	52.0	100.1	100
Social Work	16.9	41.2	42.0	100.1	712
Sociology	16.6	35.7	47.7	100.0	373
Other Humanities	15.5	52.5	32.0	100.0	194
Biology	14.0	44.7	41.3	100.1	358
Education	13.6	39.9	46.5	100.0	11,523
Business	13.2	37.2	49.6	100.0	4,503
Other Health	6.6	40.2	53.3	100.1	655

N	39,167
NA API Only	559
NA Graduate Field Only	2,087
NA Both	40
Excluded from Table:	
Not Going to Graduate School	12,383
NA Plans Index	2,428
Total Weighted N	56,664

(Table 4.2 continued)

Table 4.2. Continued

b. Grouped by Division

Per cent Top Fifth on API	Professions	Physical Science	Biological Science	Social Science	Humanities
50 –					
48 –					
46 –					
44 –					English
42 –	Medicine	Physics			Philosophy
40 –					Languages
38 –				Political Science	
36 –			Biochemistry		
34 –		Other			History
32 –		Math			
30 –	Nursing			Clinical Psychology	Art
28 –	Engineering	Chemistry	Microbiology	Psychology, Other	
26 –	Law		Zoology	Other, Economics	
24 –					
22 –					
20 –			Other, Physiology		
18 –	Other	Earth			
16 –	Social Work		Botany	Sociology	
14 –	Education		Biology		
12 –	Business				Other
10 –					
8 –					
6 –	Health				
4 –					
2 –					
0 –					

→ All Future Graduate Students

→ All Seniors

Division

manities and sociology had a smaller proportion of high API students than college seniors in general.

By the use of the proportion of top fifth students as the Index of Academic Performance, we may have slighted any field that attracts a disproportionate number of "Above Average" students but has relatively few from the very top or the bottom half. However, when the fields are ranked in terms of the per cent from top fifth *or* above average, the ordering of fields remains quite similar (Chart 4.1).

We have shown that lower API levels were associated with postponement of graduate study, the superior academic performers tending to be going on the next year rather than later. Therefore, it is worthwhile to see whether the ranking of fields holds when plans are held constant. If it is assumed that only a small proportion of the "Laters" will actually enter graduate

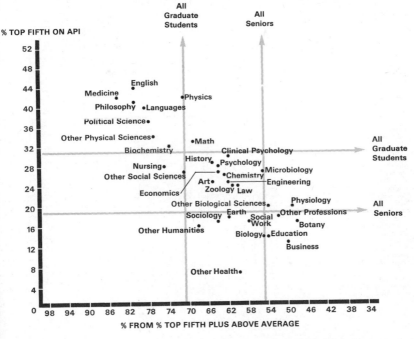

Chart 4.1. Per cent Top Fifth by Per cent Top Fifth Plus Above Average

school (an assumption previously suggested to be unwarranted), fields with high rates of postponement may have been treated unjustly in Table 4.2, their API levels being "dragged down" by less able students who may not actually go on with advanced study (Table 4.3).

When the per cent from the top fifth among the "Next Year" students was plotted against the per cent among the "Laters," a strong correlation appeared (Chart 4.2). That is, the fields that were characterized by high API levels among the students going on immediately also tended to have high API levels among

Table 4.3. Graduate Field and API, Controlling for Plans Index
(Distribution of API within Plans Groups, for Each Graduate Field)

Graduate Field	Total Per cent in Top Fifth on API	Plans								Total N
		Next Year				Later				
		Top Fifth	Above Average	Bottom Half	N	Top Fifth	Above Average	Bottom Half	N	
English	43.9	56.9	29.8	13.2	536	33.1	43.1	23.7	649	1,185
Physics	42.3	55.7	29.6	14.7	463	18.0	27.0	55.1	256	719
Medicine	42.1	46.0	42.6	11.4	1 251	12.9	40.9	46.2	171	1,422
Philosophy	40.7	61.1	24.6	14.3	126	7.7	66.7	25.6	78	204
Language	40.2	48.7	38.2	13.1	413	28.8	44.1	27.1	306	719
Political Science	36.9	44.0	42.5	13.5	341	29.8	40.1	30.1	339	680
Other Physical Sciences	34.2	45.6	45.6	8.7	92	15.8	43.8	40.4	57	149
Mathematics	33.2	49.0	34.4	16.6	410	19.8	36.1	44.1	485	895
Biochemistry	32.1	39.6	52.1	8.3	96	24.2	30.8	45.1	91	187
Clinical Psychology	29.9	35.6	35.1	29.3	205	22.9	27.1	50.0	166	371
History	28.8	40.7	40.1	19.2	511	19.1	32.4	48.5	623	1,134
Other Psychology	28.1	43.7	33.3	23.0	135	13.7	37.7	48.6	146	281
Nursing	27.6	49.3	38.7	12.0	75	22.9	49.6	27.5	353	428
Other Social Sciences	27.4	32.6	45.6	21.8	147	21.7	42.8	35.5	138	285
Economics	27.4	39.6	37.8	22.6	217	16.6	35.6	47.8	247	464
Microbiology	26.9	32.2	28.8	39.0	59	22.5	26.8	50.7	71	130
Chemistry	25.9	35.2	39.4	25.4	508	12.3	34.4	53.3	349	857
Fine Arts	25.3	36.1	38.6	25.2	595	17.3	40.8	41.8	803	1,398
Engineering	24.6	39.6	37.1	23.3	1,366	12.2	37.4	50.4	1,657	3,023
Zoology	24.4	26.0	41.0	33.0	100	21.4	28.6	50.0	56	156
Law	23.5	28.7	38.5	32.7	1,642	12.6	30.7	56.7	788	2,430
Other Biological Sciences	20.2	23.8	35.5	40.7	172	14.5	30.0	55.5	110	282
Physiology	19.6	18.9	25.7	55.4	74	–	–	–	18	92
Other Professions	17.8	23.4	35.8	40.8	1,513	12.0	32.9	55.1	1,477	2,990
Geography-Geology	17.5	29.0	46.0	25.0	124	7.6	43.1	49.3	144	268
Botany	17.0	20.9	31.3	47.8	67	–	–	–	33	100
Social Work	16.9	16.1	55.5	28.4	236	17.2	34.0	48.7	476	712
Sociology	16.6	25.6	39.3	25.0	152	10.4	26.2	63.3	221	373
Other Humanities	15.5	22.2	64.8	13.0	54	12.8	47.8	39.3	140	194
Biology	14.0	18.9	50.3	30.8	143	10.7	40.9	48.4	215	358
Education	13.6	17.8	42.9	39.2	3,391	11.9	38.6	49.5	8,132	11,523
Business	13.2	22.3	42.4	35.3	1,335	9.4	35.0	55.6	3,168	4,503
Other Health	6.6	6.2	37.9	55.9	451	7.4	45.1	47.5	204	655

N	39,167
NA, API Only	559
NA, Graduate Field Only	2,087
NA, Both	40
Excluded from Table:	
Not Going to Graduate School	12,383
NA, Plans Index	2,428
Total Weighted N	56,664

those going on later. There were exceptions, of course. In philosophy, for example, the "Next Years" were extremely high on
API and the "Laters" were quite low; but in general the rank
orders were similar.

A diagonal line has been plotted in Chart 4.2 to indicate all
points where "Next Year" and "Later" would have the same
API percentages. Except for social work and health professions,
all of the dots lie above the diagonal, which means that except
in these two fields there is a correlation between API and
immediacy of advanced study.

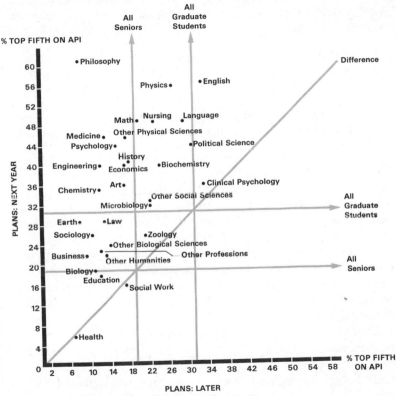

(Note: Botany and physiology excluded because of small case base)

Chart 4.2. Per cent Top Fifth API Among "Next Year," Plotted
Against Per cent Top Fifth API Among "Later"

Although the correlation between API levels in the two plans categories is high and although the "Laters" were generally below the "Next Years" in academic performance, there is enough variation to make a detailed examination worthwhile. By using the API levels of all future graduate students and all seniors as landmarks, we can locate some interesting groups. First, let us examine all the fields where those who were going on the next year ranked above the total group of graduate students in API. These are the fields above 31 per cent on the vertical axis in Chart 4.2. Although those going on later in these fields were generally better academic performers than those going on later in other fields, there is considerable variation. We can group the "Laters" as follows:

1. Better than future graduate students in general: English.
2. Better than seniors in general: physics, math, nursing, languages, political science, biochemistry, clinical psychology, other social sciences, microbiology.
3. Below seniors in general: philosophy, medicine, other physical sciences, psychology, engineering, history, economics, chemistry, art.

The quality of the future graduate students was quite different, for different fields, even though each had high academic performers among those going on immediately. The English students who were postponing graduate study were superior in academic performance to the generality of future graduate students, although not as high as the "Next Years" in English. On the other hand, in philosophy, medicine, other physical sciences, psychology, engineering, history, economics, chemistry, and art, the students who were postponing advanced study were far from outstanding, having fewer top API students among them than the graduating class in general.

Shifting to the fields in the bottom half of Chart 4.2, we see that except for zoology, the "Laters" were all inferior in API to a cross-section of the 1961 graduating class. (Both "Next Year" and "Later" zoology students were in the middle group between seniors in general and graduate students in general.) In general biology, education, social work, and health professions, those going on both the next year and later were below seniors in general, while for earth sciences, law, sociology, other biological sciences, business, other professions, and other humanities, the "Next Year" groups surpassed seniors in general but not future graduate students in general.

Assuming that postponed graduate studies are particularly undesirable for high API students, it follows that improvement of attendance rates would be most desirable in English, physics, mathematics, nursing, languages, political science, biochemistry, clinical psychology, other social sciences, microbiology, and zoology—these being the fields where the students planning to go on later had API levels superior to graduating seniors in general. On the other hand, those students who were postponing their studies in the remaining fields had an API proportion equal to or inferior to that in a class of graduating seniors, and although there was a considerable number of promising students among them, their reservoir of talent was not such that postponement had the same implication of talent loss as it did in the previous list of fields.

It has been shown that those students who expected to begin their studies immediately but who had not been accepted by June of 1961 had API levels about the same as the "Laters" and much lower than the accepted students. Let us look at the API data for the students who had been accepted for graduate school by June, 1961 (Table 4.4).

The academic performances of the accepted students were clearly superior, for in all fields except the health professions they were above the generality of graduating seniors in per cent from the top fifth in API. In 12 fields (English, philosophy, physics, other physical sciences, mathematics, foreign languages, other psychology, economics, political science, engineering, history, and medicine), half or more were from the top fifth. There were some exceptions, but considering the fields as a group, their rank order on API among those accepted was very similar to their ordering for all students expecting graduate study.

One of the exceptions deserves mention. While medicine is toward the top in API, regardless of Plans, its standing appears less impressive when only accepted students are considered. Among all students expecting graduate study, those planning to enter medicine are surpassed only by those going on in English, but when accepted students are considered, physics, other physical sciences, mathematics, engineering, psychology, economics, English, philosophy, languages, and history have greater proportion of students in the top fifth. The discrepancy arises from the fact that although the "Laters" in medicine were quite low in API, there were very few of them. In many of the arts and science fields, however, the API level of the totality expecting graduate study was diluted by high proportions of lower API students with indefinite or postponed plans for advanced study.

Table 4.4. Graduate Field and API, Among Students Accepted in Spring for Graduate Study in Fall

a. Distribution of API among Students Accepted in Spring, for Each Graduate Field

Graduate Field	API			Total	
	High	Medium	Low	Per cent	N
Chemistry	39	38	22	99	427
Physics	67	24	9	100	360
Earth (Geology-Geography)	42	48	10	100	79
Mathematics	64	27	9	100	268
Physical Sciences, Other	65	33	2	100	60
Engineering	53	34	13	100	791
Medicine	50	42	8	100	1,126
Nursing	–	–	–	–	25
Health	7	40	53	100	366
Biology	31	60	9	100	65
Biochemistry	42	51	7	100	74
Zoology	31	49	20	100	70
Other Biological Sciences*	29	34	37	100	272
Clinical Psychology	48	36	16	100	135
Psychology	56	34	10	100	95
Economics	54	37	9	100	148
Social Work	26	47	27	100	133
Political Science	52	39	9	100	253
Sociology	31	52	17	100	98
Other Social Sciences	41	42	17	100	92
Fine Arts	41	40	19	100	341
English	75	20	5	100	361
History	51	35	14	100	315
Languages	59	31	10	100	293
Philosophy	66	19	15	100	100
Humanities, Other	–	–	–	–	16
Education	28	44	28	100	1,254
Business	34	46	20	100	635
Law	34	40	26	100	1,296
Other Professions	27	37	36	100	1,036

N	10,584
Excluded:	
Not Yet Accepted to Graduate School Next Year	
and Planning Graduate School Later	28,583
NA, Graduate Field	2,087
NA, API	559
NA, Both	40
Excluded:	
Not Going to Graduate School	12,383
NA, Plans	2,428
Total Weighted N	56,664

*Botany, Microbiology, Physiology, Other.

Table 4.4. *Continued*

b. Per cent Top Fifth Among Students Accepted*

		Division		
Professions	Physical Science	Biological Science	Social Science	Humanities

				English	
	Physics Other Math			Philosophy	
				Languages	
			Psychology, Other Economics Political Science Clinical Psychology	History	
Engineering Medicine					
	Earth	Biochemistry	Other Social Sciences — Art —		→ Accepted
	Chemistry				
Business, Law		Biology, Zoology Other Biological — Sciences**	Sociology —		→ All Graduate Students
Education Other Professions Social Work					
					→ All Seniors
Health					

*Nursing and Other Humanities excluded because of small case base.
**Botany, Microbiology, Physiology, Biological Science, Other

Before concluding the analysis of API, it is necessary to consider the sex composition of the various fields (Table 4.5). Even though within a career field women were less likely to plan graduate study for the next year, over-all about the same proportion of men and women anticipated some advanced study, presumably because the concentration of men in the high attendance major professions and sciences was offset by the low attendance business fields and the lower API's of males, while the high proportion of women in education raised their contribution to those planning advanced study some time. The sex distributions have few surprises in the professions and physical sciences; nursing is quite feminine, engineering quite masculine, etc. How-

Table 4.5   Graduate Field and Sex

a. Ranked by Per cent Female

Graduate Field	Female	
	Per cent	N
Nursing	99	438
Social Work	79	724
Other Humanities	72	201
Languages	69	726
Education	65	11,691
English	65	1,201
Biochemistry	64	188
Fine Arts	63	1,429
Microbiology	54	132
Physiology	46	98
Clinical Psychology	44	375
Sociology	43	379
Other Social Sciences	42	288
Biology	42	363
History	39	1,142
Other Psychology	38	285
Other Health	38	669
Political Sciences	34	690
Other Biological Sciences	32	290
Zoology	31	158
Other Professions	31	3,038
Mathematics	28	902
Botany	27	106
Philosophy	24	205
Geology-Geography (Earth)	23	272
Chemistry	20	864
Economics	17	470
Medicine	9	1,440
Business	8	4,561
Other Physical Sciences	8	158
Physics	8	727
Law	4	2,456
Engineering	1	3,060
N		39,726
NA, Graduate Field		2,127
Excluded: Not Going to Graduate School		12,383
NA, Plans		2,428
Total Weighted N		56,664

Table 4.5. *Continued*

b. Grouped by Division (Per cent Female)

Per cent Female	Professions	Physical Science	Biological Science	Social Science	Humanities	
00–98–	Nursing					
80–78–	Social Work					
76–						
74–72–70–					Other Languages	
68–66–64–62–	Education		Biochemistry		English Art	
60–58–56–54–			Microbiology			
52–50–48–46–			Physiology	Clinical Psychology Sociology		
44–42–			Biology	Other		
40–						→ All Seniors
38–	Health			Psychology, Other	History	→ Graduate Students
36–34–				Political Science		
32–30–	Other		Other Zoology			
28–		Math	Botany			
26–24–		Earth			Philosophy	
22–20–		Chemistry				
18–16–				Economics		
14–12–10–						
8–6–	Medicine Business	Other, Physics				
4–2–	Law					
0–	Engineering					

ever, in the biological sciences there was a considerable range; biochemistry and microbiology were heavily feminine and botany, zoology, and other biological sciences were quite masculine in composition. Similarly, in the social sciences, economics stood out as an essentially masculine field while the other social science fields had a sex composition much like students in general. In the humanities, languages, English, art, and other humanities were heavily feminine fields, while history and philosophy tended to have strong male majorities.

Table 4.6 gives the API composition by sex for the graduate

fields and Chart 4.3 presents the data in chart form similar to
Chart 4.2. Referring to Chart 4.2, a number of conclusions may
be drawn:

   1) The bulk of the fields lie below the diagonal line marking
equal proportions of high API students for both sexes. In most
fields the women are higher on API than the men. Philosophy
and medicine constitute exceptions, with men being more likely
to come from the top fifth, and in law, political science, botany,

Table 4.6. Graduate Field by Academic Performance Index, Controlling
for Sex (Ranked by Per cent in Top Fifth on API)

Graduate Field	Total Per cent in Top Fifth on API	Male					Female				
		API			Total		API			Total	
		Top Fifth	Above Average	Bottom Half	Per cent	N	Top Fifth	Above Average	Bottom Half	Per cent	N
English	43.9	39.4	41.6	19.0	100.0	416	46.3	34.7	19.0	100.0	76
Physics	42.3	41.7	27.2	31.1	100.0	662	49.1	45.6	5.3	100.0	5
Medicine	42.1	43.0	42.3	14.8	100.1	1,292	33.1	43.8	23.1	100.0	13
Philosophy	40.7	45.5	34.4	20.1	100.0	154	26.0	60.0	14.0	100.0	5
Language	40.2	39.3	37.5	23.2	100.0	224	40.6	42.2	17.2	100.0	49
Political Science	36.9	37.3	37.1	25.6	100.0	450	36.1	49.6	14.3	100.0	23
Other Physical Sci.	34.2	35.3	42.6	22.1	100.0	136	–	–	–	–	1
Mathematics	33.2	28.8	33.6	37.5	99.9	642	44.3	39.5	16.2	100.0	25
Biochemistry	32.1	25.4	52.2	22.4	100.0	67	35.8	35.8	28.3	99.9	12
Clinical Psychology	29.9	13.5	35.3	51.2	100.0	207	50.6	26.8	22.6	100.0	16
History	28.8	23.9	33.2	42.9	100.0	686	36.4	40.0	23.7	100.1	44
Other Psychology	28.1	24.6	31.4	44.0	100.0	175	34.0	42.5	23.6	100.1	10
Nursing	27.6	–	–	–	–	5	27.4	48.0	24.6	100.0	42
Other Social Sciences	27.4	24.1	39.2	36.7	100.0	166	31.9	51.3	16.8	100.0	11
Economics	27.4	24.0	34.9	41.1	100.0	384	43.8	45.0	11.2	100.0	8
Microbiology	26.9	11.7	30.0	58.3	100.0	60	40.0	25.7	34.3	100.0	7
Chemistry	25.9	23.9	34.6	41.5	100.0	685	28.9	40.0	31.1	100.0	17
Fine Arts	25.3	21.8	36.7	41.6	100.1	510	27.4	41.8	30.9	100.1	88
Engineering	24.6	24.7	37.1	38.2	100.0	3,001	–	–	–	–	2
Zoology	24.4	14.8	43.5	41.7	100.0	108	–	–	–	–	4
Law	23.5	23.6	35.2	41.2	100.0	2,320	21.8	52.7	25.5	100.0	11
Other Bio. Sciences	20.2	18.5	29.1	52.4	100.0	189	23.7	41.9	34.4	100.0	9
Physiology	19.6	–	–	–	–	47	–	–	–	–	4
Other Professions	17.8	15.3	33.1	51.6	100.0	2,065	23.2	37.2	39.6	100.0	92
Geo.-Geog. (Earth)	17.5	14.1	49.0	36.9	100.0	206	29.0	29.0	41.9	99.9	6
Botany	17.0	16.9	28.6	54.5	100.0	77	–	–	–	–	2
Social Work	16.9	8.7	32.7	58.7	100.1	150	19.0	43.4	37.5	99.9	56
Sociology	16.6	9.5	37.0	53.6	100.1	211	25.9	34.0	40.1	100.1	16
Other Humanities	15.5	12.5	35.7	51.8	100.0	56	16.7	59.4	23.9	100.0	13
Biology	14.0	6.7	38.1	55.2	100.0	210	24.3	54.1	21.6	100.0	14
Education	13.6	7.7	31.5	60.8	100.0	4,027	16.8	44.4	38.8	100.0	7,49
Business	13.2	12.7	37.1	50.1	99.9	4,154	18.9	37.8	43.3	100.0	34
Other Health	6.6	6.4	30.5	63.1	100.0	407	6.9	56.0	37.1	100.0	24

N	39,167
NA, API Only	559
NA, Graduate Field Only	2,087
NA, Both	40
Excluded from Table:	
Not Going to Graduate School	12,383
NA, Plans Index	2,428
Total Weighted N	56,664

languages, and health professions the sex difference is negligible.

2) Generally speaking, the API levels of the fields are correlated in the two sexes; the fields that attract high performing men also attract high performing women.

3) The relationship is "loose" enough so that, as in the case of plans, it is useful to consider field variations. The information in Chart 4.3 can be classified as follows:

A. Lesser Sex Difference on API

1. Both sexes superior to future graduate students in general: medicine, political science, languages, English, physics.

2. Both sexes superior to seniors in general: law, chemistry, art.

3. Both sexes inferior to seniors in general: botany, other humanities, education, other health, business, social work.

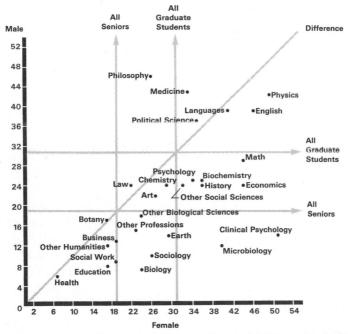

(Note: Physical science, other, engineering, zoology, physiology, and botany excluded because of small case base)

Chart 4.3. Per cent Male by Per cent Female (Per cent Top Fifth on API)

B. Women Higher than Men on API

   4. Women superior to graduate students in general, men superior to seniors in general: mathematics, economics, biochemistry, history, psychology, other social sciences.

   5. Women superior to graduate students in general, men inferior to seniors in general: clinical psychology, microbiology.

   6. Women superior to seniors in general, men inferior to seniors in general: other biological sciences, other professions, earth, sociology, biology.

C. Men Higher than Women on API

   7. Men superior to graduate students in general, women superior to seniors in general: philosophy.

From the viewpoint of social policy, it is possible to express mild regret that the sex difference runs the way it does. Although women clearly are good students, a large portion of them are destined for marriage and family life, not for full-time, long-run careers in their fields. The facts of life are that the society will get many more man years of professional work from a man than a woman.

Assuming in addition that high academic performance in undergraduate studies is predictive of greater professional potential, a more realistic index of the input into graduate fields can be made by calculating not just the per cent of students who are high on API, but the per cent who are high API men, since low API students of either sex and high API women present some drawbacks.

Table 4.7 gives the percentages of those who were high API men, high API women, and (by subtraction) low API students, for all those who were planning study in the various fields and for those who were accepted by the fall of 1961. Among "All Planning Graduate Study," those who were either in the top fifth *or* above average are considered "High"; among those "Accepted by Spring," only those in the top fifth are considered "High" because of the generally higher API levels of this group. In Chart 4.4 the same information for all future graduate students is presented in a triangular coordinate graph. The degree of scatter is considerable. For example, medicine and foreign

languages have about the same proportion of students in the top
fifth and above average API groups (84 and 81 per cent, respectively), but their sex composition varies so that 77 per cent of
the future physicians are high API men in contrast with 24 per
cent for language students. Again, foreign languages and health
professions have similar percentages of high API men (24 and 23
per cent, respectively), but they differ a lot in their percentage
of high API women. The result is that 53 per cent of those in

Table 4.7. Graduate Field and Plans, Controlling for Sex and API (All Future Graduate Students and Those Accepted by Spring)

Graduate Field	All Planning Graduate Study			Accepted by Spring		
	Male	Female	N	Male	Female	N
	Top Half			Top Fifth		
Chemistry	47	16	857	30	9	427
Physics	63	8	719	62	4	360
Geology-Geography (Earth)	48	13	268	30	11	79
Mathematics	45	24	895	48	16	268
Other Physical Sciences	71	8	149	62	3	60
Engineering	61	1	3,023	53	0	791
Medicine	77	7	1,422	46	3	1,126
Nursing	1	75	478	—	—	25
Other Health	23	24	655	5	2	366
Biology	26	32	358	9	22	65
Biochemistry	28	46	187	18	24	74
Botany	33	16	100	—	—	49
Microbiology	19	35	130	—	—	45
Physiology	14	34	92	—	—	44
Zoology	40	21	156	13	19	70
Biology, Other	46	21	282	26	2	134
Clinical Psychology	27	34	371	15	33	135
Other Psychology	35	29	281	36	20	95
Economics	49	15	464	47	7	148
Political Science	49	29	680	38	13	253
Sociology	26	26	373	15	15	98
Social Sciences, Other	37	35	285	25	25	92
Fine Arts	21	44	1,398	33	46	341
English	28	53	1,185	32	43	361
History	35	30	1,134	33	18	315
Languages	24	57	719	21	38	293
Philosophy	60	21	204	61	5	100
Other Humanities	14	54	194	—	—	16
Education	14	40	11,523	8	19	1,254
Business	46	4	4,503	30	4	635
Law	56	3	2,430	33	1	1,296
Other Professions	33	19	2,990	19	8	1,036
Social Work	9	49	712	4	22	133
Total	34	26	39,167	30	11	10,584

NA. API	559	Excluded: Not Yet
NA. Graduate Field	2,087	Accepted to Graduate
NA. Both	40	School Next Year &
Excluded:		Planning G.S. Later 28,583
Not Going to Graduate School	12,383	NA. Graduate Field 2,087
NA. Plans	2,428	NA. API 559
Total Weighted N	56,664	NA. Both 40
		Excluded: Not Going
		to Graduate School 12,383
		NA. Plans 2,428
		Total Weighted N 56,664

health professions are from the bottom half API in contrast with 19 per cent among language students.

In the graph, lines have been extended from the point describing all future graduate students so that fields can be compared on each of the three types, with the result that the fields can be classified into six groups. Group I, for example, consists of the fields with *more* high API men, *fewer* high API women, and *fewer* low API students than a cross-section of graduate students. The six groups, in turn, can be presented in the clock face diagram, similar to that used in the analysis of values (Chart 4.6).

Chart 4.5 gives similar information for the subgroup of those students who were accepted for study by the spring of 1961. Because the total group represented the pool for recruitment into the various fields, whether or not they all got to school, let

Chart 4.4. Graph of Data for All Planning Graduate Study

us consider in detail only the figures for all future graduate students. The six groups may be interpreted as follows:

Group I fields appear in many ways to be the most favorably situated in terms of their input, for compared with graduate students in general, they attracted higher proportions of high API men and lower proportions of low API students; hence more of their students had strong undergraduate records and the high performers were largely men rather than women.

Group II fields are similarly well situated, having, like Group I fields, a high percentage of high API men, but differing in having a high percentage of high API women as well. Generally, however, these fields did have somewhat fewer high API men than Group I.

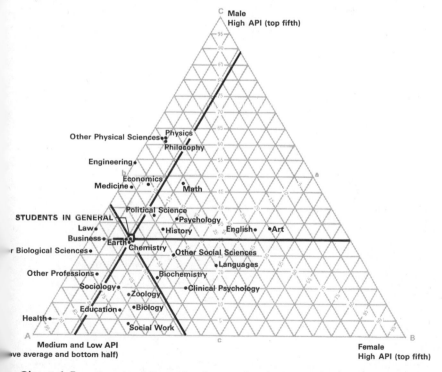

Chart 4.5. Graph of Data for Future Graduate Students Who Had Been Accepted by Spring

Group VI fields, law and business, also had a high percentage of high API men, but they had a relatively high percentage of bottom half API students in addition. That is, they gained their share of high performing men because there were very few women, with the result that although their general API levels were not too impressive, they did have a high proportion of high API males.

Group III fields were characterized by superior API levels over all, but because they were somewhat feminine, they were low on high API males. For example, 81 per cent of the students in English are top fifth and above average in API in contrast with 50 per cent of those in business, but business has a greater

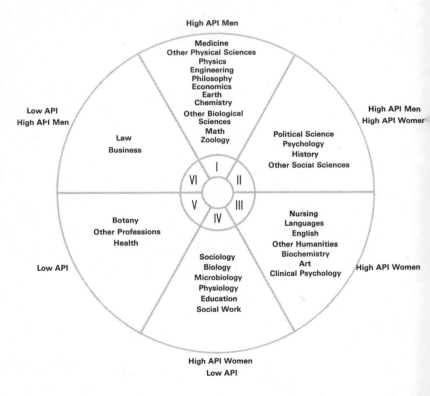

Chart 4.6. Data from Chart 4.4.

proportion of high performing men (46 versus 28) because so many high performing women are attracted to English.

Group V fields (botany, other professions, and health) had relatively fewer high API men and relatively fewer high API women; in short, they attracted students disproportionately from the bottom half in API.

Group IV fields (sociology, biology, microbiology, physiology, education, and social work) did the least well on the index, having relatively greater proportions of low API students, greater proportions of high API women, and lesser proportions of high API men.

It is odd to think that business has "better" graduate students than English, and, of course, it does not—in terms of sheer academic performance. But if one asks how much of the graduate training will be applied in long-run careers by relatively able students, a case can be made that the graduate students in business, even though a large number of mediocre academic performers are included, are a relatively promising lot, while the graduate students in English, bright as they may be in terms of undergraduate grades, include a worrisome proportion of women who may well be diverted from completion of their degrees or entrance into careers after graduate school.

Certainly, it is only "natural" that in feminine professions such as art, nursing, education, and social work, high API men constitute small fractions. When we see, however, that in arts and science fields, less than one-third of the future graduate students in botany, sociology, biology, clinical psychology, biochemistry, English, languages, microbiology, other humanities, and physiology are men from the top half of their graduating classes, some question arises as to whether the process of recruitment to postgraduate education is entirely efficient.

BACKGROUND CHARACTERISTICS

Tables 4.8, 4.9, and 4.10 distribute the future graduate students in terms of socio-economic status (SES) of their parental families, size of their hometown during high school days ("Hometown"), and the religion "in which you were reared."

In terms of SES (Table 4.8), the relatively high status origins

Table 4.8. Graduate Field and SES

a. All Fields

Graduate Field	Per cent High SES*	N
Law	70.2	2,329
Medicine	69.7	1,392
Philosophy	66.2	195
Political Sciences	63.3	670
Fine Arts	62.6	1,338
Clinical Psychology	61.6	367
English	61.4	1,124
Languages	59.9	684
Other Psychology	59.3	263
Biochemistry	56.5	186
Other Biological Sciences	56.3	288
History	56.3	1,066
Botany	55.4	101
Social Work	54.8	693
Business	54.2	4,334
Physics	53.9	698
Sociology	53.6	360
Economics	53.1	454
Other Physical Sciences	52.6	156
Microbiology	52.8	127
Health, Other	51.8	645
Other Social Sciences	51.6	274
Other Humanities	51.5	182
Zoology	50.0	146
Mathematics	49.9	879
Biology	49.3	335
Physiology	48.9	90
Other Professions	45.6	2,930
Engineering	45.6	2,938
Nursing	45.2	418
Education	43.2	11,036
Geology-Geography (Earth)	42.2	256
Chemistry	39.3	822
Total	51.5	37,776
NA, SES Only		1,950
NA, Graduate Field Only		1,989
NA, Both		138
Excluded from Table:		
Not Going to Graduate School		12,383
NA, Plans Only		2,428
Total Weighted N		56,664

*High SES = cells (a), (b), (c), and (e) in Table 2.6f.

Table 4.8. Continued

b. Grouped by Division (Per cent High SES)

		Division			
Professions	Physical Science	Biological Science	Social Science	Humanities	All Graduate Students
Law, Medicine					
			Political Science	Philosophy	
			Clinical Psychology, Psychology, Other		
	Physics, Other	Biochemistry, Other		Art, English, Languages	
Social Work, Business, Health		Botany, Microbiology	Sociology, Economics	History	
	Math	Zoology, Biology, Physiology	Other	Other	
Other, Engineering, Nursing, Education	Earth				
	Chemistry				

74 –
72 –
70 –
68 –
66 –
64 –
62 –
60 –
58 –
56 –
54 –
52 –
50 –
48 –
46 –
44 –
42 –
40 –
38 –
36 –
34 –
32 –
30 –
28 –
26 –
24 –
22 –
20 –
18 –
16 –
14 –
12 –
10 –
8 –
6 –
4 –
2 –
0 –

of future lawyers and physicians stand out here as in previous analyses. While the API level of the aspirant M.D.'s was challenged when arts and science fields were broken down into subgroups, no other field is very close to law and medicine in terms of SES origins. Within the professional fields we again see the relatively lower SES origins of students in education, engineering, and other professions, as well as the relatively low SES origins of nurses.

Within the arts and science fields, the data are suggestive of greater differences between divisions than within them, a trend which first turned up in the analysis of career choices. In the

Table 4.9. Graduate Field and Hometown

Graduate Field	Larger than 2 million	500,000- 2 million	10,000- 499,999	Less than 10,000 Farm	Total Per cent	Total N
Chemistry	19.4	31.0	17.8	31.8	100.0	830
Physics	24.0	31.1	17.4	27.5	100.0	713
Geo.-Geol. (Earth)	13.4	27.6	20.7	38.3	100.0	261
Mathematics	20.4	25.0	21.0	33.6	100.0	889
Other Phy. Sciences	22.3	31.8	21.7	24.2	100.0	157
Engineering	22.6	30.8	19.5	27.2	100.1	2,992
Medicine	27.3	32.0	21.1	19.5	99.9	1,415
Nursing	15.6	26.4	27.9	30.0	99.9	416
Other Health	16.7	22.5	25.5	35.3	100.0	652
Biology	17.0	16.4	26.4	40.2	100.0	348
Biochemistry	21.7	30.6	18.3	29.4	100.0	180
Botany	2.9	17.1	27.6	52.4	100.0	105
Microbiology	18.9	29.1	18.9	33.1	100.0	127
Physiology	37.8	11.2	16.3	34.7	100.0	98
Zoology	19.0	27.2	21.8	32.0	100.0	147
Other Bio. Sciences	18.3	23.1	25.5	33.1	100.0	290
Clinical Psychology	33.5	29.0	15.8	21.7	100.0	373
Other Psychology	33.3	24.6	23.2	18.8	99.9	276
Economics	24.7	32.8	18.8	23.8	100.1	458
Political Science	28.4	32.2	19.0	20.4	100.0	686
Sociology	20.2	35.0	16.4	28.4	100.0	377
Other Social Sciences	22.1	31.2	17.9	28.8	100.0	285
Fine Arts	19.6	29.0	25.9	25.6	100.1	1,395
English	25.5	33.4	19.7	21.4	100.0	1,163
History	20.7	31.8	22.4	25.1	100.0	1,132
Language	21.8	31.0	22.2	24.9	99.9	715
Philosophy	23.9	44.8	11.9	19.4	100.0	201
Humanities, Other	13.4	30.5	30.0	26.2	100.1	187
Education	14.2	24.2	25.7	35.9	100.0	11,390
Business	25.2	30.8	22.7	21.4	100.1	4,465
Law	28.3	30.5	23.4	17.8	100.0	2,403
Social Work	14.7	33.1	26.3	25.8	99.9	712
Other Professions	14.5	24.8	23.1	37.6	100.0	2,974

a. Size of Hometown

	N
N	38,812
NA, Graduate Field	2,070
NA, Hometown	914
NA, Both	57
Excluded:	
Not Going to Graduate School	12,383
NA, Plans	2,428
Total Weighted N	56,664

Table 4.9. Continued

b. Per cent from Hometowns of 100,000 or More, Grouped by Division

		Division			
Professions	Physical Science	Biological Science	Social Science	Humanities	
				Philosophy	
Medicine, Law			Clinical Psych. Political Sci Other Psych	English	
Business	Physics Other		Economics Sociology Other		
Engineering	Chemistry	Biochemistry Physiology		History, Languages	All Seniors
Social Work		Microbiology		Art	All Graduate Students
	Math	Zoology		Other	
Nursing Other, Health Education	Earth	Other			
		Biology			
		Botany			

humanities and social sciences no field is below the percentage for all graduate students, while in the biological sciences three out of six, and in the physical sciences two out of five fields have lesser percentages of high SES students than graduate students in general. In particular, chemistry (39 per cent high) and earth sciences (42 per cent high) have the lowest SES levels among the 33 fields in the table. At the top of the ladder of proportions from high SES families behind law and medicine, come humanities and social sciences (philosophy, political science, art, clinical psychology, English, psychology, and languages, in that order).

Turning to "Hometown" (Table 4.9) we find familiar trends, along with some new ones. As in the analysis of career choice, we note that medicine and law have high proportions from big cities, while other professions and education are relatively small town fields. The large city trend for social science seems to apply for each of the fields, all six subgroups in the social sciences being above graduate students in general in the percentage from big cities. While biological sciences as a group do not have a disproportionate small town trend, general biology, botany, and other biological fields do recruit heavily from smaller cities. In fact, 52 per cent of the botanists and 40 per cent of the biologists come from towns of under 10,000 or rural areas, compared with 30 per cent of the graduate students in general. Biological sci-

Table 4.10.   Graduate Field and Original Religion

a. Original Religion

Graduate Field	Protes-tant	Roman Catholic	Jewish	None	Other	Total Per cent	Total N
Chemistry	53.4	32.2	9.1	4.0	1.2	99.9	831
Physics	59.7	23.1	8.9	4.7	3.7	100.1	709
Geo.-Geol. (Earth)	72.6	16.2	5.0	2.7	3.5	100.0	259
Mathematics	60.8	23.6	10.8	3.4	1.4	100.0	886
Other Phy. Sciences	53.5	14.6	14.0	10.2	7.6	99.9	157
Engineering	56.7	27.0	7.9	4.2	4.3	100.1	2,993
Medicine	47.0	27.0	21.2	2.4	2.4	100.0	1,416
Nursing	68.4	24.2	1.6	1.6	4.2	100.0	430
Other Health	62.1	21.7	12.0	1.8	2.3	99.9	649
Biology	69.9	20.2	5.2	2.9	1.7	99.9	346
Biochemistry	45.2	41.9	9.7	2.9	0.5	100.2	186
Botany	74.5	7.8	1.0	6.9	9.8	100.0	102
Microbiology	64.6	21.5	11.5	2.3	0.0	99.9	130
Physiology	56.7	22.7	11.3	2.1	7.2	100.0	97
Zoology	81.5	11.6	2.1	2.1	2.7	99.9	144
Other Bio. Sciences	64.1	21.4	8.6	2.4	3.4	99.9	290
Clinical Psychology	55.9	21.0	20.2	2.4	0.5	100.0	371
Other Psychology	53.7	22.8	11.8	8.5	3.3	100.1	272
Economics	48.1	35.4	8.4	4.8	3.3	100.0	451
Political Science	52.2	30.9	9.5	4.4	2.9	99.9	68.
Sociology	58.9	23.7	11.3	2.2	4.0	100.1	372
Other Social Sciences	59.0	18.4	10.1	4.7	7.9	100.1	279
Fine Arts	67.6	16.2	9.6	4.1	2.7	100.2	1,390
English	53.3	31.3	11.2	1.8	2.4	100.0	1,160
History	58.2	28.7	7.1	3.0	3.0	100.0	1,127
Language	51.8	30.6	9.2	5.5	3.0	100.1	71
Philosophy	45.0	35.4	12.1	3.0	4.5	100.0	19
Other Humanities	58.6	27.2	5.8	5.8	2.6	100.0	19
Education	65.4	22.4	6.7	2.0	3.5	100.0	11,41
Business	53.0	34.4	8.2	2.3	2.1	100.0	4,45
Law	43.5	35.1	17.5	2.5	1.5	100.1	2,38
Social Work	62.1	24.0	9.6	1.3	3.1	100.1	71
Other Professions	72.6	16.9	4.5	2.6	3.5	100.1	2,98

N	38,80
NA, Graduate Field	2,06
NA, Religion	92
NA, Both	6
Excluded from Table:	
Not Going to Graduate School	12,38
NA, Plans	2,42
Total Weighted N	56,66

ble 4.10. *Continued*

b. Per cent Protestant (Original Religion)

Professions	Division				
	Physical Science	Biological Science	Social Science	Humanities	
		Zoology			
Other	Earth	Botany			
		Biology		Art	
Nursing		Microbiology			
Education		Other			All Graduate Students and All Seniors
Social Work, Health	Math				
	Physics		Sociology, Other	Other	
Engineering		Physiology	Clinical Psychology	History	
Business	Chem., Other		Psychology, Other		
			Political Science	English	
			Economics	Languages	
Medicine					
Law		Biochemistry		Philosophy	

(Table 4.10 continued)

ences are not thoroughly non-metropolitan, however, for biochemists, physiologists, and microbiologists have about the same proportion from larger cities as graduate students in general.

Finally, we note again that philosophers stand out as a distinctive group; 69 per cent of them are from larger cities, making them the most metropolitan field of all.

Original religion is reported in Tables 4.10a through 4.10d. Again, many of the differences are familiar. The relatively Protestant fields are mostly sciences — zoology, botany, biology, earth science, along with other professions — while all the humanities and social science fields are less Protestant than graduate students in general, as are law, medicine, and biochemistry. Biochemistry stands out, along with law, business, eco-

Table 4.10 *Continued*

c. Per cent Catholic (Original Religion)

Division

	Professions	Physical Science	Biological Science	Social Science	Humanities
54					
52					
50					
48					
46					
44					
42			Biochemistry		
40					
38					
36				Economics	Philosophy
34	Law				
32	Business	Chemistry		Political Science	Eng; Languages
30					History
28	Engineering, Med.				Other
26					← All Graduate Students
24	Soc. Work, Nursing	Math	Physiology	Sociology	
22	Health, Education	Physics	Microbiology, Other	Psychology, Other	← All Seniors
20			Biology	Clinical Psychology	
18	Other	Earth		Other	
16		Other			Art
14					
12			Zoology		
10					
8			Botany		
6					
4					
2					

Table 4.10. Continued

d. Per cent Jewish (Original Religion)

Division

	Professions	Physical Science	Biological Science	Social Science	Humanities
40—					
38—					
36—					
34—					
32—					
30—					
28—					
26—					
24—					
22—	Medicine			Clinical Psychology	
20—					
18—	Law				
16—					
14—					
12—	Health	Other	Microbiology	Psychology, Other	Philosophy
10—	Social Work	Math	Physiology	Sociology	English
	Chemistry	Physics	Biochemistry	Poli. Sci; Other	Art
8—	Engineering, Bus.	Earth	Other	Economics	Languages
6—	Education		Biology		History
4—	Other				Other
2—			Zoology		
0—	Nursing		Botany		

All Graduate Students → All Seniors

nomics, and philosophy, in the proportion of Roman Catholics, while zoology, botany, earth sciences, other physical sciences, and art have a relatively low proportion of Catholics. These figures challenge any unqualified assertion that Catholics opt for humanities and are less interested in sciences. Jews tend disproportionately to choose medicine, clinical psychology, and law, patterns that are not surprising. However, save for nursing, botany, and zoology, there do not seem to be any "non-Jewish" fields when graduate students are considered.

VALUES

The three occupational values chosen for analysis in this report are treated in Tables 4.11, 4.12, and 4.13.

"People interest," as expected, is greatest in the helping professions and least in the natural sciences. Nursing, social work, clinical psychology, education, and medicine all have 66 per cent or more endorsing this item, while in the natural science fields and engineering 43 per cent or less endorse the item. The least people-oriented field is physics, with a figure of 12 per cent.

Within this strong divisional difference there are field variations of considerable size. Within the sciences, biology, earth sciences, physiology, and zoology are *relatively* people-oriented with a third or more of their future graduate students endorsing the item. At the other extreme, less than 20 per cent of those in other physical sciences, chemistry, microbiology, engineering, and physics endorsed the value.

Although the social sciences are distinctly people-oriented in comparison with the other arts and sciences, there is a percentage range by field from 49 to 76. Economists and psychologists other than clinical are less people-oriented than graduate students in general, while clinical psychologists and sociologists are relatively high. Within the humanities, the language students are relatively people-oriented and the artists and philosophers are not, the percentage of philosophers endorsing the value being lower than biology and earth science. Again, the distinctive character of students in philosophy stands out.

The item "Opportunities to be original and creative" also

shows wide divisional differences along with considerable variation within a division. As in the previous analysis, engineering, physical sciences, and humanities are high on this indicator, while the professional fields are low. Within the physical sciences, however, it is physics, chemistry, and other physical sciences that are particularly high, while mathematics and earth sciences are close to graduate students in general. Biological sciences and social sciences cluster near the line for all graduate students, but among them psychology stands out as high, while biology is low. Among the humanities, history stands out as an exception; 50 per cent of the historians checked the item,

Table 4.11. Graduate Field and Occupational Values

a. Per cent Checking "Opportunity to Work with People Rather than Things"

Graduate Field*	Per cent	N	Grouped Graduate Field	Per cent	N
Nursing	82.0	438	Social Work	81.4	724
Social Work	81.4	724	Education	70.5	11,682
Clinical Psychology	76.0	375	Other Health	66.5	1,106
Education	70.4	11,682	Medicine	66.1	1,436
Medicine	66.1	1,436	Social Sciences	58.7	2,486
Sociology	64.1	379	Other Professions	58.4	3,037
Language	63.1	726	Law	58.2	2,455
History	58.9	1,142	Humanities	54.0	4,901
Other Professions	58.4	3,037	Business	53.2	4,557
Law	58.2	2,455	Biological Science	29.8	1,334
Political Science	58.1	689	Physical Science	20.3	2,914
English	58.0	1,199	Engineering	15.8	3,060
Other Health	56.3	668			
Other Social Sciences	55.6	288			
Other Humanities	54.7	201			
Business	53.2	4,557			
Other Psychology	49.8	285			
Economics	48.7	470			
Fine Arts	44.1	1,429			
Biology	43.2	363			
Geo.-Geol. (Earth)	40.8	272			
Philosophy	39.2	204			
Physiology	38.8	98			
Zoology	34.8	158			
Botany	29.2	106			
Mathematics	25.1	900			
Biochemistry	20.2	188			
Other Biological Sciences	20.1	289			
Other Physical Sciences	19.1	157			
Chemistry	16.0	864			
Microbiology	15.9	132			
Engineering	15.8	3,060			
Physics	11.9	721			
N		39,692	N		39,692
NA, Graduate Field Only		1,986			
NA, Values		34			
NA, Both		141			
Excluded:					
Not Going to Graduate School		12,383			
NA, Plans		2,428			
Total Weighted N		56,664			

*Fields ordered on the basis of the per cent checking the given value.

(Table 4.11 continued)

Table 4.11 *Continued*

b. Grouped by Division (Per cent "Work with People Rather Than Things")

Per cent	Professions	Physical Science	Biological Science	Social Science	Humanities	
82	Nursing					
80	Social Work					
78						
76				Clinical Psychology		
74						
72						
70	Education					
68						
66	Medicine					
64						
62				Sociology	Language	
60						
58	Other, Law			Political Science	History	All
56	Health			Other	English	Senior
54	Business				Other	Graduate Students
52						
50				Psychology, Other		
48				Economics		
46						
44			Biology		Art	
42		Earth				
40						
38			Physiology		Philosophy	
36						
34			Zoology			
32						
30						
28			Botany			
26						
24		Math				
22						
20		Other	Biochem., Other			
18						
16	Engineering	Chemistry	Microbiology			
14						
12		Physics				
10						
8						
6						
4						
2						
0						

putting them well below the next lowest humanities field — languages — where 62 per cent endorsed the response.

Table 4.13 confirms the impression that law, business, engineering, health professions, and the physical sciences have more students interested in making money, while all biological sciences, social sciences, and humanities are at or below the 23 per cent line that characterizes graduate students as a whole. Note that physicists have about the same percentage interested in making money as engineers; the difference between the two is not in the degree of acquisitiveness. Note, too, that while future physicians are below students in general on this item, they do surpass all of the biological sciences, social sciences, and humanities, except for economics.

Considering our new item, "Conventionality" (Table 4.14), there is a range from 23 per cent among the philosophers to 74 per cent among nurses. Except for biology and biochemistry (high for arts and science fields) and engineering (low for professional fields), all arts and science fields are lower than all professions. Within the arts and science group there appears to be little divisional variation, but some spread within each division. Within the arts and sciences the relatively "conventional" fields are biology, biochemistry, chemistry, earth sciences, mathematics, microbiology, other biological sciences, sociology, and history. The less conventional fields are physics,

---

ble 4.12.   Graduate Field and Occupational Values

a. Per cent Checking "Opportunity to be Original and Creative"

Graduate Field*	Per cent	N	Grouped Graduate Field	Per cent	N
Fine Arts	87.0	1,429	Engineering	71.5	3,060
Physics	79.1	721	Humanities	70.8	4,901
English	77.1	1,199	Physical Science	66.3	2,914
Chemistry	77.1	861	Social Sciences	57.1	2,486
Engineering	71.5	3,060	Other Professions	53.4	3,037
Other Humanities	68.2	201	Biological Science	51.6	1,334
Other Physical Sciences	67.5	157	Education	48.4	11,682
Philosophy	66.7	204	Law	42.9	2,455
Other Psychology	64.6	285	Medicine	42.3	1,436
Language	62.3	726	Business	40.7	4,557
Botany	61.3	106	Social Work	37.8	724
Other Social Sciences	61.1	288	Other Health	32.2	1,106
Political Science	59.9	689			
Zoology	59.5	158			
Other Biological Sciences	59.2	289			
Clinical Psychology	58.9	375			
Mathematics	56.9	900			
Physiology	56.1	98			
Sociology	55.4	379			
Other Professions	53.4	3,037			
Biochemistry	52.1	188			
History	50.5	1,142			
Education	48.4	11,682			
Geo.-Geol. (Earth)	48.2	272			
Economics	45.7	470			
Microbiology	44.7	132			
Law	42.9	2,455			
Medicine	42.3	1,436			
Business	40.7	4,557			
Biology	40.5	363			
Social Work	37.8	724			
Nursing	33.8	438			
Other Health	31.1	668			
N		39,692	N		39,692
NA, Graduate Field Only		1,986			
NA, Values		34			
NA, Both		141			
Excluded from Table:					
Not Going to Graduate School		12,383			
NA, Plans		2,428			
Total Weighted N		56,664			

elds ordered on the basis of the per cent checking the given value.

(Table 4.12   continued)

Great Aspirations

Table 4.12 Continued

b. Per cent "Original and Creative," Grouped by Division

%	Professions	Physical Science	Biological Science	Social Science	Humanities	
90						
88						
86					Art	
84						
82						
80						
78		Physics				
76					English	
74						
72	Engineering	Chemistry				
70						
68		Other		Psychology,	Other	
66				Other	Philosophy	
64						
62			Botany	Other	Languages	
60			Zoology	Political Science		
58		Math	Other	Clinical Psychology		
56			Physiology	Sociology		
54	Other					Graduate
52			Biochemistry			→Students
50					History	→ All
48	Education	Earth				Seniors
46						
44	Law		Microbiology	Economics		
42	Medicine					
40	Business		Biology			
38	Social Work					
36						
34	Nursing					
32	Health					
30						
28						
26						
24						
22						
20						
18						
16						
14						
12						
10						

physiology, psychology, clinical psychology, other social sciences, English, art, and philosophy.

The differences in political ideology appear to be divisional rather than intradivisional (Table 4.15). Social scientists are the most liberal politically; all fields surpass graduate students in general. Humanities are similarly liberal, surpassing future graduate students in general, except for the other humanities. Scientific fields are considerably less liberal, for all the physical and biological science fields are the same or lower in liberalism than graduate students in general, except for the earth sciences. Within the professional fields, social workers are quite politically liberal (61 per cent high on the item) and engineers and businessmen are the lowest professions. However, it should

be noted that engineers and businessmen (among those anticipating graduate school, you will remember) are within five
percentage points of graduate students in general. Putting it
another way, while there are five fields which surpass students
in general by 10 per cent or more in the proportion of liberals
(social work, psychology, other social sciences, economics,
history), there is only one—botany—that is 10 per cent below
students in general. Thus, while there are a number of politically liberal graduate fields, there are few "un-liberal" ones.

The differences in occupational values may be summarized
by locating each of the fields on a clock diagram. Having a
higher percentage endorsing a given value than future graduate

---

Table 4.13.   Graduate Field and Occupational Values

	a. Per cent Checking "Making a Lot of Money"				
Graduate Field*	Per cent	N	Grouped Graduate Field	Per cent	N
Law	49.6	2,455	Law	49.6	2,455
Business	47.0	4,557	Business	47.0	4,557
Engineering	34.5	3,060	Engineering	34.5	3,060
Physics	32.3	721	Physical Science	28.0	2,914
Other Health	29.8	668	Medicine	21.0	1,436
Mathematics	28.7	900	Other Health	20.7	1,106
Chemistry	27.3	864	Social Sciences	17.2	2,486
Other Phy. Sciences	23.6	157	Other Professions	16.2	3,037
Economics	22.8	470	Biological Science	15.8	1,334
Medicine	21.0	1,436	Humanities	13.4	4,901
Botany	19.8	106	Education	12.1	11,682
Geo.-Geol. (Earth)	19.1	272	Social Work	8.0	724
Other Bio. Science	19.0	289			
Microbiology	18.9	132			
Other Psychology	18.6	285			
Political Science	17.9	689			
Other Professions	16.2	3,037			
Fine Arts	15.8	1,429			
Sociology	15.6	379			
Biochemistry	15.4	188			
Zoology	15.2	158			
Biology	14.0	363			
English	13.8	1,199			
Clinical Psychology	13.1	375			
Other Social Sciences	12.8	288			
Language	12.5	726			
History	12.3	1,142			
Education	12.1	11,682			
Other Humanities	8.5	201			
Philosophy	8.3	204			
Social Work	8.0	724			
Nursing	6.8	438			
Physiology	6.1	98			
N		39,692	N		39,692
NA, Graduate Field Only		1,986			
NA, Values		34			
NA, Both		141			
Excluded from Table:					
Not Going to Graduate School		12,383			
NA, Plans		2,428			
Total Weighted N		56,664			

*Fields ordered on the basis of the per cent checking the given value.

(Table 4.13 continued)

Table 4.13 Continued

b. Per cent "Making a Lot of Money" by Division

Division

	Professions	Physical Science	Biological Science	Social Science	Humanities
56 —					
54 —					
52 —					
50 —	Law				
48 —	Business				
46 —					
44 —					
42 —					
40 —					
38 —					
36 —					
34 —	Engineering				
32 —		Physics			
30 —	Health				
29 —		Math			
28 —		Chemistry			
26 —		Other			
24 —				Economics	
22 —					
20 —	Medicine				
18 —		Earth	Botany / Other, Microbiology	Psychology, Other / Political Science	
16 —	Other			Sociology / Clinical Psych, Other	
14 —			Biochemistry, Zoology / Biology		Art / English / Lang., History
12 —	Education				
10 —					Other, Philosophy
8 —	Social Work		Physiology		
6 —	Nursing				
4 —					
2 —					

← All Seniors

← All Graduate Students

Table 4.14. Graduate Field and Attitudes

a. Per cent "Conventional"

Graduate Field	Per cent	N
Chemistry	50.4	863
Physics	36.0	711
Geo.-Geol. (Earth)	49.8	271
Mathematics	49.1	897
Other Physical Sciences	42.4	158
Engineering	50.2	3,029
Medicine	51.7	1,430
Nursing	74.2	430
Other Health	61.9	651
Biology	55.5	344
Biochemistry	55.5	182
Botany	45.7	105
Microbiology	51.1	131
Physiology	38.8	98
Zoology	46.8	158
Other Biology	50.2	287
Clinical Psychology	31.6	373
Other Psychology	35.9	281
Economics	42.5	445
Political Science	41.9	677
Sociology	47.5	364
Other Social Sciences	33.2	280
Fine Arts	36.0	1,413
English	37.0	1,177
History	50.2	1,124
Language	40.8	708
Philosophy	23.3	202
Other Humanities	40.0	200
Education	64.7	11,275
Business	57.5	4,488
Law	51.2	2,415
Social Work	50.9	713
Other Professions	54.0	2,974

N	38,854
NA, Attitudes	872
NA, Graduate Field	2,033
NA, Both	94
Excluded from Table:	
Not Going to Graduate School	12,383
NA, Plans	2,428
Total Weighted N	56,664

(Table 4.14 continued)

Table 4.14 *Continued*

b. Per cent "Conventional," Grouped by Division

	Professions	Physical Science	Biological Science	Social Science	Humanities	
			Division			
76–						
74–	Nursing					
72–						
70–						
68–						
66–						
64–	Education					
62–	Health					
60–						
58–	Business					
56–			Biology, Biochemistry			All Seniors
54–	Other———					All Graduate Students →
52–	Medicine					
50–	Social Work, Law	Chem., Earth	Microbiology / Other		History	
48–	Engineering	Math	Zoology	Sociology		
46–			Botany			
44–						
42–		Other				
40–				Econ., Poli. Sci.	Languages / Other	
38–			Physiology		English	
36–		Physics		Psychology, Other	Art	
34–				Other		
32–				Clinical Psychology		
30–						
28–						
26–						
24–						
22–					Philosophy	
20–						
18–						
16–						
14–						
12–						
10–						
8–						
6–						
4–						
2–						
0–						

students in general is defined as "plus," and all but six fields can be allocated to sectors of the clock. (Graph 4.4).

The results need little interpretation. Why history is located in the helping profession sector is puzzling at first, but later on in this chapter it will be shown that a high proportion of future history graduate students plan careers in secondary education where the "helping pattern" is characteristic. We also note that the frequent assignment of psychology to natural science, rather than the social sciences, can be justified by the fact that their high "original," low "people," low "money" classification is more characteristic of natural science than social science fields. Similarly, we note that art and philosophy are set off from their humanities neighbors by a lesser interest in people and hence

Table 4.15. Graduate Field and Attitudes

a. Per cent "Liberal"

Graduate Field	Per cent	N
Chemistry	49.4	851
Physics	47.9	725
Geography-Geology, (Earth)	53.7	272
Mathematics	46.7	890
Other Physical Sciences	40.5	158
Engineering	44.2	3,019
Medicine	50.1	1,432
Nursing	47.1	425
Other Health	47.3	653
Biology	49.0	347
Biochemistry	41.0	188
Botany	38.0	100
Microbiology	49.2	132
Physiology	44.6	92
Zoology	44.3	158
Other Biological Sciences	42.9	289
Clinical Psychology	57.9	373
Other Psychology	63.9	274
Economics	62.3	453
Political Science	55.3	680
Sociology	55.8	364
Other Social Sciences	63.0	281
Fine Arts	52.5	1,397
English	55.9	1,189
History	61.2	1,125
Language	53.2	712
Philosophy	55.2	203
Other Humanities	48.2	197
Education	48.3	11,291
Business	44.4	4,459
Law	53.1	2,431
Social Work	61.1	715
Other Professions	49.2	2,979

N	38,854
NA, Graduate Field	2,034
NA, Attitudes	872
NA, Both	93
Excluded from Table:	
Not Going to Graduate School	12,383
NA, Plans	2,428
Total Weighted N	56,664

(Table 4.15 continued)

Table 4.15 *Continued*

b. Per cent "Liberal," Grouped by Division

Division

	Professions	Physical Science	Biological Science	Social Science	Humanities	
70–68–66–64–				Psychology		
62–60–	Social Work			Other / Economics	History	
58–				Clinical Psychology		
56–				Sociology	English	
54–	Law	Earth		Political Science	Philosophy	
52–	Medicine				Languages	
50–	Other				Fine Arts	All Graduate Students
48–		Chemistry	Biology; Microbiology			
46–	Education	Physics			Other	All Seniors
44–	Nursing; Health	Math	Physiology			
42–	Engin.; Business		Zoology			
40–		Other	Other			
38–			Biochemistry			
36–			Botany			
34– down to 0–						

a more purely intellectual orientation. Among the natural science fields, none of the biological sciences have the "achievement" pattern of high "original," high "money," low "people," which is characteristic of engineering, mathematics, chemistry, and physics, although physiology, zoology, botany, and other biological sciences have the "original only" pattern characteristic of science fields. Note, too, that the lesser interest in originality of biology, biochemistry, earth sciences, and microbiology makes them (---) on the typology and thus unclassifiable on this circle diagram.

In order to summarize the findings, the differentiating characteristics of each field will be reviewed, following the arbitrary rule that a field is "high" or "low" on a characteristic if it differs from future graduate students in general by 10 per cent or more in terms of the per cent possessing the characteristic.

Professional Fields

1. *Medicine* . . . high API, high male, high SES, larger hometown, low Protestant, high Jewish, high "people," low "original."

2. *Nursing* . . . low male, high "people," low "original," low "money," high "conventional."

3. *Engineering* . . . high male, low "people," high "original," high "money."

4. *Law* . . . high male, high SES, larger hometown, low Protestant, low "original," high "money."

5. *Other Professions* . . . low API, high Protestant.

6. *Social Work* . . . low API, low male, high "people," low "original," low "money," high "liberal."

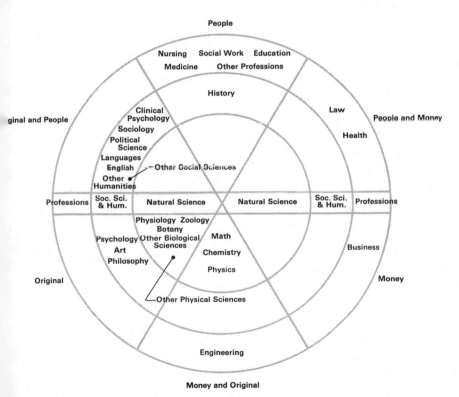

Chart 4.7. Classification of Graduate Fields* on Value Typology

*Excluded: biology, biochemistry, earth sciences, microbiology, economics, other social sciences.

7. *Education* . . . low API, low male, smaller hometown, high "people," low "money," high "conventional."

8. *Business* . . . low API, high male, low "original," high "money."

9. *Health Professions* (other than medicine and nursing) . . . low API, low "original."

Natural Sciences

10. *Physics* . . . high API, high male, low "people," high "original," low "conventional."

11. *Other Physical Sciences* . . . low Catholic, low "people," high "original," low "conventional."

12. *Mathematics* . . . high male and low "people."

13. *Biochemistry* . . . low male, low Protestant, high Catholic, low "people."

14. *Microbiology* . . . low male, low "people."

15. *Chemistry* . . . high male, low SES, low "people," high "original."

16. *Zoology* . . . high Protestant, low "people."

17. *Other Biological Sciences* . . . low API, low "people."

18. *Physiology* . . . low API, low "people," low "money," low "conventional."

19. *Earth* . . . low API, high male, high Protestant, low Catholic.

20. *Botany* . . . low API, high male, smaller hometown, high Protestant, low Catholic, low "people," low "original," low "liberal."

21. *Biology* . . . low API, smaller hometown, high Protestant, low Catholic, low "people," low "original."

Social Sciences and Humanities

22. *English* . . . high API, low male, larger hometown, high "original," low "conventional."

23. *Philosophy* . . . high API, high male, high SES, larger hometown, low Protestant, low "people," high "original," low "money," low "conventional."

24. *Languages* . . . low male, low "money," low "conventional."

25. *Political Science* . . . high SES, larger hometown, low "conventional."

26. *Clinical Psychology* . . . high SES, larger hometown, high Jewish, high "people," low "money," low "conventional."

27. *Psychology other than Clinical* . . . larger hometown, high "original," low "conventional," high "liberal."

28. *History* . . . low "money," high "liberal."

29. *Other Social Sciences* . . . low "money," low "conventional," high "liberal."

30. Economics . . . high male, low "people," low "conventional," high "liberal."

31. Art . . . low male, high SES, low Catholic, low "people," high "original," low "conventional."

32. Sociology . . . low API, high "people."

33. Humanities, Other . . . low API, low male, high "original," low "money," low "conventional."

ACADEMIC PLANS

In June, 1961, when the questionnaires were completed, none of the students had entered graduate study (although 14 per cent reported taking one or more graduate courses while under-graduates — RSS). Data on actual rates of entry and reactions to graduate study will have to come from NORC's continuing follow-up study of the sample. Information is available, though, on the students' plans and on the anticipated financial situations of those planning to go on immediately. In this section we shall review, field by field, the available information on these matters.

Postponement

Perhaps the single most important fact of the survey is that 45 per cent of the sample and 58 per cent of those anticipating graduate study fell into the group called "Later" on the Plans Index. We have previously noted that in fields where graduate study is essential for entry, postponement is rare, while in fields where postgraduate study is more of an option, rates of postponement are higher. The data on future graduate students enable us to examine postponement for a more detailed breakdown of fields (Table 4.6).

While the professional fields show both the highest (79 per cent for nursing) and lowest (11 per cent for medicine) rates for postponement, the arts and science fields generally range from 35 to 65 per cent of the future graduate students who planned to begin their studies after the fall of 1961. Within the arts and sciences, higher rates of postponement are found for other humanities, biology, sociology, art, English, history, earth sciences, mathematics, psychology, and economics, all of which have more than 50 per cent postponement. At the other extreme, physiology, physics, zoology, botany, and philosophy have postponement rates of less than 40 per cent.

The very strong association between plans and API has been noted already, and is spelled out in detail in Table 4.17. For example, while 54 per cent of the historians are postponing studies, the percentages are 36 per cent among the top fifth in API, 50 per cent among above average, and 76 per cent among those from the bottom half. Except for social work and health professions, the relationships are quite strong. However, as in the case of the analysis of broad groups of fields in chapter 3, API does not explain differences in postponement rates. In chart 4.8 the postponement rate for each field is plotted against the postponement that would be expected if the field consisted

Table 4.16. Graduate Field and Plans Index

a. Graduate Field, Graduate Plans, and Acceptance Status

Graduate Field*	Per cent Planning to Go to Graduate School		Total		Per cent Planning to Go to Graduate School Next Fall and Accepted
	Next Fall	Later	Per cent	N	
Medicine	88	12	100	1,440	79
Physiology	76	24	100	98	45
Other Health	68	32	100	669	55
Law	68	32	100	2,456	53
Zoology	65	35	100	158	46
Physics	64	36	100	727	50
Botany	63	37	100	106	46
Philosophy	62	38	100	205	49
Other Biological Sciences	60	40	100	290	47
Chemistry	59	41	100	864	50
Language	58	42	100	726	41
Other Physical Sciences	58	42	100	158	38
Clinical Psychology	55	45	100	375	36
Other Social Sciences	52	49	101	288	33
Biochemistry	51	49	100	188	39
Other Professions	50	50	100	3,038	34
Political Science	50	50	100	690	37
Geography-Geology (Earth)	47	53	100	272	30
Other Psychology	47	53	100	285	33
Economics	47	53	100	470	33
Mathematics	46	54	100	902	30
English	46	54	100	1,201	31
Microbiology	45	55	100	132	34
History	45	55	100	1,142	28
Engineering	45	55	100	3,060	26
Fine Arts	43	57	100	1,429	24
Sociology	40	60	100	379	26
Biology	40	60	100	363	18
Social Work	33	67	100	724	19
Business	30	70	100	4,561	14
Education	29	71	100	11,691	11
Other Humanities	27	73	100	201	8
Nursing	18	82	100	438	6
N				39,726	
NA, Graduate Field				2,127	
Excluded from Table:					
Not Going to Graduate School				12,383	
NA, Plans				2,428	
Total Weighted N				56,664	

*Ordered on the basis of per cent planning graduate school in the fall.

Table 4.16 *Continued*

b. Per cent "Later" on Plans, Grouped by Division

	Professions	Physical Science	Biological Science	Social Science	Humanities	
	Nursing					
					Other	
	Education; Bus.					
	Social Work					
			Biology	Sociology		→ All Graduate Students
					Art	
	Engineering	Earth; Math	Microbiology		English; History	
				Psych, Other; Econ.		
	Other		Biochemistry	Political Science / Other / Clinical Psychology		
		Other Chemistry	Other		Languages	
		Physics	Botany / Zoology		Philosophy	
	Law / Health					
			Physiology			
	Medicine					

of equal proportions from the three API groups, a way of controlling for API. The correlation is very high, which means that we get essentially the same rank of postponement when API is controlled. A hand-drawn line has been passed through the points where the raw and adjusted figures are identical. Any field lying well above the line can be interpreted as one where low API levels contribute to postponement; any point below the line can be interpreted as indicating high API levels bringing down the rate of postponement. The discrepancies are few, but chemistry, sociology, and business do lie four points or more above the line, indicating some of the postponement in these fields comes from low API; medicine, physics, languages, and English lie four or more points below the line, and thus receive some additional "boost" from their high API levels.

Because of the great field variations in sex and API and the correlation between sex and API, it is difficult to find sufficient fields with enough cases in each subgroup to examine field differences in postponement when sex and API are both controlled. Table 4.18 gives detailed information for 33 fields. For the 11 fields with sufficient cases, Chart 4.9 plots raw postponement figures against the rates to be expected if each field were com-

Table 4.17. Graduate Field, API, and Postponement of Graduate Studies (Per cent of Each API Group Planning Graduate School Later)

Graduate Field	API						Adjusted for API*
	High		Medium		Low		
	Per cent	N	Per cent	N	Per cent	N	
Chemistry	19.4	222	37.5	320	59.0	315	29.5
Physics	15.1	304	33.5	206	67.5	209	38.7
Geo.-Geol. (Earth)	—	47	52.1	119	69.6	102	—
Mathematics	32.3	297	55.4	316	75.9	282	54.5
Other Physical Science	17.6	51	37.3	67	—	31	—
Engineering	27.2	743	55.0	1,127	72.4	1,153	51.5
Medicine	3.7	598	11.6	603	35.7	221	17.0
Nursing	68.6	118	85.8	204	91.5	106	82.0
Other Health	—	43	35.0	263	27.8	349	—
Biology	46.0	50	55.0	160	70.3	148	57.1
Biochemistry	36.7	60	35.9	78	—	49	—
Botany	—	17	—	31	38.5	52	—
Microbiology	—	35	—	36	61.0	59	—
Physiology	—	18	—	27	—	47	—
Zoology	—	38	28.1	57	45.9	61	—
Other Biological Science	28.1	57	35.1	94	46.6	131	36.6
Clinical Psychology	34.2	111	38.5	117	58.0	143	43.6
Other Psychology	25.3	79	55.0	100	69.6	102	50.0
Economics	32.3	127	51.8	170	70.6	167	51.6
Political Science	40.2	251	48.3	281	68.9	148	52.5
Sociology	37.1	62	43.6	133	78.6	178	53.1
Other Social Science	38.5	78	46.8	126	60.5	81	48.9
Fine Arts	39.3	354	58.8	558	69.1	486	55.7
English	41.3	520	63.6	440	68.4	225	57.8
History	36.4	327	49.6	407	75.5	400	53.8
Language	30.4	289	46.1	293	60.6	137	45.7
Philosophy	7.2	83	62.6	83	—	38	—
Other Humanities	—	30	65.7	102	88.7	62	—
Education	61.5	1,571	68.3	4,596	75.1	5,356	68.3
Business	49.9	595	66.2	1,674	78.9	2,234	65.0
Law	17.3	571	27.7	874	45.4	985	30.1
Social Work	68.3	120	55.3	293	77.6	299	67.1
Other Professions	33.3	531	47.3	1,027	56.8	1,432	45.8

N	39,167
NA, Graduate Field	2,087
NA, API	559
NA, Both	40
Excluded from Table:	
Not Going to Graduate School	12,383
NA, Plans	2,428
Total Weighted N	56,664

*Expected per cent if equal proportions from each API group.

posed of equal proportions of high API men, above average API men, bottom half men, high API women, and above average API women. As in the case of API, the ranks are very similar for the raw and adjusted figures.

In sum, the field differences in postponement of graduate studies are not to be explained by variations in their sex or API

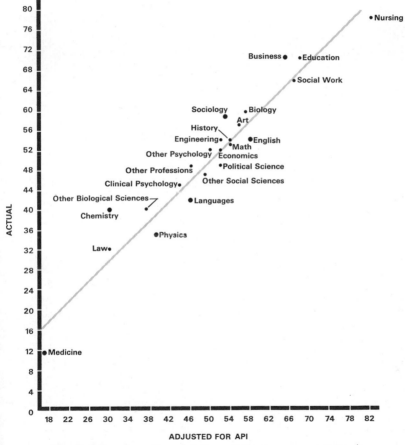

Chart 4.8. Actual and Adjusted Postponement Rates*

*Excluded because of small case base: Earth, other physical sciences, health, botany, zoology, microbiology, physiology, philosophy, other humanities, and biochemistry.

composition. Let us then examine the rates of postponement for the strategic group of men from the top fifth in API (Table 4.19b). Because of small sample sizes, all of the biological science fields had to be combined and a number of fields were excluded from the table, but the results are clear. While the high API men have much lower rates of postponement than future graduate students in general, delay in beginning graduate studies

Table 4.18. Graduate Field and Plans, Controlling for Sex and API (Per cent Postponing Graduate Studies, Among Those Planning to Go to Graduate School)

Graduate Field*	Male						Female					
	API						API					
	Top Fifth		Above Average		Bottom Half		Top Fifth		Above Average		Bottom Half	
	Per cent	N	Per cent	N	Per cent	N	Per cent	N	Per cent	N	Per cent	N
Medicine	3	555	8	546	32	191	—	43	47	57	—	30
Physiology	—	5	—	9	—	33	—	13	—	18	—	14
Other Health	—	26	25	124	31	257	—	17	44	139	18	92
Law	17	547	27	816	45	957	—	24	38	58	—	28
Zoology	—	16	—	47	—	45	—	22	—	10	—	16
Physics	12	276	33	180	68	206	—	28	—	26	—	3
Botany	—	13	—	22	—	42	—	4	—	9	—	10
Philosophy	4	70	47	53	—	31	—	13	—	30	—	7
Other Bio. Science	—	35	27	55	43	99	—	22	—	39	—	32
Chemistry	16	164	31	237	57	284	28	58	57	83	—	31
Languages	24	88	38	84	69	52	33	201	49	209	55	85
Other Phy. Science	—	48	33	58	—	30	—	3	—	9	—	1
Clinical Psychology	—	28	25	73	58	106	40	83	—	44	—	37
Other Soc. Science	—	40	40	65	66	61	—	38	54	61	—	20
Biochemistry	—	17	—	35	—	15	—	43	—	43	—	34
Other Professions	26	316	37	683	50	1,066	44	215	68	344	77	366
Political Science	32	168	51	167	67	115	57	83	45	114	—	33
Geo.-Geol. (Earth)	—	29	53	101	62	76	—	18	—	18	—	26
Other Psychology	—	43	36	55	66	77	—	36	—	45	—	25
Economics	23	92	47	134	70	158	—	35	—	36	—	9
Mathematics	18	185	45	216	76	241	55	112	77	100	—	41
English	23	164	50	173	54	79	50	356	72	267	76	146
Microbiology	—	7	—	18	—	35	—	28	—	18	—	24
History	29	164	42	228	73	294	44	163	60	179	82	106
Engineering	27	740	55	1,114	72	1,147	—	3	—	13	—	6
Fine Arts	29	111	51	187	65	212	44	243	63	371	73	274
Sociology	—	20	33	78	74	113	—	42	58	55	86	65
Biology	—	14	49	80	70	116	—	36	61	80	—	32
Social Work	—	13	—	49	61	88	69	107	61	244	84	211
Business	51	529	66	1,542	80	2,083	44	66	67	132	62	151
Education	47	309	58	1,268	72	2,450	65	1,262	72	3,328	78	2,906
Other Humanities	—	7	—	20	—	29	—	23	65	82	—	33
Nursing	—	2	—	1	—	2	69	116	86	203	93	104

N	39,167
N.A. Graduate Field	2,087
N.A. API	559
N.A. Both	40
Excluded from Table:	
Not Going to Graduate School	12,383
N.A. Plans	2,428
Total Weighted N	56,664

*Ranked by per cent planning graduate school the next fall.

is still considerable in this group. Except for philosophy and physics, between 15 and 32 per cent of the high API men are postponing their studies in the arts and sciences in the table, a figure that indicates considerable inefficiency in graduate school recruitment.

When one turns to the reasons given for not going on, as an aid in explaining field differences in postponement, they turn out to be of little help. Table 4.20 gives the per cent who are postponing their studies and who give selected reasons. There is surprisingly

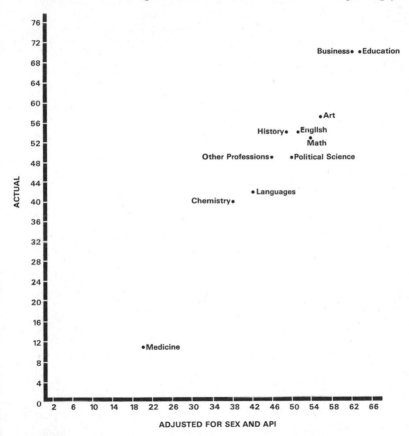

Chart 4.9. Per cent Postponing Graduate Studies, Actual and Adjusted for Sex and API

little field difference. Of the 231 percentages in the table, there are only *six entries* where a given field exceeds the figure for all graduate students by 10 per cent or more. Nursing and education stand out on "practical experience"; other humanities and biology on "financial obstacles"; other humanities on "Tired of being a student," and business on "military service."

Table 4.19. Graduate Field and Plans, Controlling for Sex and API

a. Per cent Postponing Graduate Studies

Graduate Field	All Future Graduate Students	High API Men	
		Per cent	N
Chemistry	40	16	164
Physics	35	12	276
Mathematics	53	18	185
Engineering	54	27	740
Medicine	11	3	555
Biological Sciences (All)	46	16	107
Economics	52	23	92
Political Science	49	32	168
Fine Arts	57	29	111
English	54	23	164
History	54	29	164
Language	42	24	88
Philosophy	38	4	70
Education	70	47	309
Business	70	51	529
Law	32	17	547
Other Professions	49	26	316

N	4,585
Excluded from Table:	
*Other Fields	256
All Women, Medium and Low API Men	34,326
Not Going to Graduate School	12,383
NA, Plans	2,428
NA, Graduate Field	2,087
NA, API	559
NA, Both	40
Total Weighted N	56,664

*Earth, other physical science, nursing, clinical psychology, psychology, sociology, other social sciences, other health, other humanities, and social work excluded because of small case base.

b. Per cent Postponing Graduate Studies Among High API Males, Grouped by Division

Division

Value	Professions	Physical Science	Biological Science	Social Science	Humanities
60					
58					
56					
54					
52	Business				
50					
48	Education				
46					
44					
42					
40					
38					
36					
34					
32					
30					
28	Engineering				
26	Other Professions				
24					History
22				Political Science	Art
20			All Biological Science		
18		Math			Languages
16	Law	Chemistry		Economics	English
14					
12		Physics			
10					
8					
6					Philosophy
4	Medicine				
2					
0					

Great Aspirations

Putting it another way, the fields with high rates of postpone-ment do not have spectacularly high percentages for any partic-ular reason, but rather are a little higher on each of a number of reasons.

When one considers how the fields vary in length of training, financing of training, competition for places in graduate school, and career structures, it is surprising that sharper differences do not turn up in the reasons given by those who are postponing.

Table 4.20. Graduate Field and Reasons for Not Planning Graduate Stud Next Fall

Graduate Field	Per cent Postponing	Reasons*							N	Average No of Reasons from Complete Se of 12 Checked by Postponers
		Practical Experience	Financial Obstacles	Tired of Being a Student	Family Responsibilities	Good Job	Military Service	Low Grades		
Nursing	79	49.9	27.6	17.6	14.5	14.0	1.6	3.9	435	1.83
Other Humanities	72	27.4	32.5	28.4	19.8	13.1	3.0	5.1	197	2.12
Education	70	36.5	23.4	16.0	14.3	13.3	3.2	3.5	11,559	1.78
Business	70	21.2	24.7	13.3	13.6	10.1	19.9	9.5	4,495	1.81
Social Work	66	33.0	29.3	18.6	12.8	4.8	1.6	10.7	709	1.83
Biology	60	26.5	32.1	6.1	6.1	12.8	2.0	3.1	358	1.68
Sociology	59	24.4	25.5	15.3	9.7	9.1	5.1	7.0	373	1.92
Fine Arts	57	23.8	22.5	12.9	6.2	7.9	4.6	4.9	1,425	1.70
Engineering	54	22.0	20.1	14.0	11.6	8.6	10.4	9.0	3,025	1.99
English	54	22.2	24.0	17.5	7.9	7.2	2.4	2.4	1,191	1.77
Microbiology	54	19.2	13.8	8.5	5.4	10.8	7.7	13.1	130	1.91
History	54	20.9	22.0	15.7	7.4	5.8	8.1	3.9	1,114	1.76
Mathematics	53	15.7	17.8	15.2	8.3	8.2	8.8	7.2	888	1.91
Geo.-Geol. (Earth)	53	21.6	23.0	10.8	11.2	6.7	10.8	3.0	269	1.84
Economics	52	16.2	18.1	12.2	9.0	4.1	13.0	5.5	469	1.65
Psychology	52	20.2	20.2	15.2	9.6	5.7	7.8	4.6	282	1.99
Political Science	49	16.1	18.9	13.5	4.5	6.5	12.8	4.8	682	1.80
Other Professions	49	22.3	20.4	9.5	9.1	6.8	6.9	4.3	3.004	1.36
Biochemistry	49	27.3	21.9	16.0	4.3	5.9	4.3	8.0	187	1.90
Other Social Sciences	47	18.3	23.9	13.0	11.3	4.9	3.9	3.5	284	1.84
Clinical Psychology	45	12.6	20.9	12.8	9.9	8.0	7.2	6.4	374	2.03
Languages	42	17.9	17.1	13.7	6.2	4.9	3.6	1.7	715	1.80
Other Physical Science	41	18.5	17.2	8.3	10.2	8.3	10.2	3.2	157	1.74
Chemistry	40	13.4	17.4	10.3	7.4	3.8	7.2	6.6	860	1.93
Other Biological Science	40	13.1	19.0	12.8	9.3	5.2	6.9	8.3	289	2.07
Philosophy	38	13.7	15.6	8.8	8.8	2.0	5.4	2.4	205	1.84
Botany	37	11.3	18.9	3.8	4.7	1.9	2.8	4.7	106	1.45
Zoology	35	12.0	13.9	10.8	7.6	3.2	3.2	6.3	158	1.97
Physics	35	10.3	14.6	10.4	5.7	3.8	5.4	6.1	717	1.81
Law	32	5.2	13.6	5.9	5.1	2.3	12.4	3.8	2,442	1.78
Health	30	11.9	12.1	6.6	3.8	6.6	4.7	2.8	654	1.80
Physiology	24	17.3	12.2	2.0	3.1	1.0	1.0	11.2	98	2.25
Medicine	11	1.3	3.7	1.4	0.8	1.4	0.8	3.4	1,430	1.57
Total		24.2	21.2	13.6	10.7	9.1	7.4	5.5	39,281	

N.A, Graduate Field 2,078
N.A, Reasons for Not Going 445
N.A, Both 49
Excluded from Table:
   Not Going to Graduate School 12,383
   N.A, Plans 2,428
Total Weighted N 56.664

*Shading identifies cells above the average for future graduate students in general.

Beyond the obvious fact that the fields with more men (business, political science, law, engineering, economics) are higher on "military service" as a reason, the reasons analysis sheds little light on the problem.

SUMMARY

1. Fifty-eight per cent of the students who anticipated graduate study did not plan to be in graduate school in the fall of 1961.

2. Specific fields vary in their postponement rates from 11 per cent for medicine to more than two-thirds in social work, education, business, other humanities, and nursing, with the great bulk of the fields falling between 30 and 60 per cent.

3. Differences in sex and API composition do not explain the field variation in postponement, although they add or subtract to the rates for different fields.

4. For the arts and sciences with sufficient cases to tabulate, nine out of 11 fields have postponement rates of 15 per cent for men in the top fifth in API.

5. Students in fields with high postponement rates did not differ in the kinds of reasons for postponement when compared with those in low postponement rate fields. That is, they did not cite different obstacles, merely more obstacles.

STIPENDS AND FINANCES

Except in the sense that public colleges are heavily subsidized from tax funds and private schools receive gifts and grants so that students do not pay the full cost of study, undergraduate training is not heavily subsidized in modern America. As a benchmark figure, about 20 per cent (RSS) of the seniors reported receiving a scholarship at any time during their undergraduate studies.

When we turn to advanced study, rates of stipend help are generally higher, but we shall see wide differences between fields of study because the level of stipend support for graduate study does not represent the application of any general national policy, but stems from the individual decisions of graduate schools, graduate departments, foundations, federal agencies, and individual donors.

Table 4.21a summarizes, by field, the results of the answers on stipends, given by those students who expected to begin advanced study in the fall of 1961. Considering first the expectation of any stipend, regardless of type, Table 4.21b shows striking differences. While an overall total of 42 per cent expected something, the range is from 78 per cent in chemistry to 8 per cent in nursing. The major patterns are these:

1) Although there are some arts and sciences fields with lower stipend rates than some professions, arts and sciences students,

Table 4.21. Graduate Field and Stipends

a. Graduate Field, Stipend Application Status, and Stipend Type (Among Those Going to Graduate School Next Year)

Graduate Field	Did Not Apply	Scholarship: Part Tuition	Scholarship: Full Tuition	Fellowship: Tuition Plus Less Than $1,000	Fellowship: Tuition Plus Greater Than or Equal to $1,000	Assistantship: Teaching	Assistantship: Research	None of This Type	Don't Know Yet	Total Per cent	Total N	Per cent Expect a Stipend Next Year
Chemistry	18.4	0.8	9.8	1.0	18.8	58.2	5.9	1.0	2.5	116.4	512	78.
Physics	21.0	0.9	13.3	1.7	23.6	39.1	9.2	6.2	5.6	120.6	467	67.2
Geo.-Geol. (Earth)	36.2	–	3.2	–	9.4	37.0	6.3	7.9	7.1	107.1	127	48.
Mathematics	36.1	1.0	6.7	1.4	16.6	24.3	5.1	4.1	11.1	106.4	415	48.
Other Phy. Science	28.3	3.3	7.6	–	23.9	7.6	30.4	8.7	4.3	114.1	92	58.
Engineering	49.0	1.5	5.8	1.4	13.5	12.6	12.3	5.8	6.0	107.9	1,373	39.
Medicine	68.4	8.3	3.9	0.3	0.9	0.6	1.0	5.6	12.7	101.7	1,258	13.
Nursing	81.8	–	6.5	–	2.6	–	–	1.3	9.1	101.3	77	7.
Other Health	72.3	7.3	1.5	1.5	3.5	0.9	0.4	3.5	9.7	100.6	455	14.
Biology	57.9	0.7	3.4	–	11.0	18.6	2.1	0.7	9.0	103.4	145	32.
Biochemistry	16.7	4.2	14.6	2.1	18.6	22.9	30.2	2.1	6.3	117.7	96	74.
Botany	43.3	–	–	1.5	–	28.3	11.7	6.7	1.7	106.0	67	44
Microbiology	25.0	–	3.3	–	28.3	28.3	11.7	6.7	1.7	105.0	60	66.
Physiology	58.1	–	4.1	1.4	16.2	10.8	10.8	5.4	–	106.8	74	36.
Zoology	24.5	5.9	2.0	2.0	7.8	37.3	16.7	5.9	9.8	111.9	102	59.
Other Bio. Science	33.3	–	4.1	1.8	24.6	8.2	21.6	0.6	14.0	108.2	171	52.
Clinical Psychology	40.3	5.8	1.5	–	15.0	6.8	19.9	1.9	20.9	112.1	206	36.
Other Psychology	30.6	0.7	5.2	3.7	20.9	14.9	16.4	4.5	13.4	110.3	134	51.
Economics	41.7	2.2	3.6	5.4	24.7	5.4	4.5	8.1	7.6	103.2	223	42.
Political Science	42.1	6.4	7.9	5.0	11.4	5.3	4.4	12.0	9.9	104.4	342	36.
Sociology	47.4	0.7	2.0	0.7	15.1	17.1	13.8	7.2	10.5	114.5	152	34.
Other Soc. Science	50.0	3.3	4.0	4.7	15.3	6.7	5.3	11.3	6.0	106.6	150	32
Fine Arts	56.7	5.7	5.2	1.8	6.0	11.4	0.7	6.0	13.8	107.3	614	23.
English	38.5	2.6	7.5	3.3	16.3	13.7	0.6	12.5	8.4	103.4	546	40.
History	48.8	5.3	4.7	3.9	17.6	6.6	0.2	8.6	7.8	103.5	512	34.
Languages	38.3	3.4	7.9	2.4	17.2	12.7	1.9	10.3	12.9	107.0	418	38.
Philosophy	33.1	3.9	7.9	3.9	26.0	3.9	2.4	10.2	9.4	100.7	127	47.
Other Humanities	60.0	–	10.9	–	5.5	–	1.8	12.7	9.1	100.0	55	18.
Education	79.2	2.8	2.3	1.0	2.7	5.0	0.2	4.4	4.4	102.0	3,414	12.
Business	74.5	2.0	3.9	2.2	2.4	3.2	3.8	4.9	5.8	102.7	1,355	14.
Law	72.0	5.0	7.2	2.2	0.4	0.4	0.5	6.4	7.4	101.5	1,655	14.
Social Work	44.7	3.8	10.0	7.1	13.8	1.7	0.4	0.4	23.8	105.7	239	31
Other Professions	53.8	8.8	9.3	4.2	5.3	4.6	5.8	5.2	7.7	104.7	1,513	33
Total	42.0	3.7	5.1	1.9	7.5	8.7	4.0	6.5	8.6		17,146	42

NA, Graduate Field	436
NA, Stipend Type	72
NA, Both	1
Excluded from Table:	
Planning Graduate School Later	24,198
Not Going to Graduate School	12,383
NA, Plans	2,428
Total Weighted N	56,664

ble 4.21   *Continued*

b. Per cent Expecting a Stipend Among Those Going to Graduate School Next Year, Grouped by Division

| | | Division | | |
Professions	Physical Science	Biological Science	Social Science	Humanities
	Chemistry			
		Biochemistry		
	Physics	Microbiology		
	Other	Zoology		
		Other	Other Psychology	
	Earth; Math			
		Botany		Philosophy
			— Economics —	
Engineering				English
		Physiology	Clinical Psychology Political Science	Languages
Other Social Work		Biology	Sociology Other	History
				Art
Business Health; Law Medicine Education				Other
Nursing				

All → Next Year

(Table 4.21   Continued)

generally speaking, have a distinct advantage in securing financial aid. All the fields with 40 per cent or more expecting a stipend are arts and sciences, while all the fields with 15 per cent or less are professional fields.

2) Within the arts and sciences, the physical and biological science fields considerably surpass the social sciences and humanities, all five physical sciences exceeding the percentage for students in general, as do five out of seven biological science fields. This contrasts to one out of six fields in the social sciences and one out of six in the humanities.

3) The fields in which 50 per cent or more of "next year's" students (among June, 1961, graduates) expect a stipend are: chem-

Table 4.21. *Continued*

c. Graduate Field and Stipend Type: Summary

Any Stipend	RA	TA	Fellow	Fields
+	+	+	+	Biochemistry
+	+	−	+	Other Physical Sciences; Other Biological Sciences; Clinical Psychology
+	+	+	−	Botany
+	+	−	−	–
+	−	+	+	Microbiology; Physics; Psychology; Sociology
+	−	−	+	Philosophy; Economics; English; Languages; Physiology; History
+	−	+	−	Chemistry; Zoology; Earth; Mathematics; Biology
+	−	−	−	Engineering; Political Science; Other Professions
−	−	−	−	Social Work; Art; Other Humanities; Business; Health; Law; Medicine; Education; Nursing

+ RA, TA, Fellow = 15 per cent or greater.
+ Any Stipend   = 32 per cent or greater.

istry, biochemistry, physics, microbiology, zoology, other biological sciences, and psychology other than clinical.

4) Among the professional fields, engineering, other professions, and social work all have percentages between 30 and 40, while business, health, law, medicine, education, and nursing all have 15 per cent or less.

Shifting our attention to the type of stipend, we find that there is considerable variation such that although the fields that are "low" on stipends tend to be low on all types, the fields that are "high" are not necessarily high on every kind.

Considering three types of aid—fellowships worth an amount equivalent to tuition plus $1,000 or more, teaching assistantships, and research assistantships—fields can be classified simultaneously in terms of a student's chances for particular types of stipend and for any kind of aid (Table 4.21c).

Only one field, biochemistry, is high on all three types of stipend. The remaining fields where 32 per cent or more expect some support can be classified in terms of their special forms of aid as follows:

1. Fellowships and Teaching Assistantships: microbiology, physics, psychology, sociology.

2. Fellowships and Research Assistantships: physical science, other, other biological science, clinical psychology.

3. Teaching Assistantships and Research Assistantships: botany.

4. Fellowships Only: philosophy, economics, English, languages, physiology, history.

5. Teaching Assistantships Only: chemistry, zoology, earth sciences, mathematics, biology.

6. Not High on any Particular Type: engineering, political science, other professions.

The remaining fields – social work, art, other humanities, business, health, law, medicine, education, nursing – are low on stipends in general and also relatively low on these three forms of aid.

Viewed this way, the picture changes a little, for these findings tell us that a good deal of the support for arts and sciences students comes in the form of part-time jobs – research and teaching assistantships – which have a training focus, but hardly represent free gifts to the students. There are only two fields in the table (microbiology, 28 per cent, and philosophy, 26 per cent) where as many as a quarter of the students expect a duty-free stipend that pays their full tuition and a living allowance of $1,000 or more. Thus, while many students receive aid, the American graduate student is seldom "totally supported" during his studies.

Turning to the application status data in Table 4.21, we see clearly that the decision to apply, not acceptance or rejection, is the major factor producing the field differences (Chart 4.10). The triangular coordinate graph shows that variations in the per cent who did not apply for a stipend are much greater than variations in the per cent of applications that were turned down. Does this mean that if graduate students in business were to increase their application rates they could be supported like science students? Probably not. No one knows, of course, but when analysis is limited to students who were planning graduate school next year and applied for a stipend, the figures do not look encouraging

(Table 4.22b). While the great majority of stipend applicants in each field were not turned down, the rejection rates are very similar to the rates of over-all support. Thus in all 10 science fields with sufficient cases for tabulation, rejection rates were below 15 per cent, while in all five humanities fields, three out of five social sciences fields, and four out of eight professional fields (business, education, law, and medicine) the rejection rates were 15 per cent or more. The suggestion is that even if application rates were increased in all fields, the observed field differences would remain.

Sex and academic performance, as in so many analyses in this research, also played a crucial role in stipend allocation. Table 4.23a gives the stipend information by sex and API for a grouped

Chart 4.10. Graduate Field, Stipend Application Status, and Receipt of Stipend

Table 4.22. Graduate Field and Stipend

a. Graduate Field, Stipend Application Status, and Stipend Type (Among Those Planning to Go to Graduate School Next Year Who Applied for a Stipend)

Graduate Field	Scholarship		Fellowship		Assistantship		None of This Type	Don't Know Yet	Total Per cent Applying for a Stipend	N
	Part Tuition	Full Tuition	Tuition Plus Less Than $1,000	Tuition Plus Greater Than or Equal to $1,000	Teaching	Research				
Chemistry	1.0	12.0	1.2	23.0	71.3	7.2	1.2	3.1	91.6	418
Physics	1.1	16.8	2.2	29.8	49.3	11.7	7.9	7.0	79.0	369
Geo.-Geol. (Earth)	—	4.9	—	14.8	58.0	9.9	12.3	11.1	63.8	81
Mathematics	1.5	10.6	2.3	26.0	38.1	7.9	6.4	17.4	63.9	265
Other Phy. Science	4.5	10.6	—	33.3	10.6	42.4	12.1	6.1	71.7	66
Engineering	3.0	11.4	2.7	26.6	24.7	24.1	11.3	11.7	51.0	700
Medicine	27.0	12.3	1.0	2.8	1.8	3.3	17.6	40.3	31.6	397
Nursing	—	—	—	—	—	—	—	—	18.2	14
Other Health	26.2	5.6	5.6	12.7	3.2	1.6	12.7	34.9	27.7	126
Biology	1.6	8.2	—	26.2	44.3	4.9	1.6	21.3	42.1	61
Biochemistry	5.0	17.5	2.5	22.5	27.5	36.2	2.5	7.5	83.3	80
Botany	—	—	—	—	—	—	—	—	56.7	38
Microbiology	—	—	—	—	—	—	—	—	75.0	45
Physiology	—	—	—	—	—	—	—	—	41.9	31
Zoology	7.8	2.6	2.6	10.4	49.4	23.4	7.8	13.0	75.5	77
Other Bio. Science	—	6.1	2.6	36.8	12.3	32.5	0.9	21.1	66.7	114
Clinical Psychology	9.8	2.4	5.4	25.2	11.4	33.3	3.3	35.0	59.7	123
Other Psychology	1.1	7.5	9.2	30.1	21.5	23.7	6.5	19.4	69.4	93
Economics	3.8	6.2	8.6	42.3	9.2	7.7	13.8	13.1	58.3	130
Political Science	11.1	13.6	1.2	19.7	9.1	7.6	20.7	17.2	57.9	198
Sociology	1.2	3.8	9.3	28.8	32.5	26.2	13.8	20.0	52.6	80
Other Social Science	6.7	8.0	4.1	30.7	13.3	10.7	22.7	12.0	50.0	75
Fine Arts	13.2	12.0	5.4	13.9	26.3	1.5	13.9	32.0	43.3	266
English	4.2	12.2	7.6	26.5	22.3	0.9	20.2	13.7	61.5	336
History	10.3	9.2	7.6	34.4	13.0	0.4	16.8	15.3	51.2	262
Languages	5.4	12.8	3.9	27.9	20.5	3.1	16.7	20.9	61.7	258

(Table 4.22 continued)

Table 4.22. Continued

Graduate Field	Per cent of Those Who Applied for a Stipend Who Expect to Receive. . . .									
	Scholarship		Fellowship		Assistantship		None of This Type	Don't Know Yet	Total Per cent Applying for a Stipend	N
	Part Tuition	Full Tuition	Tuition Plus Less Than $1,000	Tuition Plus Greater Than or Equal to $1,000	Teaching	Research				
Philosophy	5.9	11.8	5.9	38.8	5.9	3.5	15.3	14.1	66.9	85
Other Humanities	—	—	—	—	—	—	—	—	40.0	22
Education	13.4	11.3	4.8	13.0	24.1	0.8	21.2	21.3	20.8	709
Business	7.8	15.3	8.7	9.5	12.4	15.0	19.4	22.8	25.5	346
Law	17.9	25.6	7.8	1.5	1.5	1.9	22.8	26.5	28.0	464
Other Professions	19.0	20.2	9.0	11.4	9.9	12.4	11.2	16.7	56.6	699
Social Work	6.8	18.2	12.9	25.0	3.0	0.8	0.8	43.2	55.3	132

N 7,160
N.A. Graduate Field 72
N.A. Stipend Type 115
N.A. Both 1
Excluded from Table:
Those Planning Graduate School Later 24,198
Those Who Didn't Apply for a Stipend 10,307
Those Not Going to Graduate School 12,383
N.A. Plans 2,428

Total Weighted N 56,664

Table 4.22 Continued

b. Per cent "None" Among Those Accepted by School and Who Applied for a Stipend

Division

	Professions	Physical Science	Biological Science	Social Science	Humanities
30–					
28–					
26–					
24–					
22–	Law			Other Social Science	
20–	Education			Political Science	
18–	Business Medicine				English History; Language Philosophy Arts
16–					
14–	Other Health	Earth; Other		Econ.; Sociology	
12–	Engin; Other Prof.				
10–					
8–		Physics Math	Zoology	Other Psychology	
6–				Clinical Psychology	
4–					
2–	Social Work	Chemistry	Biology; Biochem. Other Bio. Science		
0–					

classification of the graduate fields among students accepted for study in the fall of 1961.

The first step in the process, application for a stipend, is summarized in Table 4.23b. Both sex and API made a considerable difference. Except among high API social science students and health professions, women were less likely to apply for aid than men of similar academic performance accepted for study in the same fields. Thus, for example, among high API students accepted in humanities, 80 per cent of the men applied for aid in comparison with 67 per cent of the women. API made an even greater difference. For example, among men in physical science, 91 per cent of the top fifth, 71 per cent of the above average, and 52 per cent of the bottom half applied for aid. At the same time, within a sex and API grouping, application rates varied by field, the general rank order being natural sciences, social sciences and humanities, engineering and other professions, health, education, business, and finally, law and medicine. Considering only top fifth males, 90 per cent applied in the natural sciences and 80 in the social sciences and humanities, as compared with 56 to 72 in education, other professions and engineering, and less than half in business, law, and medicine.

Table 4.23c indicates the outcomes of these requests, the majority of which were granted regardless of sex, field, and API. Rejection rates tended to be higher in groups with lesser academic performance, particularly in the arts and sciences, but those bottom half students who did apply came out pretty well. (Of course, applicants from the bottom half were probably not by any means representative of bottom half students.) Sex made little difference in the nine cells where there were enough female applicants to percentage, the women's rejection rates being neither systematically higher nor lower. Field of study did make a difference, however, for rejection rates were lowest in the natural sciences, next lowest in social sciences, humanities, other professions and engineering, and highest in education, business, law, and medicine. More top fifth men were rejected in education, business, law, and medicine than bottom half men in natural science fields.

Table 4.23. Graduate Field, Stipend Status, and Plans, Controlling for Sex and API

a. Among Those Already Accepted to Graduate School for Next Year

Graduate Field	Sex	API*	Stipend Status				Total	
			Didn't apply	None of this type	Don't know yet	Received stipend	Per cent	N
Other Professions	Male	High	34.8	4.8	8.7	51.7	100.0	230
		Medium	48.6	3.8	5.0	42.7	100.1	424
		Low	63.1	6.8	8.9	21.1	99.9	526
	Female	High	40.0	4.2	6.7	49.2	100.1	120
		Medium	59.5	8.1	15.3	17.1	100.0	111
		Low	83.1	—	3.6	13.3	100.0	83
Social Work	Male	High	—	—	—	—	—	5
		Medium	—	—	—	—	—	36
		Low	—	—	—	—	—	34
	Female	High	—	—	—	—	—	33
		Medium	42.1	—	28.4	29.5	100.0	95
		Low	—	—	—	—	—	33
Physical Science	Male	High	9.2	3.2	4.0	83.5	99.9	595
		Medium	28.9	5.9	7.0	58.2	100.0	488
		Low	47.5	4.9	10.6	37.0	100.0	284
	Female	High	15.8	4.2	7.5	72.5	100.0	120
		Medium	53.9	2.2	—	43.8	99.9	89
		Low	—	—	—	—	—	20
Engineering	Male	High	27.6	7.8	5.0	59.5	99.9	536
		Medium	53.4	5.4	7.9	33.3	100.0	496
		Low	77.5	2.5	4.8	15.2	100.0	315
	Female	High	—	—	—	—	—	3
		Medium	—	—	—	—	—	10
		Low	—	—	—	—	—	2

*High = Top fifth; Medium = Above average; and Low = Bottom half.

(Table 4.23 continued)

Table 4.23. Continued

Graduate Field	Sex	API	Stipend Status				Total	
			Didn't apply	None of this type	Don't know yet	Received stipend	Per cent	N
Medicine	Male	High	62.2	5.9	14.3	17.4	99.8	538
		Medium	73.1	6.2	10.8	10.0	100.1	502
		Low	80.0	2.4	11.9	5.6	99.9	126
	Female	High	—	—	—	—	—	37
		Medium	—	—	—	—	—	24
		Low	—	—	—	—	—	13
Health	Male	High	—	—	18.1	13.8	100.0	20
		Medium	66.0	2.1	18.1	13.8	100.0	94
		Low	79.3	5.6	3.4	11.7	100.0	179
	Female	High	—	—	—	—	—	45
		Medium	69.8	7.5	0.9	21.7	99.9	106
		Low	80.5	—	15.9	3.7	100.1	82
Biological Science	Male	High	10.0	2.2	6.7	81.1	100.0	90
		Medium	26.1	2.7	10.3	60.9	100.0	184
		Low	65.2	4.0	7.6	23.2	100.0	198
	Female	High	16.9	3.4	1.1	78.7	100.1	89
		Medium	30.9	—	12.4	56.7	100.0	97
		Low	70.0	2.0	14.0	14.0	100.0	50
Social Science	Male	High	19.5	9.2	6.1	65.2	100.0	293
		Medium	37.0	6.6	16.3	40.1	100.0	332
		Low	69.9	6.8	10.2	13.1	100.0	206
	Female	High	11.9	10.0	20.6	57.5	100.0	160
		Medium	76.3	11.2	3.9	8.6	100.0	152
		Low	92.0	—	4.0	4.0	100.0	50
Humanities	Male	High	20.5	12.0	10.3	57.2	100.0	458
		Medium	44.1	9.4	12.5	33.9	99.9	392
		Low	64.6	11.1	8.4	15.9	100.0	226
	Female	High	33.2	9.7	10.2	47.0	100.1	558
		Medium	62.2	4.5	15.8	17.5	100.0	423
		Low	86.0	8.1	1.7	4.1	99.9	172

Table 4.23 *Continued*

Graduate Field	Sex	API	Stipend Status				Total	
			Didn't apply	None of this type	Don't know yet	Received stipend	Per cent	N
Education	Male	High	43.8	11.1	10.5	34.6	100.0	162
		Medium	72.7	5.0	6.9	15.3	99.9	535
		Low	87.6	3.1	3.6	5.7	100.0	685
	Female	High	51.8	12.3	8.9	27.0	100.0	440
		Medium	84.4	2.5	3.5	9.5	99.9	913
		Low	95.8	0.6	0.2	3.5	100.1	637
Business	Male	High	57.1	7.7	7.3	28.0	100.1	261
		Medium	71.4	5.2	5.6	17.9	100.1	521
		Low	87.0	2.7	4.8	5.6	100.1	414
	Female	High	–	–	–	–	–	37
		Medium	–	–	–	–	–	44
		Low	98.2	–	–	1.8	100.0	57
Law	Male	High	52.0	9.5	9.9	28.6	100.0	454
		Medium	72.9	6.2	8.7	12.1	99.9	595
		Low	90.4	1.9	4.3	3.4	100.0	529
	Female	High	–	–	–	–	–	16
		Medium	–	–	–	–	–	36
		Low	–	–	–	–	–	9

	N
Excluded: Planning Grad School Later	16,929
NA Stipend	22,167
NA API	70
NA Field	559
NA Two or More	2,087
Excluded: Not Going to Grad School	41
NA Plans	12,383
	2,428
Total Weighted N	56,664

(Table 4.23 *continued*)

Table 4.23. Continued

b. Per cent Applying for a Stipend

Graduate Field	API					
	Top Fifth		Above Average		Bottom Half	
	Male	Female	Male	Female	Male	Female
Arts and Science						
Biological Science	90 (90)	83 (89)	74 (184)	69 (97)	35 (198)	30 (50)
Physical Science	91 (595)	84 (120)	71 (488)	46 (89)	52 (284)	— (20)
Social Science	80 (293)	88 (160)	63 (332)	24 (152)	30 (206)	8 (50)
Humanities	80 (458)	67 (558)	56 (392)	38 (423)	35 (226)	14 (172)
Professions						
Other	65 (230)	60 (120)	51 (424)	40 (111)	37 (526)	17 (83)
Engineering	72 (536)	— (3)	47 (496)	— (10)	22 (315)	— (2)
Health	— (20)	— (45)	34 (94)	30 (106)	21 (179)	20 (82)
Education	56 (162)	48 (440)	27 (535)	16 (913)	12 (685)	4 (637)
Business	43 (261)	— (37)	29 (521)	— (44)	13 (414)	2 (57)
Law	48 (454)	— (16)	27 (595)	— (36)	10 (529)	— (9)
Medicine	38 (538)	— (37)	27 (502)	— (24)	20 (126)	— (13)

N	16,693
Excluded: Social Work	236
Planning Graduate School Later	22,167
NA Stipend	70
NA API	559
NA Grad field	2,087
NA Two or More	41
Excluded: Not Going to Grad School	12,383
NA Plans	2,428

c. Per cent "Refused" (None/All, except those who "Didn't Apply")

Graduate Field	API					
	Top Fifth		Above Average		Bottom Half	
	Male	Female	Male	Female	Male	Female
Arts and Science						
Biological Science	2.4 (81)	4.1 (74)	3.7 (136)	0.0 (67)	11.5 (69)	— (15)
Physical Science	3.5 (540)	5.0 (106)	8.3 (347)	— (41)	9.3 (149)	— (5)
Social Science	11.4 (236)	11.4 (141)	10.5 (209)	— (36)	22.6 (62)	— (4)
Humanities	15.0 (364)	14.5 (373)	16.8 (219)	11.9 (160)	31.4 (80)	— (24)
Professions						
Other	7.4 (150)	7.0 (72)	7.4 (218)	— (45)	18.4 (194)	— (14)
Engineering	10.8 (388)	— (3)	11.6 (231)	— (0)	11.1 (71)	— (0)
Education	19.7 (91)	25.5 (212)	18.3 (146)	16.0 (142)	25.0 (85)	— (27)
Business	17.9 (112)	— (22)	18.2 (149)	— (4)	20.8 (54)	— (1)
Law	19.8 (218)	— (7)	22.9 (161)	— (22)	19.8 (51)	— (0)
Medicine	15.6 (203)	— (22)	23.0 (135)	— (3)	— (25)	— (4)

N   6,820
                                                     9,839
Didn't Apply
Excluded:
  Social Work and Health   270
  Planning Grad School Later   22,167
  NA Stipend   70
  NA API   559
  NA Grad Field   2,087
  NA Two or More   41
Excluded: Not going to Grad School   12,383
  NA Plans   2,428
                                                     _____
Total Weighted N   56,664

(Table 4.23 continued)

Table 4.23. Continued

d. Per cent with a Stipend

Graduate Field	API					
	Top Fifth		Above Average		Bottom Half	
	Male	Female	Male	Female	Male	Female
Arts and Science						
Biological Science	81 (90)	79 (89)	61 (184)	57 (97)	23 (198)	14 (50)
Physical Science	84 (595)	72 (120)	58 (488)	44 (89)	37 (284)	– (20)
Social Science	65 (293)	58 (160)	40 (332)	9 (152)	13 (206)	4 (50)
Humanities	57 (458)	47 (558)	34 (392)	18 (423)	16 (226)	4 (172)
Professions						
Other	52 (230)	49 (120)	43 (424)	17 (111)	21 (526)	13 (83)
Engineering	60 (536)	– (3)	33 (496)	– (10)	15 (315)	– (2)
Health	– (20)	– (45)	14 (94)	22 (106)	12 (179)	4 (82)
Education	35 (162)	27 (440)	15 (535)	10 (913)	6 (685)	4 (637)
Business	28 (261)	– (37)	18 (521)	– (44)	6 (414)	2 (57)
Law	29 (454)	– (16)	12 (595)	– (36)	3 (529)	– (9)
Medicine	17 (538)	– (37)	10 (502)	– (24)	6 (126)	– (13)

	N
Excluded: Social Work	16,693
Planning Grad School Later	236
NA Stipend	22,167
NA API	70
NA Grad Field	559
NA Two or More	2,087
Excluded: Not going to Grad School	41
NA Plans	12,383
	2,428
Total Weighted N	56,664

SUMMARY

1. Low API students are considerably less likely to apply for a stipend and a little less likely to receive one if they apply.

2. Women are less likely to apply for stipends, but have no disadvantage or advantage in offerings among those who apply.

3. Fields of study show a generally similar trend in applications and acceptance of applications, the situation being most favorable in the natural sciences and the least favorable in the professional fields of medicine, law, business, education, and health professions; social sciences, humanities, engineering, and other professions lie between these extremes.

The joint result of self-selection and stipend allocation is that aid varies tremendously when sex, API, and field of study are considered simultaneously for students who were accepted to begin study in the fall of 1961 (Table 4.23d). The percentages increase quite consistently across rows and up columns. Thus, in all the arts and sciences fields, more than half of the top fifth API men expected stipend aid in contrast to 15 per cent or less of the bottom half women; and at the same time, the per cent of top fifth men with a stipend ranges from more than 80 in the natural sciences to 17 in medicine.

It is apparent that in 1961 as in the past, there was great variation in the financing of studies in different graduate fields. While science majors and the pre-meds had essentially similar academic situations for undergraduate study, advanced study in different fields means quite dissimilar ways of life.

Information on expected sources of money other than stipends helps to underline the variety of financial situations for students in different fields. Table 4.24a gives the percentages expecting income from various sources among those students who planned to attend school in the fall of 1961.

Let us focus on three of the sources of income — stipends, full-time work, and aid from parents or relatives — calling a field "high" if its percentage is equal to or greater than future graduate students in general for that source and calling it "low" if its percentage is below all future graduate students. When field scores are intercorrelated it turns out that there are strong negative relationships (Q for "stipend" and "parental" $= -.69$; "stipend" and "full-time work" $= -.78$; "parental and full-time work" $= -1.00$); fields that tend to be characterized by one of these types of support tend to be low on the other two. The relationships are so strong that 28 out of the 33 fields can be classified as "high" on one of these three sources and "low" on the other two (Table 4.24b). Except for mathematics, sociology, other profes-

Table 4.24. Graduate Field and Financial Sources Next Year (Among Those Planning Graduate School in the Fall)

a. Graduate Field and All Sources of Support

Graduate Field	Full-time Job	Part-time Job	Savings	NDEA Loan	Other Loan	Parents, Relatives	Income from Spouse	Other	Per cent	N
Chemistry	16	15	29	4	0	24	18	31	137	447
Physics	22	18	31	3	2	23	14	33	146	432
Geo.-Geol. (Earth)	17	23	42	12	2	26	17	21	160	115
Mathematics	31	21	24	3	2	22	18	22	148	387
Other Phy. Science	22	14	17	7	4	22	11	47	144	83
Engineering	45	19	22	2	3	18	12	21	142	1,315
Medicine	3	32	42	8	15	80	14	14	208	1,261
Nursing	53	4	21	4	11	13	20	22	148	76
Other Health Prof.	11	30	33	7	13	66	17	24	201	440
Biological Science	35	18	18	12	2	29	13	17	144	136
Biochemistry	3	35	15	12	8	41	12	20	146	74
Botany	10	14	34	2	0	42	22	22	146	59
Microbiology	4	30	23	2	2	30	14	45	150	56
Physiology	34	19	23	0	4	36	20	18	154	73
Zoology	16	26	17	22	4	34	18	33	170	90
Other Bio. Science	14	34	27	6	4	37	13	31	166	167
Clinical Psychology	13	31	34	10	8	45	19	30	190	201
Other Psychology	19	22	25	7	2	34	26	28	163	125
Economics	17	25	34	5	4	35	13	28	161	208
Political Science	14	28	35	10	6	51	13	18	175	338
Sociology	28	31	25	9	6	26	24	25	174	150
Other Social Science	14	28	34	10	8	42	17	21	174	145
Fine Arts	21	41	28	10	7	43	15	17	182	612
English	24	24	22	6	3	39	17	21	156	526
History	31	23	21	8	8	35	18	21	165	480
Languages	21	18	19	9	5	42	8	23	145	396
Philosophy	10	26	26	2	6	28	22	35	155	125
Other Humanities	48	20	17	6	4	22	19	6	142	54
Education	52	19	14	5	2	25	17	9	143	3,377
Business	41	26	24	4	8	36	13	11	163	1,334
Law	15	35	31	6	6	68	13	12	186	1,643
Social Work	15	29	27	5	13	41	16	25	171	234
Other Professions	21	39	23	4	8	31	17	24	167	1,500
Total	29	26	25	6	6	38	15	18		16,664

NA, Graduate Field Only   33
NA, Sources of Finances Only   55
NA, Both   9
Excluded from Table:
   Not Planning to Go to Graduate School This Fall   36,583
   NA, Plans   2,421
Total Weighted N   56,664

Table 4.24 *Continued*

b. Income from Stipends, Full-time Work, and Parents or Relatives, by Graduate Field

Full-time Employment	Parental Support			
	Low		High	
	Stipend			
	Low	High	High	Low
High	Engineering Physiology History Biology Other Humanities Business Education Nursing	Mathematics		
Low	Sociology Other Professions	Chemistry Physics Microbiology Zoology Other Phy. Sci. Psychology Other Bio. Sci. Earth Philosophy Economics	Biochemistry Botany	English Languages Clinical Psych. Pol. Science Other Soc. Sci. Social Work Fine Arts Health Law Medicine

(Table 4.24 continued)

sions, biochemistry, and botany, each field can be characterized by "stipend support," "parental aid," or "self-support." Table 4.24c arrays the fields simultaneously by support type and division with some interesting differences. Professional fields divide between "self-support" (engineering, business, education, nursing) and "parental support" (medicine, law, social work, health); science fields are generally "stipend-supported"; social sciences and humanities students have more "parental support."

Another set of facts, and then we can attempt to pull all of this together. In Table 4.25 the fields are classified by support type and whether their students tend to be high or low on API, SES, and postponement of graduate study.

Table 4.24. Continued

c. Income from Stipends, Full-Time Work, and Parents or Relatives,
by Graduate Field, Grouped by Division

Financial Support	Professions	Division			
		Physical Science	Biological Science	Social Science	Humanities
Self-Support	Engineering − Business + Education − Nursing −		Physiology − Biology −		History + Other +
Self and Stipend		Math −			
Stipend		Chemistry − Physics + Other Phy. Sci. + Earth −	Microbiology + Zoology − Other Bio. Sci. +	Psychology + Economics +	Philosophy+
Stipend and Parental			Biochemistry + Botany +		
Parental	Medicine + Law + Social Work + Health +			Clinical Psych + Political Sci. + Other +	English + Languages + Art +

Note: Sociology and Other Professions are unclassified.
  + = Greater than or equal to graduate students in general on high socio-economic status.
  − = Less than graduate students in general on high socio-economic status.

The "parental" and "stipend" fields are relatively high in API while the "self-support" fields are low. "Parental" fields are highest in SES while "self-support" fields are lowest. "Stipend" and "parental" fields are low in postponement of graduate study, while "self-support" fields are high.

We must remember that these data treat fields, not people, and that in every field there are students with every support type, SES origin, and API. At the same time, the general outline of these findings suggests the following interpretation.

In terms of recruitment and financing, there appear to be four kinds of graduate fields: 1) the elite professions, 2) the minor professions, 3) the natural sciences, and 4) the humanities and social sciences, each characterized by a particular pattern of support and recruitment.

In the elite professions, of which law and medicine are the prototypes, the period of study is long, "evening courses" are out

---

Table 4.25. Distribution of Graduate Fields by Type of Support, API, SES, and Postponement of Graduate Studies

Variables	Type of Support[a]		
	Self-Support	Stipend	Parental
A P I[b]			
High	0	4	4
Low	8	6	6
Total	8	10	10
SES[c]			
High	3	7	10
Low	5	3	0
Total	8	10	10
Postponement[d]			
High	4	0	1
Low	4	10	9
Total	8	10	10

[a]From Table 4.24c
[b]From Table 4.2b
[c]From Table 4.8b
[d]From Chart 4.8

of the question, and stipend help is negligible. However, entry into the field is barred to anyone who has not passed through graduate study (even though technically one can still "read law" in some states) and the attraction of fields in terms of eventual income and prestige is very high. Thus, students and their families are quite willing to invest a considerable sum in the costs of school. However, because of the costs involved, low SES families are unlikely to have the funds to support their sons. Therefore, as we have seen, law and medicine recruit predominantly high SES students, who pay full fare and consider it a good investment. Entry is seldom postponed in these fields.

In the minor professions, of which engineering, business, and education are typical, graduate study is an advantage for eventual promotions and higher salaries. However, entry into the field with a bachelor's degree is permissible and normal, and stipend support is very small. Thus, many students begin full-time work and expect to begin their studies after they have earned some money or they attend part time. As such a career pattern requires little or no capital beyond the costs of a bachelor's degree, these professions attract a disproportionate number of low SES students.

In the natural sciences, for reasons which reflect the high priority given to applied science in America, stipends are available on a widespread scale. Since advanced degrees are advantageous in scientific careers and capital investment is negligible, considerable proportions enter graduate school immediately, although, because jobs are available for bachelor's degree holders, postponement is common too. As in the minor professions, the sciences provide attractive careers for lower SES students, six out of 12 science fields being classified as low in SES.

The social sciences and humanities have a less clear-cut pattern. Compared with the professions, chances for stipend support are high, but compared with science fields the pickings are considerably slimmer. On the other hand, career opportunities for students with only a bachelor's degree are limited in these fields. However, the status guaranteed by advanced degrees in these fields and the presumably greater interest in intellectual matters of upper SES families means that parental support may be forthcoming for those with sufficient resources, while stipend support means that the investment is seldom as staggering as for the elite professions. It is thus not surprising that every field in the social sciences and humanities is high on SES, but none is as high as law or medicine.

At the very least it appears that advanced study, unlike undergraduate study (whose simple structural components consist of varying quality schools and the economic distinction between public and private), is an exceedingly complicated and differentiated structure, whose patterns of recruitment involve interrelationships of career structures, academic ability, patterns of financing, and class differences, always compounded by the confusing propensity of women to have better academic records and less strong motivations for advanced study.

CAREER PLANS

Passing quickly over the time between entry into graduate school and completion of graduate study, a period running between one and ten years depending on the field, the analysis of future graduate students will be concluded by examining the students' long-run career plans. Since a career is a complicated matter, attention will be given to three different aspects: a) the intended career field of students in various graduate fields, b) the activities anticipated, and c) future employer.

CAREER FIELD

That there is a positive correlation between field of graduate study and long-run career field is a fact so obvious that it would not be worth reporting, except that there are some interesting variations in the correlation (Table 4.26). Eighty per cent or more of the students planning study in nursing, medicine, chemistry, health professions, social work, engineering, clinical psychology, physics, and other professions give identical code numbers from the questionnaire for their graduate and career fields, but in all the remaining fields more than one out of five students have a less than perfect match.

Primary and secondary education are the most common career fields where a discrepancy exists, and in 10 of the graduate fields

20 per cent or more of the graduate students anticipated careers in education. These fields, ordered by per cent planning careers in education are history (42), biology (40), English (31), other humanities (30), languages (30), other social sciences (27), zoology (26), arts (24), sociology (21), and botany (21).

Here are 15 other instances in Table 4.26 where more than 10 per cent of the graduate students in a given field expected careers in other fields or groups of fields:

Graduate Field	Career Field	Per cent
Political Science	Other Professions	28*
Economics	Business	25
Botany	Other Bio. Sciences	21
Physiology	Other Bio. Sciences	21
Physiology	Medicine	16
Philosophy	Other Professions	16**
Zoology	Other Bio. Sciences	14
Other Humanities	Humanities	14
Biochemistry	Health	13
Other Physical Science	Engineering	12
Sociology	Social Work	12
Microbiology	Health	11
Other Social Science	Humanities	11
Humanities	Other Professions	11

*Presumably heavily Public Administration
**Presumably heavily Religion

If a pattern is sought in these differences, the underlying factor seems to be divisional. In Table 4.26b fields are arrayed by division and by the per cent with career field identical to graduate field. Drawing a cutting point at 64 per cent, it is seen that: 1) the professions and physical sciences are all above the line; 2) all humanities fields are below the line, 3) the biological sciences, microbiology, and biochemistry are above, all other fields below, 4) all fields in the social sciences are below except for clinical psychology.

Strong percentage differences are always interesting, but these are particularly interesting, for among the arts and sciences they are rather like the rank order on postponement in graduate study, a phenomenon previously resistant to correlations. Chart 4.11

Table 4.26. Graduate Major and Future Career Field

a. Per cent in Given Future Career Field When the Career Field is Not Identical[a] to the Graduate Major

Graduate Major	Identical to Graduate Major	Nat. Sci.	Bio. Sci.	Soc. Sci.	Humanities	Eng.	Med.	Edu.	Bus.	Law	Soc. Work	Other Health	Other Profs.	Per cent	N
Chemistry	91	1	0	0	0	0	0	5	0	0	0	0	2	99	861
Physics	81	3	1	0	0	6	0	4	1	0	0	1	4	101	721
Geo., Geol. (Earth)	65	1	0	3	2	1	0	19	1	0	0	0	8	100	271
Mathematics	68	3	0	0	0	6	1	15	4	0	0	0	4	101	898
Other Physical Sci.	65	2	1	0	0	12	1	13	1	1	0	0	4	100	156
Engineering	85	1	0	0	0	8	0	0	3	0	0	0	3	100	3,041
Medicine	97	0	0	0	0	0	0	1	0	0	0	1	1	100	1,431
Nursing	98	0	0	0	0	0	0	1	0	0	0	0	0	99	400
Other Health	88	0	0	1	0	0	0	4	0	0	0	4	2	99	663
Biology	46	0	6	0	2	0	4	40	1	0	0	0	1	101	360
Biochemistry	71	9	2	0	0	0	4	1	0	0	0	13	2	102	182
Botany	48	1	21	0	0	0	0	21	0	0	0	0	9	100	103
Microbiology	79	0	3	0	0	0	2	2	0	0	0	11	2	99	131
Other Biology	62	0	9	0	0	2	1	10	0	0	0	7	8	99	287
Physiology	46	0	21	0	0	0	16	7	0	0	0	10	0	100	96
Zoology	48	1	14	0	0	0	3	26	0	0	0	1	8	101	157
Other Professions	80	0	0	1	1	1	0	9	2	0	0	1	4	99	2,988
Clinical Psychology	84	0	0	1	0	0	1	10	2	0	1	0	2	101	366
Other Psychology	61	1	0	5	0	1	0	12	13	1	0	1	4	99	281
Economics	52	0	0	2	1	2	0	5	25	2	0	0	10	99	455
Political Science	53	1	0	1	1	0	0	10	6	1	0	0	28	101	676
Sociology	49	0	0	1	0	0	0	21	7	0	12	0	9	99	362

[a]In some cases (e.g., education) it is possible to find that people "changed" from a given graduate major to the identical category on "Future Career Field." This seeming inconsistency is explained by the fact that those categories frequently include sub-categorizations (e.g., 25 per cent of those with graduate majors in one educational field actually expect to teach in another).

Graduate Major	Identical to Graduate Major	Nat. Sci.	Bio. Sci.	Soc. Sci.	Humanities	Eng.	Med.	Edu.	Bus.	Law	Soc. Work	Other Health	Other Profs.	Per cent	N
Other Social Sciences	41	1	0	8	11	0	0	27	2	0	0	1	8	99	270
Fine Arts	62	1	0	0	3	1	0	24	3	0	0	0	5	99	1,407
English	55	0	0	0	2	0	0	31	4	0	0	0	7	99	1,172
Languages	48	1	0	1	3	0	0	30	4	1	0	1	10	100	700
History	41	0	0	2	1	0	0	42	3	1	1	0	10	101	1,121
Philosophy	62	1	0	1	3	0	0	13	4	0	0	0	16	100	193
Humanities, Other	28	0	0	1	14	2	0	30	6	1	0	9	11	102	176
Education	68	0	0	0	1	0	0	25	1	0	0	0	3	99	11,469
Business	74	0	0	0	0	6	0	2	10	0	0	0	7	99	4,526
Law	79	0	0	2	0	1	0	1	11	0	0	0	6	100	2,434
Social Work	86	0	0	0	0	0	0	9	2	0	0	0	1	98	705

N	39,059
NA, Future Career Field	667
NA Graduate Field Only	1,622
NA Both	505
Excluded from Table:	
Not Going to Graduate School	12,383
NA Plans	2,428
Total Weighted N	56,664

(Table 4.26 continued)

Table 4.26. *Continued*

b. Per cent with Identical Graduate Field and Career Field, Grouped by Division

		Division			
	Professions	Physical Science	Biological Science	Social Science	Humanities
100— 98— 96— 94— 92— 90— 88— 86— 84— 82— 80— 78— 76— 74— 72— 70— 68— 66—	Nursing Medicine Health Social Work Engineering Other Law Business Ed:cation	Chemistry Physics Math Earth; Other	 Microbiology Biochemistry	 Clinical Psychology	
64— 62— 60— 58— 56— 54— 52— 50— 48— 46— 44— 42— 40— 38— 36— 34— 32— 30— 28— 26— 24— 22— 20—			Other Botany; Zoology Biology; Physiology	Psychology Political Science Economics Sociology Other	Art; Philosophy English Languages History Other

→ All Graduate Students

correlates the percentage postponing graduate study with the percentage of those in the arts and sciences who reported a career field outside of arts and sciences. The correlation is far from perfect, but of the fields with 26 per cent or fewer "mismatches," four out of five have less than 50 per cent postponement; of the fields with between 26 and 45 per cent discrepancies, six out of 13 have a 50 per cent postponement rate, while in the fields with a discrepancy percentage of 46 or more, four out of five have postponement rates over 50 per cent.

While these are ecological correlations (correlations between properties of groups, not individuals) and do not prove that it is the student with a "discrepancy" who is more likely to postpone, the following interpretation is suggested.

One of the great (and generally ignored) problems in arts and sciences fields other than the physical sciences is the desultory fashion in which students enter and complete their studies. While the faculties in schools teaching the elite professions are a little like train crews who pick up passengers at a particular time and deliver them to a particular place within a specified interval of time, faculties in arts and sciences are more like men who sit at the information booth giving out knowledge to people who wander in at various times and depart for quite different destinations at quite different times. The data in chart 4.11 suggest that a major part of the reason is that arts and sciences faculties, particularly in the humanities and the social sciences, do not control a body of knowledge organized around a particular career, as law school is adapted to the legal profession and medical school to the medical profession. Rather they are masters of a body of lore that is relevant for a variety of professional contexts. Graduate study in history is a necessity for the future professional historian, but a great proportion of the graduate students in history appear to be high school teachers for whom advanced study in history is useful, but hardly necessary. Similarly, political science feeds government, economics is useful collateral reading for businessmen, English is good for secondary English teachers, and the biological sciences service health professions and secondary education. At the same time, in curriculum and legislation these fields are "supposed" to train historians, economists, literary specialists, and biological scientists. It is instructive to compare clinical psychology, an arts and sciences field with a clear-cut professional structure, and other psychology, a more amorphous academic discipline. In many cases instruction was in the same department in the same institution; yet 32 per cent of the future graduate students in other psychology gave a different profession as their career field in contrast with 16 per cent of the clinical psychologists. It is perhaps no coincidence that more other psychologists were postponing their studies than were clinical psychologists, even though the latter field included more women and low API men.

Whether or not such a development would be desirable, the suggestion is that postponed and intermittent graduate study will

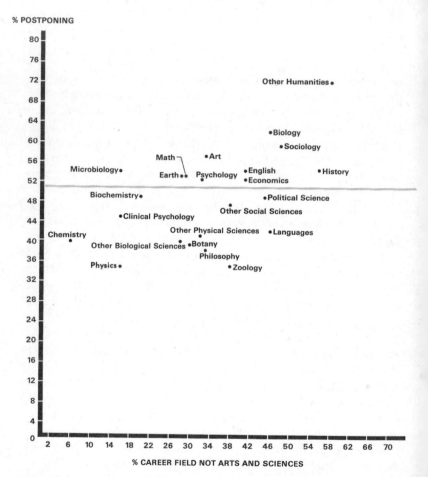

Chart 4.11. Per cent Postponing Graduate Studies in Arts and Sciences Fields by Per cent Planning Career Outside of Arts and Sciences

continue in the arts and sciences until advanced study in these fields is prerequisite for entry into employment for their students.

ACTIVITIES

Cutting across the content of a given occupation are certain functions which transcend particular fields. Whether the content area is arc welding or brain surgery, some people within the field make their living teaching it and some do not, and in an age of increasing organization there are few fields where some men and women do not work at administration. For the graduate fields in the survey four activities were selected as of particular importance — teaching, research, administration, and "service to patients or clients" — and each future graduate student was asked "Which ones do you anticipate will be an important part of your long-run career work? (Circle any which apply.)" The generality of the functions is such that there was only one field where more than nine per cent circled "None of these," the field being fine arts where 17 per cent circled the negative response.

Table 4.27a gives the distribution of responses, which are often multiple, the percentages in social work totalling 139, biochemistry 158, education 131, etc. As is so often the case, the differences are clearer when the distributions are seen within and between divisions (Tables 4.27b, 4.27c, 4.27d, 4.27e).

"Teaching" was extremely popular (Table 4.27b). Obviously, 94 per cent of those in education anticipated teaching, but it is interesting that with the two exceptions of business and law, 20 per cent or more of the graduate students in each field expected to teach, although it should be noted that no information on level (college, primary, or secondary) was given by this question. As one would expect, the arts and sciences ran high, but 66 per cent of the nurses (not, of course, all nurses, but those students with bachelor's degrees who expected graduate study in nursing) and 54 per cent of those in other professions were planning to do some teaching, and about a quarter of those in social work, medicine, and other professions also circled the item. Within the arts and sciences fields, teaching interest is greatest in humanities, all six fields being over 70 per cent, and lowest in physical sciences, four out of five fields being 51 per cent or lower. The biological sciences and social sciences scattered considerably, for more than 60 per cent anticipated teaching in biology, other social sciences, other biological sciences, zoology, sociology, psychology, and physiology, while less than 54 per cent circled the item in botany, political science, biochemistry, economics, clinical psychology, and microbiology – that is, mostly in the fields just observed to have a heavy professional tinge.

Turning to research, (Table 4.27c) we see that there is a range from 92 per cent in biochemistry to 9 per cent in education. Predictably, the science fields are high, all being 70 per cent or higher except in mathematics, earth sciences, and biology. Humanists

Table 4.27. Graduate Field and Career Activities

a. Per cent Checking Each Career Activity

Graduate Field	Career Activities					N
	Teaching	Research	Adminis-tration	Service	None of Preceding	
Chemistry	39.3	84.3	15.2	2.9	2.0	840
Physics	50.9	87.0	23.6	1.9	1.7	721
Geology, Geography	68.5	48.1	18.5	3.3	6.3	270
Mathematics	47.2	61.4	21.3	6.3	5.4	875
Other Physical Science	45.1	77.1	20.9	3.3	3.9	153
Engineering	20.0	59.3	48.3	10.5	8.8	3,031
Medicine	25.3	41.6	6.0	95.3	0.6	1,438
Nursing	65.7	17.9	29.6	80.1	0.5	402
Other Health	24.0	23.2	13.2	85.1	1.3	638
Biology	78.2	40.5	8.6	6.7	0.3	326
Biochemistry	46.2	92.4	8.2	10.9	0.0	184
Botany	52.9	74.0	14.4	1.0	2.9	104
Microbiology	37.3	90.0	4.8	26.2	0.8	126
Physiology	61.7	83.0	3.2	27.7	0.0	94
Zoology	68.4	70.3	11.0	5.2	2.6	155
Other Biological Science	71.7	78.5	11.6	11.6	2.1	284
Clinical Psychology	44.5	48.0	12.6	85.2	0.8	357
Other Psychology	62.7	65.9	23.6	30.4	0.7	276
Economics	45.6	38.7	57.1	9.8	3.4	450
Political Science	49.7	39.5	54.1	11.4	8.3	640
Sociology	63.5	39.7	18.3	30.1	1.7	345
Other Social Sciences	77.1	50.5	15.4	8.6	6.5	279
Fine Arts	70.4	15.7	12.6	14.7	16.7	1,336
English	83.8	25.9	12.2	4.1	7.8	1,109
History	87.8	30.1	18.7	6.4	2.5	1,102
Language	83.9	30.2	16.0	9.6	4.1	638
Philosophy	83.2	36.6	17.8	10.5	4.2	191
Other Humanities	76.7	17.0	23.3	20.5	6.8	176
Education	93.7	9.3	18.7	7.9	1.0	10,573
Business	12.6	14.6	80.1	21.4	4.0	4,492
Law	10.0	17.5	40.3	68.3	5.7	2,428
Social Work	28.1	10.7	13.4	83.2	2.5	644
Other Professions	53.9	24.8	42.9	36.4	8.7	2,887
All Graduate Students	55.4	22.7	31.6	–	–	–

N	37,564
NA Career Activities Only	2,162
NA Graduate Field Only	1,786
NA Both	341
Excluded: Not Going to Graduate School	12,383
NA Plans Index	2,428
Total Weighted N	56,664

Table 4.27 Continued

b. Per cent Checking "Teaching," Grouped by Division

		Division			
	Professions	Physical Science	Biological Science	Social Science	Humanities
94—	Education				
90—					
86—					History
82—					Engl., Lang. Philosophy
78—			Biology	Other	
74—			Other		Other
70—		Earth	Zoology		Art
66—	Nursing				
62—			Physiology	Sociology Other Psychology	
58—					
54—	Other				
50—		Physics	Botany	Political Science	
46—		Math Other	Biochemistry	Economics Clinical Psychology	
42—		Chemistry			
38—			Microbiology		
34					
30—	Social Work				
26—	Medicine				
22—	Health Engineering				
18—					
14—	Business				
10—	Law				

→ All Graduate Students

(Table 4.27 continued)

are relatively uninterested in research, for in their top field, philosophy, 37 per cent circled the item. Social sciences fields span the range between the natural sciences and the humanities, psychology having 66 per cent while political science, sociology, and economics are just a hair above philosophy. In the professional fields, engineers (59 per cent) and physicians (42 per cent) stand out, for while all other professions are 25 per cent or less, engineering and medicine have percentages between the natural sciences and humanities.

Chart 4.12 correlates the per cent interested in teaching and the per cent interested in research for the arts and sciences fields. Despite the oft-claimed ideal of combining teaching and research,

Table 4.27. Continued

c. Per cent Checking "Research," Grouped by Division

%	Professions	Physical Science	Biological Science	Social Science	Humanities
94 –					
90 –			Biochemistry Microbiology		
86 –		Physics			
82 –		Chemistry	Physiology		
78 –			Other		
74 –		Other	Botany		
70 –			Zoology		
66 –				Other Psychology	
62 –					
58 –	Engineering	Math			
54 –					
50 –				Other	
46 –		Earth		Clinical Psychology	
42 –	Medicine				
38 –			Biology	Poli. Sci; Soc. Economics	
34 –					Philosophy
30 –					History, Lang.
26 –					English
22 –	Other Health				
18 –	Nursing, Law Business				
14 –	Social Work				Other Art
10 –	Education				

→ All Graduate Students

the correlation is negative; the research fields are low on teaching and the teaching fields are low on research. Clinical psychology, political science, and economics, the professionalized social science fields, have 50 per cent or less on both functions. Using 50 per cent as a cutting point, the fields high on research and low on teaching in the arts and sciences are biochemistry, chemistry, microbiology, other physical sciences, and mathematics; the fields high on both are physics, physiology, botany, other biological sciences, zoology, psychology, and other social sciences. The fields high on teaching and low on research are earth sciences, sociology, biology, philosophy, languages, history, En-

Table 4.27 *Continued*

d. Per cent Checking "Administration" Grouped by Division

Professions	Division			
	Physical Science	Biological Science	Social Science	Humanities
Business				
			Economics	
			Political Science	
Engineering				
Other				
Law				
Nursing					→ All Graduate Students
	Physics		Psychology, Other	Other
	Math, Other			History
Education	Earth		Sociology	Philosophy
	Chemistry		Other	Languages
Soc. Work; Health		Botany	Clinical Psychology	Art
		Other		English
		Zoology		
Medicine		Biology		
		Biochemistry		
		Microbiology		
		Physiology		

(Table 4.27 continued)

glish, art, and other humanities. The professors of English and history who are so willing to speak up in the mass media about the dangers of research might note that their graduate students are a somewhat extreme group — no fields are higher in teaching and only two fields are lower in research interest than are English and history.

Administrative proclivities (Table 4.27d) are oddly distributed. Business (80 per cent) is very high, of course; among the professions, engineering (48 per cent), other professions (43 per cent), law (40 per cent), and nursing (30 per cent) are relatively high. All other fields have less than 25 per cent checking the item, ex-

Table 4.27. *Continued*

e. Per cent Checking "Service," Grouped by Division

	Division				
	Professions	Physical Science	Biological Science	Social Science	Humanities
96 –	Medicine				
92 –					
88 –					
84 –	Health / Social Work			Clinical Psychology	
80 –	Nursing				
76 –					
72 –					
68 –	Law				
64 –					
60 –					
40 –					
36 –	Other				
32 –				Psych; Sociology	
28 –			Physiology / Microbiology		
24 –					
20 –	Business				Other
16 –					Art
12 –	Engineering / Education		Biology; Other / Biochemistry	Political Science / Economics / Other	Lang; Phil. / History
8 –		Math	Biology / Zoology		
4 –		Chem.; Earth; Other			English
0 –		Physics	Botany		

cept for two quasi-professional social sciences – political science and economics, where a little over 50 per cent circle the item. The least organizational-minded fields are medicine, biology, biochemistry, microbiology, and physiology, each with a figure of less than 10 per cent.

The fourth function, "service to patients or clients," is a specialty of the service professions. Medicine, clinical psychology, health professions, social work, and nursing are all over 75 per cent on the item, although the fact that nurses are as low as 78, along with their interest in teaching and administration, underlines the idea that graduate work in nursing leads away from the traditional bedside functions. Among less service-oriented fields, psychology, sociology, physiology, and microbiology all have about a quarter of their students checking the item; in law the percentage is 68.

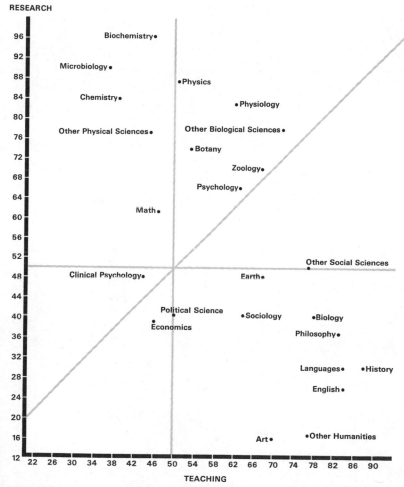

Chart 4.12. Per cent "Research" by Per cent "Teaching," for Arts and Science Fields Research

Since recruitment to research is one of the major foci of this research, let us return to that function and consider the field differences in the light of sex and academic performance. In most fields (but not chemistry, biology, other biological sciences, art, and other humanities) the per cent who circled research increases with API (Table 4.28). Nevertheless, field differences in research interest are not a function of API variation. Chart 4.13 plots the raw percentage interested in research against the percentage to be expected if each field consisted of equal proportions from the

Table 4.28. Graduate Field, Career Activities, and Academic Performance Index: Per cent Checking "Research"

Graduate Field	Academic Performance Index					
	Top Fifth		Above Average		Bottom Half	
	Per cent	N	Per cent	N	Per cent	N
Chemistry	87	220	80	307	87	306
Physics	96	303	86	202	75	208
Geology, Geography	–	47	56	117	36	102
Mathematics	72	279	61	309	51	280
Other Physical Sciences	92	50	79	63	–	31
Engineering	73	737	58	1,123	51	1,135
Medicine	51	597	36	602	30	221
Nursing	23	105	17	188	11	99
Other Health	–	41	24	246	20	337
Biology	–	48	24	136	50	137
Biochemistry	93	60	97	77	–	46
Botany	–	17	–	29	81	52
Microbiology	–	32	–	36	77	56
Physiology	–	18	–	24	–	46
Zoology	–	36	79	56	54	61
Other Biological Sciences	95	56	69	93	80	127
Clinical Psychology	56	108	53	112	36	133
Other Psychology	84	77	66	93	54	102
Economics	55	114	36	167	29	163
Political Science	49	223	37	263	32	144
Sociology	56	52	49	127	28	166
Other Social Sciences	69	75	56	124	25	77
Fine Arts	17	327	18	519	11	459
English	34	477	21	415	15	203
History	49	317	31	391	14	392
Languages	39	262	32	250	8	120
Philosophy	42	77	34	77	–	36
Other Humanities	–	22	11	88	22	59
Education	12	1,381	10	4,134	8	4,904
Business	22	590	14	1,639	13	2,206
Law	25	569	17	858	14	975
Social Work	22	106	12	258	6	268
Other Professions	31	501	28	991	20	1,353

N	37,042
NA Graduate Field Only	1,758
NA API Only	522
NA Both	28
NA Career Activities	2,503
Excluded: Not Going to Graduate School	12,383
NA Plans Index	2,428
Total Weighted N	56,664

three API levels. The rank order is very similar in both cases, so API composition does not alter the field differences much. Languages and medicine do lie a little above the line drawn through the points where raw and adjusted figures are identical, suggesting that the research level of these fields is pulled up by their high API levels, while sociology and other biological sciences are a

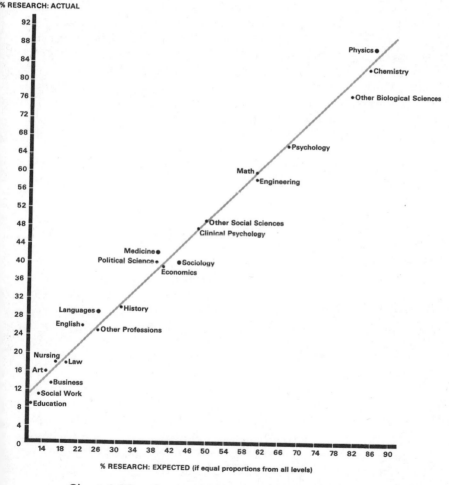

Chart 4.13. Per cent Research: Actual by Expected

little below the line, suggesting that their lower API levels pull their research interest down. The differences are small, but it is interesting that while for the raw figures medicine is slightly above sociology in research interest, sociology is a little above medicine when API is controlled.

Within a given field and API level, women are somewhat less research-oriented than men, so that when graduate field, sex, and API are considered simultaneously (Table 4.29) a wide range appears. Thus, in physical sciences the per cent rises from 43 among females from the lowest API level to 87 among top fifth men. Considering top fifth men, there is a range from over 80 in physical and biological sciences to 21 in education.

Despite all the variation, it still can be said that research is a widespread interest of the future graduate students. Except for education and social work from the bottom half in API, each cell in Table 4.29 is 12 per cent or more. In every field, at least a fifth of the highest API men express an interest in research work of some kind, and in natural sciences, engineering, social sciences, and medicine, more than half of the top fifth men circled this item.

FUTURE EMPLOYER

Along with field and activity, the type of employer constitutes a third dimension of occupational classification, for such a specialized line of work as medical research is found in universities, government, and private corporations. The schedule asked students who would be "your most likely employer when you begin full-time work in your anticipated career field? (If you have a definite expectation, circle one; if not, circle the most likely possibilities.)" Twelve possibilities were listed: "Private company with 100 or more employees;" "Private company with fewer than 100 employees or professional partnership;" "Family business;" "Self-employed;" "Research organization or institute;" "College or university or junior college;" "Elementary or secondary school or school system;" "Other educational institutions;" "Federal government (U.S.);" "State or local government;" "Hospital-church-clinic-welfare organization, etc.;" and "Other."

Among graduate students, the most frequent responses were:

Table 4.29. Graduate Field, Career Activities, Sex, and API (Per cent Checking "Research")

Graduate Field	Over-all Per cent "Research"	API					
		Top Fifth		Above Average		Bottom Half	
		Male	Female	Male	Female	Male	Female
Phy. Sciences	74	87 (698)	73 (201)	74 (789)	66 (209)	70 (833)	43 (94)
Bio. Sciences	70	84 (104)	82 (163)	68 (265)	60 (186)	65 (384)	82 (141)
Engineering	59	73 (734)	– (3)	58 (1,110)	– (13)	51 (1,130)	– (5)
Social Sciences	45	60 (383)	56 (266)	49 (566)	40 (320)	35 (625)	26 (160)
Medicine	42	52 (554)	– (43)	36 (545)	35 (57)	26 (191)	– (30)
Other Professions	25	32 (316)	28 (185)	30 (674)	24 (317)	21 (1,060)	17 (293)
Humanities	25	39 (601)	32 (881)	28 (740)	21 (1,000)	13 (690)	13 (579)
Health	21	– (27)	27 (119)	22 (125)	20 (309)	13 (256)	26 (180)
Law	18	25 (547)	– (22)	18 (809)	– (49)	13 (949)	– (26)
Business	15	23 (528)	19 (62)	14 (1,536)	12 (103)	13 (2,064)	15 (142)
Social Work	11	– (13)	22 (93)	– (49)	13 (209)	7 (83)	5 (185)
Education	9	21 (307)	9 (1,074)	9 (1,257)	10 (2,877)	8 (2,426)	9 (2,478)

N	37,042
NA, Career Activities Only	2,125
NA, Graduate Field Only	1,758
NA, API Only	522
NA, on Two or More Items	406
Excluded from Table:	
Not Planning Graduate School	12,383
NA, Plans Index	2,428
Total Weighted N	56,664

"Elementary or secondary education," 35 per cent; "Large business," 24 per cent; "College or university," 15 per cent; and "Federal government," 14 per cent. The total for all responses is 134 per cent which means considerable multiple checking.

Table 4.30 gives the distributions for the 33 graduate fields. Because of the wide scatter, it will perhaps be useful to review the leading choices for each field. (Numbers in parentheses are per cents.)

Professional Fields
  1. Engineering—Large business (69), Federal government (20)
  2. Medicine—Self-employed (76), Hospital or welfare organization (34)

Table 4.30. Graduate Field and Career Employer

Graduate Field	Private Company 100 or More Employees	Less Than 100 Employees	Family Business	Self-Employed	Research Organization	College	Elementary, Secondary School	Other Educational	Federal Government	State or Local Government	Hospital, Church Welfare	Other	Per cent	N
Chemistry	58	8	0	0	43	30	6	0	17	3	2	1	168	839
Physics	44	5	1	2	47	42	8	0	33	0	1	0	183	721
Geology-Geog.	27	10	0	5	13	39	33	0	34	14	4	1	180	270
Mathematics	43	5	1	1	20	26	18	1	24	2	0	1	142	870
Other Phy. Science	29	5	0	9	42	35	12	3	39	5	2	1	182	153
Engineering	69	10	1	3	14	8	1	0	20	6	0	2	134	3,036
Medicine	1	5	1	76	16	9	1	0	6	2	34	2	153	1,438
Nursing	0	0	0	0	2	9	5	2	8	12	75	3	116	402
Other Health	5	5	1	46	10	5	7	0	7	3	35	2	126	636
Biology	7	1	1	5	20	12	61	1	11	3	2	1	125	325
Biochemistry	23	2	2	2	61	36	4	0	22	1	19	0	172	185
Botany	8	2	0	0	36	34	28	0	31	9	0	0	148	104
Microbiology	21	4	1	2	55	32	4	1	18	11	27	0	176	126
Physiology	13	5	1	7	52	50	4	7	11	3	22	0	175	94
Zoology	6	1	0	5	27	39	30	0	22	14	6	6	156	155
Other Bio. Science	20	5	1	5	46	34	15	0	29	15	8	1	179	285
Clinical Psychology	6	3	0	15	24	26	15	2	20	18	64	1	194	357
Other Psychology	23	3	2	7	37	45	15	1	24	7	17	0	181	275
Economics	40	7	2	3	8	31	5	0	36	6	1	4	143	450
Political Science	12	6	3	3	7	26	15	0	58	13	2	9	154	650
Sociology	12	6	0	3	15	32	27	2	14	18	20	0	149	348
Other Soc. Science	9	2	3	3	25	44	35	0	23	7	3	4	158	280
Fine Arts	16	16	2	13	2	33	36	2	6	1	5	8	140	1,339
English	11	5	0	5	2	45	42	1	6	2	3	3	125	1,105
History	6	2	0	2	2	37	53	2	17	4	6	3	134	1,099
Languages	12	3	1	2	3	42	35	1	17	0	2	6	124	643
Philosophy	6	3	0	3	2	75	9	0	3	1	9	4	115	190
Other Humanities	21	9	1	5	2	27	35	0	14	6	17	2	139	170
Education	3	1	0	1	1	7	88	1	3	3	4	1	113	10,599
Business	68	18	5	6	3	3	2	0	16	3	1	3	128	4,498
Law	27	44	6	30	1	3	2	0	28	11	0	5	157	2,426
Social Work	3	2	1	1	5	3	10	0	13	33	66	3	140	644
Other Professions	16	11	1	6	7	15	17	1	15	11	32	5	137	2,888
All Grad. Students	24	9	2	9	8	15	35	1	14	5	10	2	–	–

N 37,600
NA Career Employer Only 1,790
NA Graduate Field Only 2,126
NA Both 337
Excluded: Planning Never to Go to Graduate School 12,383
NA Plans 2,428

Total Weighted N 56,664

3. Nursing—Hospital or welfare (75)

4. Health—Self-employed (46), Hospital or welfare (35)

5. Education—Education (88)

6. Business—Large business (68), Federal government (16)

7. Law—Small business (44), Self-employed (30), Federal government (28)

8. Social Work—Hospital or welfare (66), State or local government (33)

9. Other Professions—Hospital or welfare (32)

Natural Science

10. Chemistry—Large business (58), Research organization (43), College (30)

11. Physics—Research organization (47), Large business (44), College (42), Federal government (33)

12. Earth sciences—College (39), Federal government (34), Education (33), Large business (27)

13. Mathematics—Large business (43), College (26), Federal government (24), Research organization (20)

14. Other Physical Science—Research organization (42), Federal government (39), College (35), Large business (29)

15. Biology—Education (61), Research organization (20)

16. Biochemistry—Research organization (61), College (36), Large business (23), Federal government (22)

17. Botany—Research organization (36), College (34), Federal government (31), Education (28)

18. Microbiology—Research organization (55), College (32), Hospital or welfare organization (27), Large business (21)

19. Physiology—Research organization (52), College (50), Hospital or welfare organization (22)

20. Zoology—College (39), Education (30), Research organization (27), Federal government (22)

21. Other Biological Sciences—Research organization (46), College (34), Federal government (29), Large business (20)

Social Sciences and Humanities

22. Clinical Psychology—Hospital or welfare organization (64), College (26), Research organization (24), Federal government (20)

23. Psychology—College (45), Research organization (37), Federal government (24), Large business (23)

24. Economics—Large business (40), Federal government (36), College (31)

25. Political Science—Federal government (58), College (26)

26. Sociology—College (32), Education (27), Hospital or welfare organization (20)

27. Other Social Sciences—College (44), Education (35), Research organization (25), Federal government (23)

28. Arts—Education (36), College (33)

29. English—College (45), Education (42)

30. History—Education (53), College (37)

31. Languages—College (42), Education (35)

32. Philosophy—College (75)

33. Other Humanities—Education (35), College (27), Large business (21)

The variety is such as to defy easy generalizations, but we noted several themes. The large variety of employers mentioned in the natural and social sciences contrasts with the humanities and professions; Federal government, while the leading employer in only one field—political science—is among the most popular in 17 out of the 33 fields, especially among the natural sciences; while arts and sciences graduate training, by tradition and structure, is designed to prepare students for college and university careers, it is seldom the most common future employer for graduate students, except for those in the humanities; "Research organization or institute" is tremendously popular among students in the natural sciences and the social sciences.

Whether these expectations will be realized or not is open to question (and research), but it is clear that in most fields of study, the students see a number of alternative employers. Thus, it is interesting to conclude this section and the research report by considering how—if the expectations of the students are fulfilled—talent as measured by our ubiquitous API index will be shared among future employers. Will private business be able to outbid non-profit and government organizations? Will colleges and universities get a fair share of the talent they have nurtured? Will self-employment attract the high or low API student? Table 4.31 gives the per cent in the top fifth in API among men by career field and future employer in order to answer these questions. (Because of multiple answers, the same student may appear in several cells of the table.) Even limiting the table to eight future employers makes a complicated set of figures, and the situation varies with the field. Nevertheless, some generalizations may be drawn.

Table 4.31. Graduate Field, Career Employer, and Academic Performance Index Among Men* (Per cent Top Fifth API)

Graduate Field	Self-Employed	Private Company		Elementary of Secondary Educational System	Hospital, Church or Welfare Organization	Federal Government	Research Organization	College or University
		Less than 100 Employees	100 or More Employees					
Medicine	43 (1,011)	25 (63)	– (13)	– (11)	44 (430)	30 (100)	52 (202)	69 (118)
Engineering	21 (94)	31 (316)	26 (2,059)	– (32)	– (8)	17 (768)	46 (420)	52 (244)
Physical Science	14 (147)	20 (291)	20 (1,576)	8 (420)	3 (60)	23 (848)	38 (842)	49 (873)
Humanities	23 (145)	12 (122)	15 (202)	18 (645)	22 (100)	21 (254)	– (14)	45 (1,007)
Social Science	20 (97)	13 (87)	16 (321)	8 (204)	13 (184)	24 (740)	31 (207)	37 (553)
Law	25 (688)	31 (195)	20 (627)	– (29)	– (10)	25 (857)	– (24)	31 (70)
Other Professions	15 (143)	22 (251)	14 (344)	11 (160)	14 (750)	12 (572)	13 (126)	31 (307)
Business	7 (268)	12 (727)	14 (2,889)	– (40)	– (40)	7 (710)	18 (90)	24 (127)
Biological Science	– (45)	– (22)	9 (94)	5 (191)	– (33)	11 (261)	17 (261)	23 (250)
Education	2 (63)	8 (77)	6 (170)	7 (3,390)	10 (180)	11 (288)	– (36)	17 (424)

*The following categories are excluded: Women; graduate fields of health and social work, because of small case base; career employer categories of family business, state and local government, and other; and those not planning to go to graduate school.

**Individuals may be included in more than one "career employer" category.

Beginning with the "non-profit" sector, a distinct rank order appears. "Colleges and universities" has the highest API levels, "Research organization" the second highest, and "Education" the lowest. Thus, in the physical sciences, 49 per cent of the prospective college staffs are in the top fifth, 38 per cent of research organization people are in the top fifth, and 8 per cent are in education. Federal government and private welfare organizations fall in between, generally above education but below the research organizations in API level.

There is no distinct pattern among the private sector employers—large business, small business and professional partnership, and self-employment. These three types are generally, but not always, superior to education in API levels, and in all comparisons save one below the levels for "College" or "Research organization." There certainly is no evidence that big business has a greater attraction than the federal government for the high API student, for there are just about as many comparisons favoring the one as the other.

The general picture, then, is that the academic world that produced them has the greatest attraction for the students who are most successful in its eyes; the elementary and secondary schools that prepared them attract the less successful grade-getters; other employers fall in between without much systematic difference.

Thus we end our analysis of advanced study as we began it, with the over-riding fact of this research. Despite the harsh criticism of higher education from within and without, American colleges and universities are a tremendous success, judged by the market research criterion of satisfied customers. A surprisingly high proportion of their customers are demanding still more after four years of undergraduate study, and the most promising of these by the standards of academia show a disproportionate tendency toward the academy, which suggests that higher education has an addictive quality.

Appendix 1

Selected Tabulations By Undergraduate Major

In the text of this report, the undergraduate major fields of the students were not treated as variables in the analyses. Since undergraduate major field is strongly correlated with career preference, it was felt that career preference would be more important of the two. That is, it was assumed that in the case of a discrepancy, education majors aiming for careers in engineering would behave more like engineers than like educators.

Because of the large amount of research and official statistics reported by undergraduate major, we felt that it would be useful to make available selected tabulations by undergraduate major.

The following data are included:

Sex

Per cent female for detailed breakdown of undergraduate majors (A-1.1) and for the dichotomy, arts and sciences v. professional (A-1.5b).

Academic Performance Index

Distribution by detailed breakdown of undergraduate majors (A-1.1) and for the dichotomy, arts and sciences v. professional (A-1.5b).

Sex by Academic Performance Index

Not reported separately, but can be calculated for detailed undergraduate major field in A-1.3, grouped undergraduate major in A-1.4, and for arts and sciences v. professional in A-1.5c.

239

Plans

Distribution by detailed undergraduate major (A-1.2), grouped major (A-1.4), and arts and sciences v. professional (A-1.5a).

Per cent planning graduate school next year, controlling for sex and API, by detailed undergraduate major (A-1.3), grouped undergraduate major (A-1.4), and arts and sciences v. professional (A-1.5).

Graduate Major

Graduate and undergraduate major fields are cross-tabulated in Tables A-1.6 and A-1.7 for those students classified as "Next Year" or "Later" on the Plans Index.

Table A – 1.1. Undergraduate Major and Sex; Undergraduate Major and Academic Performance

Undergraduate Major	Per cent Female	Academic Performance Index			Total	
		Top Fifth	Above Average	Bottom Half	Per cent	N
Pre-medical	6.0	32.2	49.0	18.6	99.8	487
Physics	7.7	43.2	28.3	28.4	99.9	830
Other Biological Sciences[a]	33.1	26.0	30.6	43.3	99.9	738
Chemistry	25.2	27.7	36.1	36.1	99.9	1,482
Biology	41.4	19.0	39.9	41.0	99.9	1,318
Psychology[b]	43.9	25.3	37.2	37.4	99.9	1,336
Humanities[c]	53.3	30.4	38.5	31.0	99.9	8,560
Other Social Sciences[d]	33.1	21.6	38.9	39.4	99.9	4,334
Mathematics	32.8	31.1	33.5	35.2	99.8	1,298
Other Physical Sciences[e]	9.2	18.2	38.3	43.4	99.9	467
Engineering	6.0	19.7	34.6	45.6	99.9	4,967
Other Professions[f]	51.2	14.7	33.9	51.2	99.8	2,081
Agriculture[g]	0.7	8.9	28.8	62.1	99.8	734
Not elsewhere classified (NEC)	20.2	13.1	25.4	61.4	99.9	679
Education	68.6	12.7	39.8	47.4	99.9	14,393
Business[h]	9.2	8.5	30.1	61.3	99.9	7,038
Other Health[i]	76.2	18.1	42.4	39.3	99.8	1,753

	N	52,495
	NA. Plans	2,428
	NA. API	830
	NA. Field	911
	Total Weighted N	56,664

[a]Anatomy, Biochemistry, Botany, Biophysics, Entomology, Genetics, Microbiology, Pathology, Pharmacology, Other Biological Science, Physiology, Zoology.

[b]Clinical Psychology, Social Psychology, Industrial and Personal Psychology, Experimental Psychology, Other Psychology.

[c]Fine and Applied Arts, English, Creative Writing, Classical Language and Literature, History, Modern Foreign Language and Literature, Philosophy, Humanities, General.

[d]Anthropology, Archeology, Economics, Area and Region Study, Political Science and Government, Sociology, Social Science, General.

[e]Astronomy, Astrophysics, Geography, Geology, Geophysics, Oceanography, Metallurgy, Meterology, Physical Science, General.

[f]Architecture, City Planning, Journalism, Radio-Television-Communication, Library Science, Archives, Theology, Religion, Foreign Service, Law, Pre-law, Social Group Work, Home Economics.

[g]Veterinary and Pre-veterinary, Agricultural Science, Forestry, Farming.

[h]Advertising, Public Relations, Other Business, Accounting, Public Administration, Secretarial Science, Military Service.

[i]Dentistry and Pre-dentistry, Nursing, Optometry, Pharmacy, Physical Therapy, Occupational Therapy, Medical Technology, Dental Hygiene, Other Health.

Table A–1.2. Undergraduate Major and Plans

Undergraduate Major	Per cent of Sample	Plans Index				Total		Total Per cent Next Year
		Next Year		Per cent Later	Per cent Never	Per cent	N	
		Per cent Accepted	Per cent Other					
Pre-Med	0.9	80.6	9.8	7.4	2.2	100.0	500	90.4
Physics	1.5	50.5	14.5	29.9	4.8	99.7	838	65.1
Other Bio. Sciences	1.4	47.0	12.3	27.9	12.6	99.8	761	59.3
Chemistry	2.8	46.3	9.5	33.5	10.5	99.8	1,491	55.9
Biology	2.5	42.2	13.1	32.0	12.6	99.9	1,343	55.3
Psychology	2.5	33.4	13.4	31.6	21.5	99.9	1,347	46.8
Humanities	16.3	30.0	13.3	36.4	20.1	99.8	8,680	43.4
Other Soc. Sciences	8.2	31.6	11.1	38.9	18.2	99.8	4,367	42.7
Mathematics	2.4	28.5	13.2	38.7	19.5	99.9	1,310	41.7
Other Phy. Sciences	0.9	25.4	11.2	46.5	18.7	101.8	479	36.7
Engineering	9.2	18.8	13.9	45.9	21.2	99.8	5,030	32.8
Other Professions	4.0	21.8	10.4	39.4	28.2	99.8	2,127	32.3
Agriculture	1.4	16.9	8.2	29.0	45.7	99.8	750	25.2
NEC	1.3	10.0	12.4	38.2	39.2	99.8	698	22.4
Education	27.6	7.4	14.2	61.3	16.8	99.4	4,646	21.7
Business	13.3	7.8	9.0	42.4	40.7	99.9	7,151	16.8
Other Health	3.3	9.7	6.9	37.4	45.7	99.7	1,773	16.7
Total	99.5						N 53,291	
N	55,546						N.A. Plans 2,428	
N.A. Field	1,118						N.A. Field 945	
Total Weighted N	56,664					Total Weighted N	56,664	

Table A—1.3. Undergraduate Major and Plans, Controlling for Sex and Academic Performance

Undergraduate Major	Male			Female		
	Top Fifth	Above Average	Bottom Half	Top Fifth	Above Average	Bottom Half
Pre-Med	98.7 (154)	92.9 (227)	81.8 (77)	— (3)	— (12)	— (14)
Physics	85.5 (325)	65.7 (207)	37.6 (234)	— (34)	— (28)	— (2)
Other Bio. Sciences	94.6 (113)	84.1 (139)	53.3 (242)	48.1 (79)	37.9 (87)	23.0 (78)
Chemistry	85.2 (285)	73.9 (384)	38.8 (440)	53.1 (126)	32.4 (151)	14.5 (96)
Biology	93.2 (149)	73.7 (270)	51.6 (354)	53.9 (102)	37.1 (256)	38.5 (187)
Psychology	78.5 (149)	65.0 (272)	42.6 (328)	58.4 (190)	24.0 (225)	17.4 (172)
Humanities	74.6 (1,130)	55.1 (1,409)	36.8 (1,456)	48.3 (1,476)	31.4 (1,887)	20.8 (1,202)
Other Soc. Sciences	70.0 (612)	55.9 (1,096)	33.0 (1,192)	44.4 (326)	27.9 (591)	21.0 (517)
Mathematics	81.0 (238)	52.8 (280)	21.7 (354)	39.1 (166)	21.7 (156)	23.0 (104)
Other Phy. Sciences	76.7 (73)	40.6 (160)	23.0 (191)	— (12)	— (19)	— (12)
Engineering	61.7 (972)	35.9 (1,709)	18.2 (2,256)	— (12)	— (19)	— (11)
Other Professions	64.8 (125)	42.1 (332)	44.0 (559)	23.0 (182)	25.6 (375)	13.9 (508)
Agriculture	51.5 (64)	33.0 (212)	17.4 (453)	— (2)	— (0)	— (3)
NEC	45.4 (66)	44.4 (117)	15.3 (359)	— (23)	12.5 (56)	12.0 (58)
Education	43.8 (319)	39.9 (1,393)	23.0 (2,810)	22.0 (1,511)	20.1 (4,343)	14.3 (4,017)
Business	37.8 (526)	23.2 (1,913)	11.8 (3,954)	3.8 (77)	14.4 (207)	11.6 (361)
Other Health	36.8 (57)	35.7 (137)	25.4 (224)	18.7 (262)	14.3 (608)	6.6 (465)

Per cent Next Year on Plans Among . . .

N 52,495
N.A. Field 911
N.A. API 830
N.A. Plans 2,428
Total Weighted N 56,664

Table A—1.4. Undergraduate Major (Grouped) and Plans, Controlling for Sex and Academic Performance

Per cent Next Year on Plans Among . . .

Undergraduate Major	Male			Female			Total	
	Top Fifth	Above Average	Bottom Half	Top Fifth	Above Average	Bottom Half		
Biological Sciences	93.8 (262)	77.2 (409)	52.3 (596)	51.3 (181)	37.3 (343)	33.9 (265)	56.7	(2,104)
Physical Sciences	83.6 (921)	61.3 (1,031)	31.1 (1,219)	44.9 (338)	30.7 (354)	18.6 (214)	51.0	(4,118)
Social Sciences	71.7 (761)	51.9 (1,368)	35.1 (1,523)	49.6 (516)	26.8 (816)	20.1 (689)	43.7	(5,714)
Humanities	74.6 (1,130)	55.1 (1,409)	36.8 (1,455)	48.3 (1,476)	31.4 (1,887)	20.8 (1,202)	43.4	(8,680)
Other Professions	64.6 (1,372)	41.4 (2,617)	23.9 (3,569)	21.7 (456)	19.4 (1,007)	10.4 (1,001)	32.1	(10,180)
NEC	45.4 (66)	44.4 (117)	15.3 (359)	— (23)	12.5 (56)	12.0 (58)	22.4	(698)
Education	43.8 (319)	39.9 (1,393)	23.0 (2,810)	22.0 (1,511)	20.1 (4,343)	14.3 (4,017)	21.7	(14,646)
Business	37.8 (526)	23.2 (1,913)	11.8 (3,954)	3.8 (77)	14.4 (207)	11.6 (361)	16.8	(7,151)

N	52,495
N.A. Field	911
N.A. API	830
N.A. Plans	2,428
Total Weighted N	56,664

Table A-1.6 percentages the data to show the undergraduate origins of those planning graduate study in a particular field, reported in detail in A-1.6a and with undergraduate major grouped in A-1.6b.

Table A-1.7 percentages the same data to show the graduate destinations of particular undergraduate majors, destinations reported in detail in A-1.7a and grouped in A-1.7b.

Table A—1.5. Undergraduate Major (Arts and Science vs. Professional) Plans, Sex and Academic Performance Index

a. Undergraduate Major and Plans

Undergraduate Major	Per cent of Sample	Plans Index				Total		Total Per cent Next Year
		Next Year		Later	Never	Per cent	N	
		Accepted	Other					
Arts and Science	38.8	33.8	12.5	35.9	17.6	99.8	20,616	46.3
Professional	59.8	11.7	12.1	50.3	25.7	99.8	31,977	23.9
NEC	1.3	10.0	12.4	38.2	39.2	99.8	698	22.4
Total Per cent	99.9							

N 55,546
NA, Field 1,118
Total Weighted N 56,664

N 53,291
NA, Field 945
NA, Plans 2,428
Total Weighted N 56,664

b. Undergraduate Major and Sex; Undergraduate Major and Academic Performance

Undergraduate Field	Per cent Female	Academic Performance Index			Total	
		Top Fifth	Above Average	Bottom Half	Per cent	N
Arts and Science	40.7	27.4	37.4	35.1	99.9	20,363
Professional	41.3	13.5	36.4	49.9	99.8	31,453
NEC	20.2	13.1	25.4	61.4	99.9	679

N 52,495
NA, Field 911
NA, Plans 2,428
NA, API 830
Total Weighted N 56,664

c. Undergraduate Major and Plans, Controlling for Sex and API

Undergraduate Major	Per cent Next Year on Plans Among					
	Male			Female		
	Top Fifth	Above Average	Bottom Half	Top Fifth	Above Average	Bottom Half
Arts and Science	78.2 (3,074)	59.6 (4,217)	36.7 (4,791)	48.3 (2,511)	30.8 (3,400)	21.9 (2,370)
Professional	55.2 (2,217)	35.0 (5,923)	19.1 (10,333)	21.2 (2,044)	19.7 (5,557)	13.4 (5,379)
NEC	1.3 (66)	44.4 (117)	15.3 (359)	— (23)	12.5 (56)	12.0 (58)

N 52,495
NA, Field 911
NA, API 830
NA, Plans 2,428
Total Weighted N 56,664

Table A—1.6. Undergraduate Major of Students Expecting to Enter Various Graduate Fields

a. Detailed Fields (Per cent of Prospective Graduate Students Whose Undergraduate Major Was . . .)

Anticipated Graduate Field	Chemistry	Physics	Earth	Math.	Other Phy. Sci.	Biology	Bio. Chem.	Botany	Microbio.	Physiology	Zoology	Other Bio. Sci.	Clinical Psychology	Other Psych.	Economics	Pol. Sci.	Sociology	Other Soc. Sci.	Fine Arts	English	Language	History	Philosophy	Other Humanities	Engineer.	Medicine	Nursing	Other Health	Education	Business	Law	Social Work	Other Profes.	Per cent*	N
Chemistry	89	0	0	1	0	0	0	0	0	0	0	0	0	0	0	0	0	0	0	0	0	0	0	0	2	0	0	0	5	0	0	0	1	100	857
Physics	1	74	0	8	0	0	0	0	0	0	0	0	0	0	0	0	0	0	0	0	0	0	0	0	9	0	0	0	5	0	0	0	1	100	726
Geol.—Geog. (Earth)	0	0	69	0	3	0	0	0	0	0	0	0	0	0	1	0	0	0	0	0	0	5	0	0	2	0	0	0	16	0	0	0	0	100	272
Mathematics	1	8	0	68	0	0	0	0	0	0	0	0	0	0	0	0	0	0	0	0	0	0	0	0	7	0	0	0	13	0	0	0	3	100	899
Other Physical Sciences	3	19	10	4	26	0	0	0	0	0	0	0	0	0	0	0	0	0	0	0	0	0	0	0	9	0	0	0	11	0	0	0	2	102	158
Biology	11	0	0	0	0	65	1	0	0	0	2	0	0	0	0	0	0	0	0	0	0	0	0	0	0	1	0	0	22	0	0	0	1	100	363
Biochemistry	55	0	0	0	0	11	7	0	2	0	6	0	0	0	0	0	0	0	0	0	0	0	0	0	0	0	0	0	6	0	0	0	4	102	188
Botany	2	0	0	0	0	35	0	41	0	0	7	0	0	0	0	0	0	0	0	0	0	0	0	0	0	0	0	0	2	0	0	0	7	102	106
Microbiology	2	0	0	0	0	34	2	3	36	0	8	0	0	0	0	0	0	0	0	0	0	0	0	0	0	4	0	0	6	0	0	0	1	101	130
Physiology	8	0	0	0	0	48	1	0	0	14	13	0	0	0	0	0	0	0	0	0	0	0	0	0	0	0	0	0	11	0	0	0	2	99	92
Zoology	0	0	0	0	0	51	0	1	0	0	35	0	0	0	0	0	0	0	0	0	0	0	0	0	0	0	0	0	7	0	0	0	0	100	158
Other Biological Sciences	3	0	0	0	0	34	1	2	1	0	17	13	0	0	0	0	0	0	0	0	0	0	0	0	0	0	0	0	11	0	0	0	6	97	290
Clinical Psychology	3	0	0	0	0	0	0	0	0	0	0	0	44	28	0	0	1	0	0	0	0	0	0	0	0	0	0	0	11	0	0	2	1	99	371
Other Psychology	0	0	0	0	0	0	0	0	0	0	0	0	1	59	0	1	6	2	0	0	0	0	1	0	0	3	0	0	4	0	0	9	3	100	285
Economics	0	0	0	0	0	0	0	0	0	0	0	0	0	0	61	2	2	4	0	0	0	2	0	0	0	0	0	0	12	8	0	0	1	99	458
Political Science	0	0	0	0	0	0	0	0	0	0	0	0	0	1	2	52	2	1	0	0	0	7	0	0	0	0	0	0	24	2	0	0	3	99	688
Sociology	0	0	0	0	0	0	0	0	0	0	0	0	0	1	4	1	56	1	0	0	0	2	0	0	0	0	0	0	11	0	0	0	5	102	376
Other Social Sciences	0	0	0	0	0	1	0	0	0	0	0	0	0	3	0	9	5	28	0	0	0	2	0	0	0	0	0	0	14	0	0	0	4	98	286
Fine Arts	0	0	0	0	0	0	0	0	0	0	0	0	0	0	0	0	0	0	61	2	1	1	0	0	0	0	0	0	15	0	0	0	2	99	1,413
English	0	0	0	0	0	0	0	0	0	0	0	0	0	0	0	0	0	0	2	78	1	2	1	0	0	0	0	0	7	0	0	0	3	100	1,192
Languages	0	0	0	0	0	0	0	0	0	0	0	0	0	0	0	0	0	0	2	6	62	2	1	0	0	0	0	0	35	0	0	0	5	97	718
History	0	0	0	0	0	0	0	0	0	0	0	0	0	0	0	2	0	0	3	9	1	68	1	0	0	0	0	0	1	0	0	0	2	102	1,124
Philosophy	0	0	0	0	0	0	0	0	0	0	0	0	0	1	0	1	0	0	2	5	1	3	50	0	0	0	0	0	3	0	0	0	3	104	202
Other Humanities	0	0	0	0	0	0	0	0	0	0	0	0	0	0	0	0	0	0	6	16	2	2	1	16	0	0	0	0	13	0	0	0	5	103	201
Engineering	1	9	2	6	2	0	0	0	0	0	1	0	0	0	0	0	0	0	0	0	0	0	0	0	90	0	0	0	4	0	0	0	4	99	1,436
Medicine	13	0	0	0	0	20	2	0	2	0	8	2	0	3	0	0	0	0	0	0	0	0	0	0	0	30	0	0	3	0	0	0	2	102	655
Nursing	0	0	0	0	0	1	0	0	0	0	1	0	0	0	0	0	0	0	0	0	0	0	0	0	0	0	91	0	0	0	0	0	1	100	429
Other Health	5	0	0	0	0	20	2	0	0	0	7	0	0	3	0	0	0	0	0	0	0	0	0	0	0	30	2	33	0	0	0	0	6	100	3,043
Education	1	0	0	1	0	2	0	0	0	0	0	0	0	2	0	2	2	4	2	15	7	14	1	0	3	0	0	0	13	2	0	0	4	98	1,436
Business	0	0	0	0	0	0	0	0	0	0	0	0	0	2	8	2	2	1	1	2	1	4	0	0	5	0	0	0	2	59	5	0	2	98	11,572
Law	1	0	0	0	0	2	0	0	0	0	0	0	0	2	0	19	2	4	0	2	1	6	0	0	0	0	0	0	3	2	0	0	2	100	4,519
Social Work	1	0	0	0	0	0	0	0	0	0	0	0	2	9	0	3	36	4	0	2	1	2	0	0	0	0	0	0	11	0	0	20	4	98	2,440
Other Professions	1	0	0	1	0	0	0	0	0	0	0	0	1	1	1	3	3	4	2	5	1	6	4	1	3	1	0	0	17	2	0	20	42	101	721

N.A. Undergraduate Major — 39,371
N.A. Graduate Major — 355
N.A. Undergraduate Major and Graduate Major — 1,792
Excluded from Table: — 335
Not Planning Graduate School Ever — 12,383
N.A. Plans — 2,428
Total Weighted N — 56,664

(Table 1.6 *continued*)

*Due to rounding, total percentages deviate from 100 in some cases.

Table 1.6. Continued

b. Data in Table 1.6a Grouped

Anticipated Graduate Field / Arts and Science	Undergraduate Major					Total		Other Undergraduate Majors Contributing 10 Per cent or More of Prospective Graduate Students
	Phy. Sci.	Bio. Sci.	Soc. Sci.	Hum.	Prof.	Per cent	N	
Chemistry	90.7	0.4	0.2	0.8	7.8	99.9	857	—
Physics	82.8	1.7	0.0	0.2	15.3	100.0	726	—
Geog., Geol. (Earth)	69.8	0.4	4.7	7.1	18.0	100.0	272	Education (158)
Mathematics	71.8	0.0	1.1	0.8	26.2	99.9	899	Education (13.0)
Other Physical Sciences	61.4	3.8	0.0	0.6	34.1	99.9	158	Physics (19.0), English (19.0), Education (11.4)
Biology	2.2	68.4	1.2	3.0	25.4	100.2	363	Education (21.5)
Biochemistry	54.8	27.0	0.0	0.0	18.1	99.9	188	Chemistry (54.8), Biology (10.6)
Botany	2.8	84.0	0.9	0.0	12.3	100.0	106	Biology (34.9)
Microbiology	2.3	82.3	0.0	2.3	13.1	100.0	130	Biology (33.8), Health (10.0)
Physiology	8.7	77.1	2.2	0.0	12.0	100.0	92	Biology (47.8), Zoology (13.0)
Zoology	1.9	86.7	0.0	0.6	10.8	100.0	158	Biology (51.3), Education (10.8)
Other Biological Sciences	6.8	67.9	0.6	0.6	23.7	99.6	290	Biology (34.1), Zoology (17.2)
Clinical Psychology	0.6	0.0	72.8	9.8	17.0	100.2	371	Psychology (27.5), Education (11.3)
Other Psychology	4.3	0.7	65.7	4.3	25.4	100.4	285	Education (10.9)
Economics	3.3	0.4	66.5	8.3	21.4	99.9	458	Business (15.7)
Political Science	1.8	0.0	57.1	28.4	12.7	100.0	688	History (20.2)
Sociology	2.7	1.6	64.0	7.8	24.3	100.4	376	Education (12.0)
Other Social Sciences	1.4	1.5	43.3	24.5	29.5	100.2	286	History (11.9), Education (24.5)
Fine Arts	1.4	1.0	2.4	70.9	24.3	100.0	1,413	Education (19.8)
English	0.8	0.1	1.3	83.8	14.3	100.3	1,192	Education (10.9)
Languages	2.7	0.1	3.9	74.3	18.9	99.9	718	Education (13.8)
History	2.1	0.1	7.4	71.9	18.5	100.0	1,124	Education (14.7)
Philosophy	7.9	1.0	1.5	68.9	20.8	100.1	202	English (14.9)
Other Humanities	0.5	0.0	2.5	47.8	49.3	100.1	201	English (16.4), Education (35.3)

Table A—1.6 Continued

Anticipated Graduate Field	Undergraduate Major			Total		Other Undergraduate Majors Contributing 10 Per cent or More of Prospective Graduate Students
Professional	Arts and Science	Same Profes.	Other Profes.	Per cent	N	
Engineering	5.9	87.9	4.3	100.1	3,043	—
Medicine	63.1	30.2	6.6	99.9	1,436	Chemistry (13.4), Biology (19.9)
Nursing	4.4	0.0	95.5	99.9	429	—
Other Health	42.8	33.3	24.0	100.1	655	Biology (19.5), Education (12.8)
Education	15.2	80.5	4.2	100.0	11,572	—
Business	20.0	59.4	20.6	100.0	4,519	Engineering (13.3)
Law	60.3	27.7	16.1	100.1	2,440	Political Science (19.3), History (14.2), Business (23.7)
Social Work	62.9	19.8	17.4	100.1	721	Sociology (36.2)
All Other Professions	33.0	41.6	25.6	100.1	3,003	Education (11.0), Education (16.6)

N 39,371
NA, Undergraduate Major 355
NA, Graduate Major 1,792
NA, Undergraduate Major and Graduate Major 335
Excluded from Table:
Not Planning Graduate School Ever 12,383
NA, Plans 2,428

Total Weighted N 56,664

Table A–1.7. Anticipated Graduate Field of Students in Various Undergraduate Fields Among Those Expecting to Go On Next Year or Later

a. Detailed Fields

Undergraduate Major	Chemistry	Physics	Earth	Mathematics	Other Phy. Sci.	Biology	Biochem.	Botany	Microbiol.	Physiology	Zoology	Other Bio. Sci.	Clinical Psychology	Other Psychology	Economics	Pol. Sci.	Sociology	Other Soc. Sci.	Fine Arts	English	Language	History	Philosophy	Other Hum.	Engineering	Medicine	Nursing	Other Health	Education	Business	Law	Social Work	Other Prof.	Per cent*	N
Chemistry	59	0	0	1	0	0	8	0	0	1	0	1	0	0	0	0	0	0	1	0	0	0	0	0	2	15	0	3	4	3	1	0	2	100	1,292
Physics	0	69	0	3	4	0	0	0	0	0	0	0	0	0	0	0	0	0	1	0	1	0	0	0	10	1	0	0	4	3	2	0	–	98	781
Geol.-Geog. (Earth)	0	0	63	0	0	0	0	0	0	0	0	2	0	0	0	0	0	0	2	0	2	2	0	0	3	0	0	0	8	3	3	0	6	100	298
Mathematics	1	6	0	58	–	0	0	0	0	0	0	0	0	0	0	0	0	0	1	0	0	0	0	0	10	2	0	0	8	6	3	0	3	100	1,042
Other Physical Sciences	0	–	0	2	47	0	2	0	0	4	0	0	0	0	0	0	0	0	0	0	0	0	0	0	10	25	0	0	2	2	3	0	–	98	88
Biology	0	0	0	0	0	20	2	3	4	2	7	9	0	0	0	0	0	0	–	0	0	0	0	0	0	47	0	1	2	2	0	0	6	102	1,150
Biochemistry	2	0	0	0	0	6	29	0	6	2	0	2	0	0	0	0	0	0	0	0	0	0	0	0	0	47	0	0	4	2	0	0	2	102	49
Botany	0	0	0	0	0	6	0	65	0	0	0	9	0	0	0	0	0	0	0	0	0	0	0	0	0	17	0	0	8	2	0	0	2	102	66
Microbiology	0	0	0	0	0	–	3	2	51	2	0	4	0	0	0	0	0	0	0	0	0	0	0	0	0	32	0	0	2	0	0	0	2	99	92
Physiology	1	0	0	0	0	–	0	0	3	48	0	14	0	0	0	0	0	0	0	0	0	0	0	0	0	22	0	0	4	0	0	0	–	100	27
Zoology	0	0	0	0	0	–	0	2	0	4	16	54	0	0	0	0	0	0	0	0	0	0	0	0	0	7	0	0	4	2	–	0	–	103	346
Other Biological Sciences	0	0	0	0	0	2	0	2	3	2	0	–	0	0	0	0	0	0	4	0	0	0	0	0	2	7	0	0	2	2	–	0	–	101	68
Clinical Psychology	0	0	0	0	0	0	0	0	0	0	0	0	66	25	0	0	0	0	0	0	0	0	0	0	0	3	0	0	5	0	0	–	–	99	247
Other Psychology	0	0	0	0	0	0	0	0	0	0	0	0	15	25	0	0	9	2	0	0	–	0	0	0	0	0	0	0	17	2	0	2	–	98	667
Economics	0	0	0	0	0	0	0	0	0	0	0	0	0	0	29	2	0	2	0	0	0	0	0	0	0	–	0	0	19	36	16	0	5	99	964
Political Science	0	0	0	0	0	0	0	0	0	0	0	0	0	0	–	30	0	2	0	0	0	–	0	0	0	0	0	0	3	6	40	–	7	99	1,185
Sociology	0	0	0	0	0	0	0	0	0	0	0	0	0	2	0	–	22	2	0	0	–	0	0	0	0	0	0	0	6	5	6	28	9	99	942
Other Social Science	0	0	0	0	0	0	0	0	0	0	0	0	0	0	2	2	3	24	–	0	0	2	0	2	0	3	0	0	17	5	7	8	7	97	329
Fine Arts	0	0	0	0	0	0	0	0	0	0	0	0	0	0	0	0	0	0	67	2	–	–	–	2	0	0	0	0	4	2	–	0	2	101	1,298
English	0	0	0	0	0	0	0	0	0	0	0	0	0	0	0	0	0	0	2	48	–	2	2	2	0	0	0	0	17	2	–	0	–	100	1,912
Language	0	0	0	2	0	0	0	0	0	0	0	0	0	0	0	0	0	0	–	–	59	–	2	6	0	0	0	0	17	2	0	0	–	102	751
History	0	0	1	0	0	0	0	0	0	0	0	0	0	0	–	3	–	2	–	2	–	35	–	2	0	0	0	0	17	5	5	0	–	100	2,178
Philosophy	0	0	0	0	0	0	0	0	0	0	0	0	0	0	0	–	–	–	–	2	–	–	27	2	0	0	0	0	33	8	8	2	11	98	367
Other Humanities	0	0	0	0	0	2	0	0	0	0	0	0	0	0	0	0	0	0	3	2	6	–	–	22	0	0	0	0	17	–	17	0	3	102	151
Engineering	2	2	0	2	0	0	0	0	0	0	0	0	0	0	0	0	0	0	0	0	0	0	0	0	72	–	0	0	7	6	3	0	6	100	3,813
Medicine	0	0	0	0	0	0	0	0	0	0	0	0	0	0	0	0	0	0	0	0	0	0	0	0	0	93	0	2	2	0	0	0	0	99	469
Nursing	0	0	0	0	0	2	0	0	4	0	0	0	0	0	0	0	0	0	0	0	0	0	0	0	0	–	72	2	12	–	0	0	2	99	547
Other Health	0	0	0	0	0	0	0	0	0	0	0	7	0	0	0	0	0	0	0	0	0	0	0	0	0	10	0	59	4	–	–	0	–	100	372
Education	2	0	0	2	0	0	0	0	0	0	0	0	–	1	0	0	0	0	2	2	2	–	0	0	0	–	0	–	80	5	0	0	4	99	11,601
Business	0	0	0	0	0	0	0	0	0	0	0	0	0	0	2	–	–	0	0	0	0	0	0	0	2	0	0	0	5	67	15	0	3	100	3,992
Law	0	0	0	0	0	0	0	0	0	0	0	0	0	0	2	3	0	2	0	0	0	0	0	0	0	0	0	0	7	7	67	0	2	102	133
Social Work	0	0	0	0	0	0	0	0	0	0	0	0	0	0	0	0	2	0	0	0	0	0	0	0	0	0	0	0	8	0	0	82	7	100	174
Other Professions	0	1	0	1	0	1	0	0	1	0	0	1	0	0	1	5	2	1	2	1	1	–	1	1	2	1	0	2	7	8	3	2	63	102	1,980

N.A. Undergraduate Major — 39,371
N.A. Graduate Field — 1,792
N.A. Undergraduate Major and Graduate Field — 335
Excluded from Table:
  Not Planning Graduate School Ever — 12,383
  N.A. Plans — 2,428

Total Weighted N — 56,664

TABLE A—1.7 continued

b. Data in Table A—1.7a Grouped

Undergraduate Major	Anticipated Graduate Field					Total		Fields Other than Original Major with 10 Per cent or More
Arts and Science	Phy. Sci.	Bio. Sci.	Soc. Sci.	Hum.	Prof.	Per cent	N	
Chemistry	60.6	9.7	0.2	1.0	28.7	100.2	1,292	Medicine (14.9)
Physics	76.3	1.9	0.3	1.6	19.7	99.8	781	—
Geog.-Geol. (Earth)	68.4	0.0	3.7	3.6	24.2	99.9	298	Education (10.1)
Mathematics	65.7	0.6	3.8	3.2	25.5	98.8	1,042	Engineering (10.2), Education (19.3)
Other Physical Sciences	51.1	2.2	1.1	1.1	44.2	99.7	88	—
Biology	1.6	48.4	0.4	1.1	48.2	99.7	1,150	Medicine (24.9), Health Fields (11.1)
Biochemistry	2.0	44.9	0.0	0.0	52.9	99.8	49	Medicine (46.9)
Botany	1.5	88.0	0.0	1.5	9.1	100.1	66	—
Microbiology	0.0	59.9	0.0	1.1	39.2	100.2	92	Medicine (17.4), Health Fields (10.9)
Physiology	0.0	55.5	3.7	0.0	40.7	99.9	27	Medicine (11.1), Education (22.2)
Zoology	0.6	44.2	0.9	0.6	53.9	100.2	346	Med. (32.1), Other Bio. Sci. (14.4), Other Health (13.6)
Other Biological Sciences	0.0	55.9	8.8	4.4	30.9	100.0	68	Medicine (22.1)
Clinical Psychology	0.0	0.0	68.0	0.8	31.1	99.9	247	Education (10.5)
Other Psychology	0.2	0.2	42.2	1.4	56.1	100.1	667	Clin. Psy. (15.3), Education (19.0)
Economics	1.0	0.2	32.0	1.0	65.6	99.8	964	Business (35.8), Law (20.6)
Political Science	0.2	0.0	33.7	5.0	61.2	100.1	1,185	Law (39.7)
Sociology	0.1	0.1	27.1	3.7	68.9	99.9	942	Education (19.2), Social Work (27.7)
Other Social Sciences	3.3	0.9	31.8	15.8	48.1	99.9	329	History (13.4), Education (18.9)
Fine Arts	0.1	0.3	2.1	70.8	26.8	100.1	1,298	Education (14.4)
English	0.5	0.2	2.5	59.3	37.7	100.2	1,912	Education (14.5)
Language	1.0	0.0	4.9	66.3	27.8	100.0	751	—
History	1.0	0.6	10.8	38.4	49.4	100.2	2,178	Education (16.9), Law (15.9)
Philosophy	0.0	0.6	8.0	35.9	55.7	100.2	367	Other Professions (33.0)
Other Humanities	0.7	0.0	5.3	38.5	55.7	100.2	151	Education (16.6), Law (17.2), Other (10.6)

(Table A—1.7 continued)

Table 1.7. *Continued*

Undergraduate Major	Anticipated Graduate Field			Total		Fields Other than Original Major with 10 Per cent or More
Professional	Arts and Science	Same Profes.	Other Profes.	Per cent	N	
Engineering	6.0	71.3	22.9	100.2	3,813	Business (15.7)
Pre-Medicine	3.8	92.5	3.5	99.8	469	—
Nursing	6.1	71.5	22.6	100.2	547	Education (11.9)
Other Health	22.6	58.6	19.0	100.2	372	—
Education	13.3	80.4	7.8	101.5	11,601	—
Business	8.3	67.3	26.1	101.7	3,992	Law (14.3)
Law	2.4	94.0	3.8	100.2	133	—
Social Work	5.7	82.2	12.1	100.0	174	—
Other Professions	13.6	63.0	24.3	100.9	1,980	—

N	39,371
NA, Undergraduate Major	355
NA, Graduate Field	1,792
NA, Undergraduate Major and Graduate Field	335
Excluded from Table:	
Not Planning Graduate School Ever	12,383
NA, Plans	2,428
Total Weighted N	56,664

Appendix 2

National Projections Of Graduate School Attendance

During the summer of 1961 we arrived at the projections in the following tables in the following manner:

1. From U.S. Office of Education publications we obtained projections of the number of bachelor's and first professional degrees awarded in 1959–60 and to be awarded in 1961–62.

2. On the basis of *1* above, the number of graduates for the year 1960–61 was interpolated.

3. First professional degrees that are not also undergraduate bachelor's degrees were subtracted from the figures arrived at in *2* above.

a. It was ascertained which institutions offer first professional degrees that are not undergraduate bachelor's degrees. Students in five-year baccalaureate programs in fields such as engineering and architecture were included. Students graduating from a professional school that required two or more years of undergraduate work prior to admission were viewed as receiving graduate degrees and were excluded.

b. The total number of first professional degrees that are not undergraduate bachelor's degrees was estimated from Office of Education reports of degrees awarded by field and institution during the academic year 1958–59.

4. On the basis of reports from the sample schools, it was estimated that approximately 25 per cent of the bachelor's degrees awarded by American colleges and universities are conferred at times other than June. The total resulting from step *3* above was therefore multiplied by 75 per cent. This resulted in an estimate of 265,000 bachelor's degrees awarded in June, 1961.

5. The projected 265,000 graduates were distributed among fields and API categories within fields according to their proportional representation in the sample.

Table A—2.1. Projected Numbers of June, 1961, College Graduates Planning Graduate or Professional Study, by Field, Among Those Who Indicated a Specific Graduate or Professional Field (Note: Projections are rounded to the nearest ten)

	a. Broad Field Groupings						
	Plans to Attend Graduate School						Total* All Times
Field of Study	Fall, 1961			Later			
	Accepted	Other	Total	Definite Date	No Definite Date	Total	
Chemistry	2,190	410	2,600	1,210	580	1,790	4,390
Math. and Statistics	1,380	730	2,110	1,630	840	2,470	4,580
Physics	1,840	540	2,380	980	340	1,320	3,700
Other Physical Sci.	720	410	1,130	760	330	1,090	2,220
Biological Sciences	2,490	1,190	3,680	2,100	1,070	3,170	6,850
Social Sciences	4,460	2,200	6,660	5,360	2,030	7,390	14,050
Humanities	7,350	4,230	11,580	9,140	4,220	13,360	24,940
Education	6,440	11,020	17,460	27,930	14,060	41,990	59,450
Engineering	4,050	2,950	7,000	5,820	2,730	8,550	15,550
Medicine	5,810	640	6,450	710	160	870	7,320
Other Health Prof.	1,920	670	2,590	1,720	1,160	2,880	5,470
Law	6,640	1,790	8,430	3,390	670	4,060	12,490
Social Work	690	520	1,210	1,800	670	2,470	3,680
Other Professions	3,990	1,690	5,680	3,330	1,620	4,950	10,630
Business	3,320	3,600	6,920	10,850	5,310	16,160	23,080
Agriculture	540	230	770	640	290	930	1,700
"No Near Equivalent"	620	330	950	700	370	1,070	2,020
Total	54,450	33,150	87,600	78,070	36,450	114,520	202,120

Total All Times	202,120	
Not Going	62,970	
Total	265,090	

*The careful reader will note that totals in Tables A—2.1 and A—2.2 are not identical. This is due to the different numbers of NA in the two tables. The totals were not corrected for these few NA's because the projections are approximations only.

able A—2.1   Continued

b. Field Groupings with Science Fields Specified

Field of Study	Plans to Attend Graduate School						Total* All Times
	Fall, 1961			Later			
	Accepted	Other	Total	Definite Date	No Definite Date	Total	
Chemistry	2,190	410	2,600	1,210	580	1,790	4,390
Math. and Statistics	1,380	730	2,110	1,630	840	2,470	4,580
Physics	1,840	540	2,380	980	340	1,320	3,700
Astrom./Astrophys.	90	50	140	40	20	60	200
Geography	180	140	320	420	160	580	900
Geol./Geophysics	230	90	320	130	30	160	480
Oceanography	60	10	70	20	30	50	120
Metallurgy	50	10	60	40	20	60	120
Meterology	60	50	110	30	50	80	190
Phy., Gen. & Other	50	60	110	80	20	100	210
Anatomy	120	20	140	80	20	100	240
Biology	340	400	740	740	370	1,110	1,850
Biochemistry	380	110	490	340	130	470	960
Botany	250	90	340	110	90	200	540
Biophysics	70	10	80	70	—	70	150
Entomology	100	20	120	90	50	140	260
Genetics	150	30	180	100	40	140	320
Microbiology	230	80	310	230	130	360	670
Pathology	—	10	10	10	10	20	30
Pharmacology	60	10	70	30	30	60	130
Physiology	220	150	370	100	30	130	500
Zoology	370	150	520	130	150	280	800
Other Biology	200	110	310	70	20	90	400
Social Sciences	4,460	2,200	6,660	5,360	2,030	7,390	14,050
Humanities	7,350	4,230	11,580	9,140	4,220	13,360	24,940
Education	6,440	11,020	17,460	27,930	14,060	41,990	59,450
Engineering	4,050	2,950	7,000	5,820	2,730	8,550	15,550
Medicine	5,810	640	6,450	710	160	870	7,320
Dentistry	950	120	1,070	170	60	230	1,300
Other Health Prof.	970	550	1,520	1,550	1,100	2,650	4,170
Law	6,640	1,790	8,430	3,390	670	4,060	12,490
Social Work	690	520	1,210	1,800	670	2,470	3,680
Other Professions	3,990	1,690	5,680	3,330	1,620	4,950	10,630
Business	3,320	3,600	6,920	10,850	5,310	16,160	23,080
Agriculture	540	230	770	640	290	930	1,700
"No Near Equivalent"	620	330	950	700	370	1,070	2,020
Total	54,450	33,150	87,600	78,070	36,450	114,520	202,120

Total All Times All Fields	202,120
Not Going	62,970
Total	265,090

Table A – 2.2. Projected Numbers of June, 1961, College Graduates Planning Graduate or Professional Study by Field and Academic Performance, Among Those Who Indicated A Specific Graduate or Professional Field (Note: Projections are rounded to the nearest ten)

Field of Study	Academic Performance*	Plans to Attend Graduate School						Total All Times
		Fall, 1961			Later			
		Accepted	Other	Total	Definite Date	No Definite Date	Total	
Chemistry	H	860	60	920	180	40	220	1,140
	M	840	190	1,030	450	170	620	1,650
	L	490	170	660	580	380	960	1,620
Math. & Stat.	H	880	150	1,030	360	130	490	1,520
	M	380	350	730	550	350	900	1,630
	L	120	230	350	740	360	1,100	1,450
Physics	H	1,240	90	1,330	230	10	240	1,570
	M	450	260	710	270	80	350	1,060
	L	160	190	350	480	250	730	1,080
Other Physical Sciences	H	370	30	400	60	40	100	500
	M	300	210	510	340	100	440	950
	L	50	150	200	310	170	480	680
Bio. Science	H	780	140	920	310	190	500	1,420
	M	1,040	400	1,440	630	410	1,040	2,480
	L	650	640	1,290	1,060	460	1,520	2,810
Social Science	H	2,090	350	2,440	990	390	1,380	3,820
	M	1,760	930	2,690	1,910	590	2,500	5,190
	L	570	910	1,480	2,450	1,030	3,480	4,960
Humanities	H	4,180	1,050	5,230	2,180	830	3,010	8,240
	M	2,260	1,950	4,210	3,800	1,670	5,470	9,680
	L	880	1,160	2,040	3,200	1,680	4,880	6,920

able A—2.2 Continued

Field of Study	Academic Performance*	Plans to Attend Graduate School						Total All Times
		Fall, 1961			Later			
		Accepted	Other	Total	Definite Date	No Definite Date	Total	
Education	H	1,780	1,330	3,110	3,510	1,450	4,960	8,070
	M	2,840	4,640	7,480	10,650	5,500	16,150	23,630
	L	1,820	5,020	6,840	13,690	7,000	20,690	27,530
Engineering	H	2,170	610	2,780	810	230	1,040	3,820
	M	1,380	1,230	2,610	2,180	1,010	3,190	5,800
	L	520	1,120	1,640	2,810	1,490	4,300	5,940
Medicine	H	2,870	90	2,960	100	10	110	3,070
	M	2,430	310	2,740	280	80	360	3,100
	L	490	240	730	340	70	410	1,140
Other Health	H	210	100	310	320	170	490	800
	M	740	240	980	820	540	1,360	2,340
	L	980	330	1,310	520	450	970	2,280
Law	H	2,280	150	2,430	490	20	510	2,940
	M	2,640	610	3,250	1,050	190	1,240	4,490
	L	1,750	1,020	2,770	1,840	460	2,300	5,070
Social Work	H	170	20	190	300	120	420	610
	M	320	350	670	580	250	830	1,500
	L	190	160	350	890	300	1,190	1,540
Other Professions	H	1,020	230	1,250	410	250	660	1,910
	M	1,370	540	1,910	1,190	460	1,650	3,560
	L	1,610	920	2,530	1,680	920	2,600	5,130
Business	H	1,150	410	1,560	1,070	420	1,490	3,050
	M	1,500	1,470	2,970	3,990	1,690	5,680	8,650
	L	680	1,720	2,400	5,800	3,180	8,980	11,380
Agriculture	H	100	40	140	60	20	80	220
	M	290	40	330	240	100	340	670
	L	150	140	290	340	170	510	800
"No Near Equivalent"	H	260	70	330	100	40	140	470
	M	220	130	350	200	110	310	660
	L	140	120	260	380	230	610	870
Total		54,420	33,010	87,430	77,720	36,260	113,980	201,410

Total All Times   201,410
Not Going   63,660
Total   265,070

* H = Top 20
M = Above Average
L = Bottom Half

Appendix 3

Notes
On the Validity
Of the Academic
Performance
Index

Throughout the report, numerous associations have been reported involving the Academic Performance Index (API), a composite measure based on the student's cumulative grade point average and the quality of his school in terms of the intellectual calibre of its freshmen. It has been shown that API is associated with sex, SES, hometown, race, career choice, plans for graduate study, award of a stipend, application for a stipend, interest in research, and type of future employer.

While the findings in themselves provide some reassurance about the validity of the measure (any measure on which higher SES students, those from larger cities, whites, future physicians, students going on for graduate study immediately, students who apply for and receive stipends, students who want to do research, etc., all tend to receive high scores, is undoubtedly getting at something like academic performance), it would be helpful to have independent evidence on its validity. We shall here present two sets of data which provide further information — that on Law School Admissions Test scores and that on National Merit Scholarship finalists.

LAW SCHOOL ADMISSIONS TEST SCORES

Since the completion of the report, it has become possible to use scores on the Law School Admissions Test of the Educational Testing Service as a validating instrument. The opportunity arose in connection with an analysis of data on recruitment to law by Seymour Warkov of NORC.

The Law School Admissions Test (LSAT) is a three and one-half hour paper and pencil test required for admission to some eighty law schools that constitute about two-thirds of the fully-accredited law schools in the United States. The test purports to measure "comprehension of written language, facility with words and with data presented in graphic form, and reasoning power,"[1] it was designed to "be a measure of aptitude for the study of law and (to) be as free as possible of questions assuming a knowledge of specific course work. . . . to make it possible for applicants having the mental abilities necessary for the study of law to make good scores on the test regardless of the undergraduate curricula they had engaged in."

As for the validity of the LSAT itself, Winterbottom and Johnson write, " . . . ETS has conducted over forty validity studies based on LSAT scores. The criterion characteristically used has been first year average grades (in law school). The range of average correlations for the years 1948–57 is .38 to .59." A 1959 study in six law schools gives an average correlation of .52 and a correlation of .64 when the data are adjusted to allow for the fact that since the test itself is used for selection, the correlations are lowered through the screening of low LSAT scorers who presumably would get very low grades in law school.[2]

The Educational Testing Service kindly searched its files for LSAT scores of men in the NORC survey who gave law as their current or sometime preference for future study or employment.

[1]Materials in quotation marks and most descriptive information on the LSAT are taken from John A. Winterbottom and A. Pemberton Johnson, "The Law School Admissions Test Program," Educational Testing Service, September, 1961 (litho.).

[2]Barbara Pitcher and Marjorie Olsen, "The Law School Admission Test as a Predictor of First-Year Law School Grades, 1957–58," Educational Testing Service, April, 1959 (mimeo.).

A weighted total of 1,595 cases with both API and LSAT scores was located.

If the assumptions underlying the API are correct (and the LSAT is a measure of academic achievement), three sets of relationships should obtain when LSAT scores are tabulated simultaneously by GPA and the School Quality Index:

1. Within a school quality level, mean LSAT scores should increase with increasing GPA.

2. Within a GPA level, mean LSAT scores should increase with school quality.

3. Considering the cutting points used (as indicated below), the following differences in LSAT should hold:

School Quality	GPA								
	A	A−	B+	B	B−	C+	C	C−	D+
I									
II	Top Fifth					Above Average			Bottom Half
III									
IV									

GPA	Quality	Should Surpass		
B−	I	B−II	B+III	A−IV
B	II		B+III	A−IV
B+	III			A−IV
C	I	C−II	C+III	B−IV
C+	II		C+III	B−IV
B−	III			B−IV

Even by lowering our criterion for cell size with weighted data from 50 to 20 cases, some cells are too small to justify tabulations, but the general nature of the relationship is clear.

Within a school quality group, the higher the GPA, the higher the LSAT. Because the LSAT has a standard deviation of 100, we can say that in A level schools there is a range in means of .73 sigma units from the A− GPA group to the C level; and in C schools, the range is 1.11 standard deviations.

Within a GPA level, the higher the school quality, the higher the mean LSAT. For cells with sufficient cases, the range from A to D school quality within a GPA group is in the neighborhood of one standard deviation.

It is interesting to note that C+ students in the A schools have means about the same as B+ and A students in C and D level schools, and C or worse students in A level schools surpass B students in levels B, C, and D.

As for the justification of the cutting points, unfortunately there are not sufficient cases to the specific hypotheses set forth. However, it may be said that no cell stands out as grossly misclassified by the cutting points. Thus, there is no cell in the "bottom half" classification with an LSAT mean as high or higher than any cell in the other two groups, and save for the B students in level II (who may represent sampling error because their LSAT is lower than for B− students in level II) there is no cell classified as "Above Average" that surpasses a cell classified as "Top Fifth."

Because LSAT takers are not representative of men in general and the validity of the LSAT is still being explored, these figures should not be taken as indicating that there are no further questions about the API. However, it is encouraging to find that the

Table A−3.1.   Mean LSAT—Weighted N

School Quality	≧ A−	B+	B	B−	C+	≦ C
				GPA		
I	621 (26)	612 (41)	588 (75)	585 (90)	574 (59)	548 ↑(37)
II	[579 (21)]		528 (31)	543 (38)	506 (33)	− (9)
III	576 (47)	551 (105)	515 (168)	491 (245)	477 (239)	465 (143)
IV	[↓574 (21)]		490 (30)	445 (55)	430 (48)	433 (34)

two components of API do correlate with an independent test that purports to tap academic potential.

UNDERGRADUATE MAJOR,
NATIONAL MERIT FINALISTS,
SEX, AND FIELD OF STUDY

One of the persistent problems involved in the API measure is that of comparability across fields of study. While the question of comparability across schools was attacked by correcting the raw GPA's by means of the School Quality Index, no assumptions were made about differences in the meaning of GPA's in various fields of study.

Although there was no practical method of establishing a discount for inflated academic currency, a number of persons in and out of NORC have been bothered about possible biases introduced by curricular differences. Although the question is usually put more diplomatically, behind it lies the ominous proposition, "You are treating a B average in 'Industrial Arts Education' as representing the same degree of academic performance as a B average in pure Mathematics." If pursued relentlessly, such a question is really unanswerable because no one can define academic achievement completely independent of subject matter and different subject matter is different. However, we can put the problem into a more realistic frame of reference by examining data on GPA, undergraduate major, school quality, sex, and National Merit Scholarship status.

To begin with, the School Quality Index itself unwittingly serves to establish a discount system, for undergraduate majors are differentially distributed according to school quality.

There is no simple rank order, but rather a series of patterns. Education students appear especially concentrated in level IV; humanities, social sciences, physical sciences, and engineering students are disproportionately concentrated in levels I and II; pre-medicine is concentrated in level III; and so on. Thus, even if there were no differences in the GPA's of students in various undergraduate majors within a quality level, education students would have to receive higher grades than physical sciences, social sciences, and humanities students to obtain the same API classification.

Table A—3.2. Undergraduate Major and School Quality

School Quality	Undergraduate Major									
	Pre-Med.	Soc. Science	Hum.	Phy. Science	Eng.	Bio. Science	All Students	Other Prof.	Bus.	Edu.
I–II	13	23	26	19	24	16	14	10	5	3
III	74	61	55	58	51	58	55	54	63	48
IV	13	16	20	23	26	26	31	36	31	49
Total N	100% (508)	100% (5,736)	101% (8,954)	100% (4,237)	101% (5,084)	100% (2,135)	100% (53,916)	100% (4,770)	99% (7,435)	100% (15,057)

Total Weighted N   53,916*

*Total differs from 56,664 because of "No answer" and "Not elsewhere classified" on undergraduate major and because of 975 NA's on grade point average, Table A—3.2 being calculated from a more complex tabulation including GPA.

More important, however, are the persistent GPA differences among various majors within a quality level. Table A-3.3 summarizes the results.

Clearly grade averages are stable across quality levels and vary by undergraduate major within quality level. At the extremes 81 per cent of the pre-medicine majors report a GPA of B— or better, in contrast with 44 per cent of the business majors. Furthermore, the rank order of fields is essentially similar in each quality level.

What is not obvious is the implication of these findings. On the one hand, they could suggest that different grade standards are being used in different curricula, but on the other hand, a case could be made that the differences reflect actual differences in achievement. The inference that business students show lower levels of academic achievement than humanities students is certainly in line with academic folklore, although the fact that education students surpass biological sciences, social sciences, and engineering students is not exactly in accord with academic opinion on these matters.

Table A—3.3. Undergraduate Major, School Quality, and GPA (Per cent Reporting a GPA of B— or Higher)

Undergraduate Major	Total		School Quality				
			I – II		III		IV
Pre-Medicine	81	(508)	79 (68)		80 (374)		88 (66)
Humanities	68	(8,954)	71 (2,289)		65 (4,917)		71 (1,748)
Phy. Science	67	(4,237)	73 (807)		63 (2,461)		67 (969)
Education	64	(15,057)	74 (443)		63 (7,244)		65 (7,370)
Bio. Science	61	(2,135)	71 (336)		56 (1,241)		63 (558)
Soc. Science	57	(5,736)	60 (1,327)		55 (3,499)		58 (910)
Other Prof.	55	(4,770)	62 (495)		55 (2,573)		53 (1,702)
Engineering	49	(5,084)	57 (1,199)		54 (2,586)		49 (1,299)
Business	44	(7,435)	50 (406)		43 (4,700)		46 (2,329)
Total	60	(53,916)*	65 (7,370)		58 (29,595)		60 (16,951)

*Cf. footnote to Table A—3.2.

Ideally we should like to have some measures known to be predictive of "true" achievement regardless of field of study. If the introduction of these measures eliminated the field differences in GPA, our confidence in the API would be doubly strengthened: 1) If the field differences disappeared when "true potential" is controlled, this would argue that there is little difference in faculty standards in different academic programs. 2) If the ordering of fields on "true potential" is correlated with their GPA order, we would have more confidence that the API index has a meaning across fields of study. No such pure measures are actually available (if they were we would have used them to begin with instead of API), but considerable light is shed on the matter when we simply consider National Merit Scholarship status and sex.

In the questionnaire, each student was asked to check whether he was a "National Merit Scholarship holder, Finalist, or Semifinalist" in high school. Since we are informed in a personal communication that some 90 per cent of our sample probably took the National Merit Scholarship examination, and since the group of semi-finalists, finalists, and scholarship holders fall above a fixed cutting point on that examination, we can assume that the students who checked this item represent a pool of uniformly high academic potential regardless of their undergraduate major. The drawback to this measure (other than an unknown degree of error in reporting) is that only three per cent of the total sample met the high cut-off point. While they undoubtedly constitute a group of very high talent, the remaining 97 per cent cover such a range in ability that the items cannot be used to "hold performance constant." The situation is somewhat akin to measuring social class by whether or not the respondents "have an income of a million dollars a year." However, if we assume that where the very, very bright students are, the very and fairly bright will tend to be also, we can use percentage of National Merit "winners" to rank order various groups.

The second measure is sex, which is introduced because, as we have seen previously, girls tend to get better grades than boys, perhaps because they are more conventionally industrious or perhaps because they are more highly selected.

Table A-3.4 shows the effect of these independent variables on GPA (there is no appreciable sex difference in National Merit status).

The differences are those we expected: Women are more likely than men to have high GPA's, although less so among the Merit winners who are all very bright; Merit winners get strikingly higher grades than the riffraff in the bottom 97 per cent in ability. Interestingly too, the Merit winners get better grades in lower quality schools, while non-Merit winners do not. Presumably the Merit winners do better in less selective schools because their *rank* standing is much higher (a Merit winner in level IV is in the top one per cent of his class, while in levels I and II he is only in the top 10 per cent). That non-Merit winners show no consistent differences by school quality is consistent with our assumption that pulling out the top 3 per cent leaves the remaining IQ's very heterogeneous.

Now, let us examine the talent differentials by field of study, within a sex grouping and quality.

Table A-3.5 contains a considerable amount of substantive information about the interrelations of school quality, undergraduate major, and the distribution of talent. We note some confirmations of folklore in the fact that, over all, the natural sciences have the greatest proportion of Merit winners, followed by the humanities and the social sciences, while business and education are the bottom ranking fields. However, we note also that the school

Table A—3.4. Per Cent With a GPA or B— or Higher

Merit Winner	Sex	School Quality			Total
		I–II	III	IV	
Yes	Female	86 (234)	98 (278)	100 (79)	
	Male	81 (529)	88 (393)	99 (138)	
No	Female	71 (2,515)	65 (12,335)	70 (6,641)	
	Male	59 (4,092)	51 (16,589)	53 (10,093)	
					3.1* (53,916)

*Cf. footnote to Table A—3.2.

Table A–3.5. Undergraduate Major, Sex, School Quality and Merit Winners

a. Per cent Merit Winners

Sex	School Quality	Undergraduate Major									Total
		Pre-Med.	Hum.	Phy. Sci.	Edu.	Bio. Sci.	Soc. Sci.	Other Prof.	Eng.	Bus.	
Male	I–II	16.2 (68)	11.2 (982)	22.2 (603)	2.9 (104)	11.0 (204)	10.4 (862)	2.8 (233)	8.4 (1,190)	3.4 (375)	11.4 (4,621)
	III	2.5 (354)	4.6 (2,187)	5.2 (1,824)	0.6 (1,773)	0.6 (676)	3.1 (2,181)	1.7 (1,155)	1.8 (2,567)	1.0 (4,265)	2.3 (16,982)
	IV	1.8 (56)	2.3 (1,024)	4.1 (876)	0.5 (2,873)	2.8 (427)	3.3 (662)	0.0 (889)	1.3 (1,296)	0.5 (2,128)	1.3 (10,231)
Female	I–II	– (0)	11.1 (1,307)	17.6 (204)	2.4 (339)	6.8 (132)	7.1 (465)	7.6 (262)	– (9)	– (31)	8.5 (2,749)
	III	– (20)	3.4 (2,730)	9.4 (637)	1.0 (5,471)	4.1 (565)	1.9 (1,318)	1.2 (1,418)	– (19)	1.1 (435)	2.2 (12,613)
	IV	– (10)	3.5 (724)	5.3 (93)	0.8 (4,497)	0.0 (131)	1.6 (248)	1.0 (813)	– (3)	0.0 (201)	1.2 (6,720)
Total		4.3 (508)	5.6 (8,954)	8.8 (4,237)	0.9 (15,057)	3.6 (2,135)	4.5 (5,736)	1.2 (4,770)	3.2 (5,084)	1.0 (7,435)	3.1 (53,916)*

b. Rank in Per cent of Merit Winners

Sex	School Quality	Pre-Med.	Hum.	Phy. Sci.	Edu.	Bio. Sci.	Soc. Sci.	Other Prof.	Eng.	Bus.
Male	I–II	2.0	3.0	1.0	8.0	4.0	5.0	9.0	6.0	7.0
	III	4.0	2.0	1.0	8.5	8.5	3.0	6.0	5.0	7.0
	IV	5.0	4.0	1.0	7.5	3.0	2.0	9.0	6.0	7.5
Female	I–II	–	2.0	1.0	6.0	5.0	4.0	3.0	–	–
	III	–	3.0	1.0	7.0	2.0	4.0	5.0	–	6.0
	IV	–	2.0	1.0	5.0	6.5	3.0	4.0	–	6.5
Total Sample		4.0	2.0	1.0	9.0	5.0	3.0	7.0	6.0	8.0

*Cf. footnote in Table A–3.2.

differences[3] are considerable, e.g., women business majors in levels I and II rank higher than every level IV field except the physical sciences.

Table A-3.6 gives the per cent of students in each of these groups reporting a GPA of B— or higher (N's are identical with Table A-3.5).

Now, if within a school quality level differences in the GPA's of students in various undergraduate fields stem only from differences in sex composition and in recruitment of talented high school seniors, then within a sex and quality grouping, ranks in GPA and in Merit winners should be similar. Tables A-3.5 and A-3.6 show that there is considerable agreement:

The relationship is not perfect by any means, but there is only one discrepancy of four ranks, and only four of three ranks, the remaining 40 cases all receiving relative GPA's within 0,1, or 2

[3]Because school quality was defined in terms of mean scores on the National Merit test for samples of freshmen, the *existence* of a school quality correlation is guaranteed. It is the degree of relationship and trends in sub-fields that can be considered "findings."

Table A—3.6. Undergraduate Major, Sex, School Quality and GPA

a. Per cent with GPA of B— or Higher

Sex	School Quality	Undergraduate Major								
		Pre-Med.	Hum.	Phy. Sci.	Edu.	Bio. Sci.	Soc. Sci.	Other Prof.	Eng.	Bus.
Male	I–II	79	68	72	67	70	56		58	49
	III	82	62	59	51	51	52	47	54	42
	IV	86	67	66	54	60	55	49	49	45
Female	I–II	—	72	77	77	72	68	72	—	—
	III	—	68	73	67	64	59	62	—	56
	IV	—	77	75	72	73	66	58	—	58

b. Rank in GPA

Sex	School Quality	Pre-Med.	Hum.	Phy. Sci.	Edu.	Bio. Sci.	Soc. Sci.	Other Prof.	Eng.	Bus.
Male	I–II	1.0	4.0	2.0	5.0	3.0	7.0	8.0	6.0	9.0
	III	1.0	2.0	3.0	6.5	6.5	5.0	8.0	4.0	9.0
	IV	1.0	2.0	3.0	6.0	4.0	5.0	7.5	7.5	9.0
Female	I–II	—	3.0	1.0	2.0	4.0	6.0	5.0	—	—
	III	—	2.0	1.0	3.0	4.0	6.0	5.0	—	7.0
	IV	—	1.0	2.0	4.0	3.0	5.0	6.0	—	7.0

steps of the prediction. What is perhaps even more important is that only two fields have consistent signs to their discrepancies . . . that is, receive better (or worse) grades in each comparison than would be predicted. Clearly students in education are more likely to report a GPA of B— or better than one would predict on the basis of their Merit winners, regardless of sex or school quality. Perhaps there is some inflation in grading standards applied to education students, or perhaps they consistently do better in their course work than their "talent" would suggest. At the opposite extreme, social sciences students are consistently lower in rank than their merit proportion predicts. Either tougher standards are being applied to social sciences majors or they are "under-achieving" in terms of their IQ. The fact that male pre-

Table A—3.7. Rank in Merit Winners (Table A—3.5) Minus Rank in GPA (Table A—3.6)

Sex	School Quality	Undergraduate Major								
		Pre-Med.	Hum.	Phy. Sci.	Edu.	Bio. Sci.	Soc. Sci.	Other Prof.	Eng.	Bus.
Male	I–II	+1.0	−1.0	−1.0	+3.0	+1.0	−2.0	+1.0	0.0	−2.0
	III	+3.0	0.0	2.0	+2.0	+2.0	−2.0	−2.0	+1.0	−2.0
	IV	+4.0	+2.0	−2.0	+1.5	−1.0	−3.0	+1.5	−1.5	−1.5
Female	I–II	—	−1.0	0.0	+4.0	+1.0	−2.0	−2.0	—	—
	III	—	+1.0	0.0	+4.0	−2.0	−2.0	0.0	—	−1.0
	IV	—	−1.0	−1.0	+1.0	+3.5	−2.0	−2.0	—	−0.5

Table A—3.8. Rank in Merit Winners by Rank in GPA

Rank in Merit Winners	Rank in GPA		Total
	1–4	5 or less	
1–4	17	7	24
5 or less	7	16	23
Total	24	23	47

$Q = 0.70$

medical students (there are too few women pre-medical majors to justify tabulations) have all positive deviations probably reflects the fact that, regardless of native ability, an undergraduate with less than a B— cumulative grade point average is probably likely to abandon "preMed" as a major field before his senior year.

Because the relationships are far from perfect and the measures crude, these findings should not be considered definitive by any means. However, it is our feeling that the following generalizations find some support:

1. Grades in education are somewhat "inflated," although our correction for school quality serves indirectly to mitigate this.

2. The grades of social sciences majors appear somewhat "deflated."

3. Although the remaining fields vary considerably in GPA levels when sex is controlled, the rank correlation between GPA level and per cent Merit winners suggests that these differences may well stem from actual differences in academic potential and thus, presumably, in actual performance.

Appendix 4

Listing of
Sample Colleges
and Universities

**SAMPLE OF COLLEGES AND UNIVERSITIES FOR SURVEY OF 1961
GRADUATING CLASS (ALPHABETICAL LISTING)**

COLLEGE OR UNIVERSITY	NUMBER ELIGIBLE STUDENTS SAMPLED	PER CENT RESPONDING
Alabama, University of— University	471	62
Albion College—Albion, Michigan	171	100
Arkansas State College— Jonesboro	197	72
Arkansas, University of— Fayetteville	365	64
Atlantic Union College—South Lancaster Massachusetts	50	98
Auburn University—Auburn, Alabama	178	82
Beloit College—Beloit, Wisconsin	147	98
Blackburn College—Carlinville, Illinois	41	100
Boston College—Chestnut Hill, Massachusetts	533	91
Boston University— Massachusetts	396	73
Briar Cliff College—Sioux City, Iowa	25	100

COLLEGES AND UNIVERSITIES — Continued

COLLEGE OR UNIVERSITY	NUMBER ELIGIBLE STUDENTS SAMPLED	PER CENT RESPONDING
Bridgewater College — Bridgewater, Virginia	74	93
Brooklyn College — New York	593	90
Brooklyn, Polytechnic Institute of — New York	209	72
Brown University (and Pembroke College) Providence, Rhode Island	584	77
California, University of — Berkeley	595	87
California, University of — Los Angeles	487	82
Carnegie Institute of Technology — Pittsburgh, Pennsylvania	230	97
Case Institute of Technology — Cleveland, Ohio	260	84
Chico State College — Chico, California	264	91
Cincinnati, University of — Ohio	762	89
Clark University — Worcester, Massachusetts	105	99
Cleary College — Ypsilanti, Michigan	19	79
Clemson Agricultural College — Clemson, South Carolina	329	99
Colorado State University — Fort Collins	427	88
Colorado, University of — Boulder	501	82
Columbia University — New York City	382	79
Concordia Teachers College — Seward, Nebraska	114	99
Cornell University — Ithaca, New York	447	84
Dartmouth College — Hanover, New Hampshire	236	91

COLLEGES AND UNIVERSITIES—Continued

COLLEGE OR UNIVERSITY	NUMBER ELIGIBLE STUDENTS SAMPLED	PER CENT RESPONDING
Delaware, University of— Newark	350	45
De Paul University—Chicago, Illinois	324	99
Detroit, University of— Michigan	177	84
Drexel Institute of Technology —Philadelphia, Pennsylvania	356	72
Eastern Michigan University— Ypsilanti, Michigan	461	86
Eastern Oregon College—La Grande	63	81
Eastern Washington College of Education—Cheney	157	79
Evansville College—Evansville, Indiana	160	99
Florence State College— Florence, Alabama	116	100
Fordham University—New York City	574	73
Fort Valley State College—Fort Valley, Georgia	98	83
Fresno State College—Fresno, California	425	68
Greenville College—Greenville, Illinois	101	100
Hamline University—St. Paul, Minnesota	146	98
Harvard University—Radcliff College—Cambridge, Massachusetts	491	75
Haverford College—Haverford, Pennsylvania	110	57
Hawaii, University of— Honolulu	624	96
Hebrew Teachers College— Brookline, Massachusetts	23	100

COLLEGES AND UNIVERSITIES—Continued

COLLEGE OR UNIVERSITY	NUMBER ELIGIBLE STUDENTS SAMPLED	PER CENT RESPONDING
Henderson State Teachers College—Arkadelphia, Arkansas	113	90
Holy Cross, College of the—Worchester, Massachusetts	353	96
Hood College—Frederick, Maryland	98	100
Hunter College—New York City	647	61
Huron College—Huron, South Dakota	38	97
Illinois Institute of Technology—Chicago	155	93
Illinois, University of—Urbana	480	76
Indiana University—Bloomington	447	77
Iowa State University of Science and Technology—Ames	437	94
Kansas, University of—Lawrence	619	94
Kentucky, University of—Lexington	427	87
Lake Erie College—Painesville, Ohio	80	86
Lake Forest College—Lake Forest, Illinois	104	94
Langston University—Langston, Oklahoma	63	86
Le Moyne College—Syracuse, New York	204	100
Long Beach State College—California	179	83
Long Island University—Brooklyn, New York	434	69
Los Angeles State College—California	309	80
Lycoming College—Williamsport, Pennsylvania	107	79
Manhattanville College of the		

COLLEGES AND UNIVERSITIES—Continued

COLLEGE OR UNIVERSITY	NUMBER ELIGIBLE STUDENTS SAMPLED	PER CENT RESPONDING
Sacred Heart—Purchase, New York	143	100
Marquette University—Milwaukee,Wisconsin	386	96
Maryland, University of—College Park	594	68
Mary Washington College—Predericksburg, Virginia	224	93
Massachusetts Institute of Technology, Cambridge, Massachusetts	206	88
McKendree College—Lebanon, Illinois	47	77
Memphis State University—Memphis, Tennessee	256	91
Merrimac College—North Andover, Massachusetts	148	92
Miami, University of—Coral Gables, Florida	419	94
Michigan State University—East Lansing, Michigan	453	94
Michigan, University of—Ann Arbor	588	93
Mills College of Education—New York City	29	100
Minnesota, University of—Minneapolis	409	88
Minnesota, University of—Duluth Campus	78	78
Mississippi Southern College—Hattiesburg	180	96
Mississippi State University—State College, Mississippi	481	86
Montclair State College—Upper Montclair, New Jersey	383	54
New York, City College of	519	95

COLLEGES AND UNIVERSITIES—Continued

COLLEGE OR UNIVERSITY	NUMBER ELIGIBLE STUDENTS SAMPLED	PER CENT RESPONDING
New York, State University of:		
College of Education at Buffalo	418	93
College of Education at Fredonia	146	92
New York University—New York City	385	74
North Carolina, University of— Chapel Hill	407	94
Northland College—Ashland, Wisconsin	53	81
Northwestern University— Evanston, Illinois	393	54
Notre Dame of Maryland, College of—Baltimore	87	100
Notre Dame University—Notre Dame, Indiana	790	85
Oberlin College—Oberlin, Ohio	288	99
Ohio State University— Columbus	504	82
Ohio Wesleyan University— Delaware	350	81
Oklahoma Baptist University— Shawnee	172	73
Oklahoma, University of— Norman	420	86
Oregon State University— Corvallis	614	88
Oregon, University of—Eugene	534	84
Pasadena College—Pasadena, California	104	99
Pembroke State College— Pembroke, North Carolina	63	100
Pennsylvania State University— University Park	624	92
Pennsylvania, University of— Philadelphia	417	70

COLLEGES AND UNIVERSITIES—Continued

COLLEGE OR UNIVERSITY	NUMBER ELIGIBLE STUDENTS SAMPLED	PER CENT RESPONDING
Pittsburgh, University of— Pennsylvania	233	71
Princeton University— Princeton, New Jersey	245	86
Rensselaer Polytechnic Institute —Troy, New York	238	81
Rochester Institute of Technology—Rochester, New York	238	75
St. Benedict, College of— St. Joseph, Minnesota	50	100
St. Bonaventure University— St. Bonaventure, New York	194	98
St. Scholastica, College of— Duluth, Minnesota	65	91
Sam Houston State Teachers College—Huntsville, Texas	221	94
San Jose State College—San Jose, California	422	93
South Dakota, State University of—Vermillion	247	92
Southeastern State College— Durant, Oklahoma	117	97
Southern California, University of—Los Angeles	297	73
Southern Illinois University— Carbondale	391	83
Southern Methodist University —Dallas, Texas	529	54
Southern University—Baton Rouge, Louisiana	180	92
Stanford University—Stanford, California	413	88
Susquehanna University— Selinsgrove, Pennsylvania	85	100
Sweet Briar College—Sweet Briar, Virginia	87	100

COLLEGES AND UNIVERSITIES—Continued

COLLEGE OR UNIVERSITY	NUMBER ELIGIBLE STUDENTS SAMPLED	PER CENT RESPONDING
Syracuse University—Syracuse, New York	294	31
Texas, University of—Austin	412	80
Tulane University—New Orleans, Louisiana	171	69
Ursinus College—Collegeville, Pennsylvania	178	100
Wagner College—Staten Island, New York	255	100
Washington University—St. Louis, Missouri	543	69
Washington, University of—Seattle	481	89
Wayne State University—Detroit, Michigan	470	89
Western Kentucky State College—Bowling Green	237	86
Western State College of Colorado—Gunnison	109	100
Williams College—Williamstown, Massachusetts	269	99
Wisconsin, University of—Madison	520	88
Wyoming, University of—Laramie	450	77
Xavier University—Cincinnati, Ohio	270	96

Summary of School Response Rates

Per cent Return	N	Per cent of Schools	Cumulative Per cent of Schools
96 – 100	37	27.2	27.2
91 – 95	24	17.6	44.8
86 – 90	21	15.4	60.2
81 – 85	16	11.8	72.0
76 – 80	12	8.8	80.0
71 – 75	11	8.1	88.9
66 – 70	6	4.4	93.3
61 – 65	3	2.2	95.5
60 or less	6	4.4	99.9
	136*	99.9%	

*Totals 136 rather than 135 because of separate field operations of University of Minnesota, Duluth, and University of Minnesota, Minneapolis.

Schools with Less Than 60 Per Cent Response

School	Per cent
Haverford College	57
Northwestern University	54
Montclair State College	54
Southern Methodist University	54
University of Delaware	45
Syracuse University	31

Appendix 5

The Sample Design

DELIMITATION OF THE UNIVERSE

The universe for the survey was defined to include:

All students completing the requirements for their baccalaureate degrees during the spring term (semester, quarter, or trimester) of 1961 and upon whom such degrees were conferred at the end of that term by an eligible institution of higher learning.

A number of the concepts employed in the foregoing are in need of explanation:

Baccalaureate recipients were here defined as including all those receiving a first-level earned degree of a type normally based on at least four years of degree-credit work beyond the high school level with the exception of those receiving a first-level degree from a professional school requiring at least two years of undergraduate work prior to admission. The decision to exclude the specified set of first professional degree recipients derived from the focus of the survey on graduate educational plans. It was felt that, in practice, the degrees granted by professional schools of the type here excluded were generally terminal. The largest groups excluded under this provision are recipients of M.D., D.D.S., L.L.B., and B.D. degrees. Groups like these did not appear to fit into the study design very well. The excluded first-level degree recipients amounted to about 8 or 9 per cent of the total first-level degree recipients during the 1960–1961 academic year. While the rule under which they were excluded was admittedly arbitrary, it most certainly served to delimit for the study a universe that was more nearly congruent with the study objectives than one in which all recipients of first professional degrees would be included.[1]

The restriction of the universe to spring convocation degree recipients was a result of two rather different considerations. First of all, many of the students who received their degrees in August of 1960 or during the winter of 1960–1961 might already have embarked, by the time of the survey in April, 1961, on some kind of postgraduate activity. Some were already serving in the military establishment, some were in graduate school, some were working at regular jobs, and others were full-time housewives. A questionnaire dealing with plans for the first year out of college did not seem appropriate for mid-year graduates; yet their special problems did not seem to be of sufficient interest to warrant the design and administration of a special retrospective questionnaire. Second, we thought it would be quite difficult to locate these individuals and to elicit their cooperation.

This combination of circumstances made it appear prudent to exclude mid-year (including summer session) graduates from the scope of the inquiry. The problem then became one of defining a mid-year graduate. A number of institutions hold only one convocation a year while others have only summer session and spring convocations. But there are students at such institutions who complete their degree requirements at the end of the autumn

[1]See W. C. Eells and H. A. Haswell, *Academic Degrees,* OE-54008, Bulletin 1960, No. 28, G.P.O., Washington, 1960, and W. E. Tolliver, *Earned Degrees Conferred 1959–1960,* OE-54013-60, Circular No. 687, G.P.O., Washington, 1962, for an elaboration of these problems. Beginning with the 1960–1961 earned degree statistics, the Office of Education will be making a distinction between baccalaureate and first professional degrees only slightly different from the one made in the present survey. Statistics for baccalaureate and first professional degrees involving four years of *academic* credit will for the first time be separated from the statistics for professional degrees requiring five or more years of *academic* credit. Thus, the only discrepancy between the NORC and the Office of Education classifications will be in the handling of participants in the relatively rare five-year programs leading to bachelor degrees in engineering and the five-year bachelor degree programs in fields like architecture and forestry. The relatively small number of recipients of degrees under such programs were considered as eligible for the NORC survey but will be combined with recipients of first professional degrees in fields such as law, medicine, dentistry, and divinity in the Office of Education Series.

semester and are then free to enter into their postgraduate activities in February. Even though they do not receive their degrees until June, their status is essentially identical to that of students who are graduated mid-year from multiple-convocation institutions. It was thus decided to include in the survey only students who were still in the process of completing their baccalaureate degree requirements during the spring term. This included all students who were formally registered as well as some students who were not registered but were working on undergraduate honor theses, engaged in required practice teaching, or fulfilling some other type of internship requirement. On the basis of a special survey of college registrars, we estimate that approximately 75 per cent of all those receiving baccalaureate degrees during the period from July, 1960, through June, 1961, did not complete the requirements for their degrees until the spring term of 1961 and were thus included within the scope of the present research. Our more detailed estimates appear in the following table:

Table A—5.1. Percentage Distribution of Students Receiving Baccalaureate Degrees from July, 1960, Through June, 1961, by Period During Which Degree Requirements Were Completed*

Summer, 1960**	12%	
"Regular students"		10
Summer session only		2
Autumn-Winter, 1960–61**	13	
Spring, 1961	75	
	100%	

*Based on March, 1961, survey of registrars at the 135 institutions in the NORC sample. The estimates are so weighted as to provide an unbiased estimate for 1960–1961 graduates of all U.S. institutions of higher learning.

**About one-sixth to one-fifth of those completing their requirements mid-year (i.e., about 4 or 5 per cent of all graduates) were in attendance at schools with a single convocation and therefore did not actually receive degrees until the end of the spring term.

The distributions of a number of characteristics among the students completing their requirements mid-year unquestionably differ appreciably from the comparable distributions among those finishing in the spring. We know, for instance, that the mid-year students were disproportionately in attendance at Southern and public institutions, while the spring students were disproportionately from Northeastern and private institutions. There are quite probably many concomitant differences between the two groups of students, arising out of the variation among institutions of regulations and customs regarding the phasing of the various academic junctures as well as more idiosyncratic factors which cause a student to deviate from the time pattern conventional to his own institution. Thus, in generalizing from the current sample, we suggest the rather conservative approach of limiting projections to those 1960–1961 graduates who completed their baccalaureate requirements during the spring term of 1961.[2]

An "eligible institution" for purposes of this study was one listed in Part 3 (Higher Education) of the 1957–1958 Office of Education *Education Directory* as being accredited by one of the six regional accrediting associations (including institutions with only provisional accreditation). Also included were those institutions granting baccalaureate degrees that were not accredited by a regional accrediting association but that were listed in the *Directory* as having an enrollment of five hundred or more students.[3]

The use of the foregoing sampling frame resulted in the ex-

[2]Some notion of the possible danger involved in projections from the present survey to the total 1960–1961 graduating class can be gained from the following rather extreme hypothetical example.

> Assume that 30 per cent of the spring students but only 10 per cent of the mid-year students planned to enroll for graduate courses during 1961–1962. Then, a projection to the entire 1960–1961 class from the survey of spring students would show 106,000 students planning to enroll while a survey of the entire class would have resulted in a projection of 88,000. Thus, the projection derived from the spring students alone would be about 20 per cent too high.

This example may be highly unrealistic. A difference of twenty percentage points in any variable of consequence may be substantially larger than one would ever find between the mid-year and spring students. Unfortunately, we are aware of no data that would enable us to estimate the magnitude of parametric differences between the two populations. Thus, caution in the scope of projections is advisable, particularly where relatively small proportions of the total population are characterized by the property in question.

[3]The enrollment figures were for the fall of 1956. They presumably included all students enrolled for courses beyond the high school level but excluded students enrolled only in correspondence courses.

clusion from the survey universe of certain types of students who might properly have been included.

1. Students who received at the end of the spring term of 1961 a baccalaureate degree from an institution that had not had a baccalaureate degree program in 1956–1957.

2. Students who received at the end of the spring term of 1961 a baccalaureate degree from an institution that was listed in the 1957– 1958 *Directory* either as not being accredited by one of the regional accrediting associations as having a total enrollment of less than five hundred students.

3. Students who received at the end of the spring term of 1961 a baccalaureate degree from an institution that had a baccalaureate degree program in 1956–1957 but did not meet the criteria for inclusion in the *Directory.*[4]

Since the statistics pertaining to earned degrees conferred during 1960–1961 will not be available until the summer of 1963, it is impossible at present to make a precise estimate of the number of legitimate baccalaureate degree recipients excluded from the survey universe. Our best guess is that the exclusions amount to somewhere between 5 and 10 per cent of the hypothetically complete universe. A more precise estimate will be made at such time as the requisite conferment data become available.

THE SAMPLE

A two-stage sampling scheme was followed in the selection of students. The first stage involved the selection of 135 of the 1,039 institutions defined as eligible for the purposes of this study.[5]

[4]See page one of the previously cited *Directory* for the criteria. Given the leniency of the standards for inclusion in the *Directory,* this source of loss was probably totally inconsequential. Excluded institutions would appear to have been primarily "diploma mills," the degrees from which were recognized as legitimate by practically no reputable institutions connected with higher education.

[5]A number of arbitrary decisions was involved in the formation of primary sampling units. It is difficult to determine the limits of a particular institution in situations where several rather distinct colleges are affiliated in such a way that they can be viewed as either components of a larger university or separate schools. Since the expected values of estimates to the universe of graduates are not affected by the manner in which primary samplings are formed, expediency in the field operation governed the process. A few examples follow:

1. Harvard and Radcliffe were treated as one.
2. Brown and Pembroke were treated as one.

Clustering by school was adopted in preference to a single stage sample wherein students would be sub-sampled from each of the 1,039 schools. One reason for this decision was the necessity of employing field representatives at each of the schools from which students were being taken in order to insure the accuracy of the subsampling process within the school and to maximize the rate of questionnaire completion. The costs of employing field representatives at all 1,039 schools would have been prohibitive. Our second reason for clustering was that we intended to analyze certain of the data on a school-by-school basis. For this purpose, it was deemed desirable to select a relatively large number of cases from each of the schools falling into the sample. Of course the fewer schools in the sample the larger the "take" from each school (given a fixed total sample size) but the larger the sampling variance of estimates pertaining to the entire universe. Balancing the two pressures toward a smaller number of primary sampling units against the pressure toward the minimization of the variance of over-all estimates, a first-stage sample of 135 was felt to be more or less optimal.

Each institution was first allocated into one of four strata on the basis of an index reflecting the postgraduate educational activities of its recent graduates. Values for each of eight variables were determined for each of the 1,039 schools. The value of a given variable for a given school was the number of individuals who had received a baccalaureate degree from that school and who:

1. were awarded a Ph.D. during 1957, 1958, or 1959 in mathematics, physics, astronomy, chemistry, or an earth science.

2. were awarded a Ph.D. during 1957, 1958, or 1959 in botany, phy-

---

3. Columbia and Barnard were treated as one.
4. Tulane and Newcomb were treated as one.
5. Brooklyn Center, Brooklyn College of Pharmacy, and C. W. Post College were treated as one.
6. The Minneapolis and Duluth Campuses of the University of Minnesota were treated separately.
7. The various branches of the University of California were treated separately.
8. The various branches of the College of the City of New York were each treated separately.

topathology, biochemistry, genetics, microbiology, physiology or a related field, zoology, in some other biological science, or in a medical science.

3. were awarded a Ph.D. during 1957, 1958, or 1959 in engineering.

4. were awarded a Ph.D. during 1957, 1958, or 1959 in sociology, anthropology, archeology, economics, geography, or psychology.

5. were awarded a Ph.D. during 1957, 1958, or 1959 in history, a foreign language, English, or philosophy.　　　·

6. were awarded a Ph.D. or Ed.D. in education during 1957, 1958, or 1959.

7. enrolled as a freshman in an American medical school during one of four selected academic years between 1949 and 1955.

8. enrolled as a freshman in an American dental school at some time between 1951 and 1957.

The schools were ranked with respect to each of these eight variables independently. The four strata were then defined as follows:

I. One of the 25 top schools in one or more of the eight variables.

II. Not in Stratum I, but with a rank between 26 and 100 in one or more of the eight variables.

III. Not in strata I or II, but had a value of two or more per year in one or more of the eight variables.

IV. Not in Strata I, II, or III.

Within each of the above strata, the institutions were allocated into two groups according to whether they were under public or private control. Within each of the resulting eight strata, the institutions were ordered according to a measure of size and institutions were generally sampled systematically with probability proportionate to the measure of size. In the case of several strata, it was necessary to sample with equal probability a substratum composed of the smallest schools, in order to avoid intricate weighting at the tabulation stage of the survey.

The measure of size was usually the number of 1958–1959 bachelor degrees awarded by that school as reported in the 1960 edition of the American Council on Education's *American Universities and Colleges*.[6] Frequently, separate figures appeared

[6]In the relatively rare instances when no data were available in the ACE volume on the number of degrees conferred by a given school, the data appearing in the Office of Education's *Earned Degrees* volume for 1957–1958 were employed.

for bachelor degrees and for first professional degrees. For institutions where *all* professional degrees granted were clearly of the type that were being treated as baccalaureate degrees in the present survey,[7] the measure of size was the sum of the bachelor and first professional figures. For each of the 111 institutions thought to grant some first professional degrees that were to be excluded from the survey, a letter was sent to the registrar requesting the total count of bachelor degrees and first professional degrees of the type to be included in the survey granted by his institution during the 1958–1959 academic year. The figure supplied by the registrar was then used as the measure of size.

The following table shows how the universe and the sample were distributed with respect to the eight strata (A–5.2).

The number of schools selected from a given stratum was arbitrary. The numbers were arrived at by trying to balance the needs of the anticipated school-by-school analysis against the need to avoid a complex system of weights.

A field representative was assigned to each of the 135 schools. His first task was to collect the previously cited data pertaining to the number of degrees of various types conferred at each convocation during the academic year. This information was necessary for the establishment of the over-all sampling rate for the survey. The next task of the field representative was to assemble a list of all seniors who were completing their baccalaureate requirements during the spring term and who, it was anticipated, were going to be graduated at the end of that term. Officials at every one of the 135 selected institutions cooperated with the field representative in assembling the list of eligible seniors and granted general approval for the survey.

Prospective baccalaureate degree recipients from institutions in Strata I and II were sampled at a rate of .288 while those from institutions in Strata III and IV were sampled at a rate of .096. The differential sampling rates were adopted because among the chief objectives of the survey was the estimation of parameters pertaining to graduating seniors who were planning to go on for

---

[7]In other words, the institution had no medical, dental, law, divinity, or other professional school that granted first professional degrees of the type being excluded from the present survey.

Table A — 5.2. Distribution of The Universe and The Sample With Respect to The Eight Strata

Index of Post Graduate Activities	Public Control				Private Control			
	Universe		Sample	Universe		Sample
	Number of Schools	Total Measure of Size	Number of Schools	Number of Schools	Total Measure of Size	Number of Schools
I	35	69,414	22	31	32,613	22
II	66	56,334	20	92	38,085	20
III	113	44,684	10	204	40,614	11
IV	138	26,571	10	360	36,592	20
Total	352	197,003	62	687	147,904	73

graduate study in particular academic fields. Even though the stratification was based on the absolute numbers of eventual Ph.D.'s produced by a school rather than its per capita productivity, there was reason to believe that the rate of graduate study would be appreciably higher among Strata I and II baccalaureates than among those from Strata III and IV. While the employment of differential sampling rates undoubtedly increased the sampling variance of most estimates pertaining to the total cohort of graduating seniors, it was felt that this disadvantage would be more than compensated by the gains in the precision of estimates pertaining to certain relatively rare graduate fields.

For any given school, the subsampling rate for students was the ratio of the over-all sampling rate for the school's stratum to the school's probability of being selected. This procedure automatically compensated for any disproportionality between the measure of size that had been assigned to the school at the primary stage of selection and the actual number of students found to be eligible for inclusion in the survey. The assigned measures of size were, of course, quite imperfectly related to the actual sizes because of differences among the schools in the magnitude of the changes which had taken place from 1958–1959 to 1960–1961 in the sizes of their graduating classes. In addition, schools varied markedly in the proportion of graduates completing the requirements for the baccalaureate degree during a term other than the spring one. Nevertheless, the disproportionality resulting from these factors introduced no appreciable bias in the estimates derived from the sample. The primary consequence was a considerable variation among schools in the number of students selected for the sample and quite probably a slight increase in the sampling variance of the survey statistics, even though they are all of the ratio type.

At sixty of the schools, *all* eligible seniors were to be taken into the sample because the probability of the school was either less than or equal to the student sampling rate which had been set for the school's stratum. At the remaining seventy-five schools, a sample of eligible seniors was drawn at a rate computed in the manner indicated in the preceding paragraph. The actual sampling procedures employed varied from school to school. A copy of the field representatives' sampling instructions appears at the end of this appendix.

As was anticipated, lists of eligible seniors assembled during March and April turned out to contain a number of false positives, individuals who failed to meet at least one of our criteria of eligibility. The most frequent types of false positives were cases where the student himself did not (in April, May, or June) think that he would be graduated at the end of the current term.[8] Of the 36,013 completed questionnaires returned prior to the survey deadline, 2,231 were from individuals who appeared to be ineligible for the survey. These questionnaires were omitted from all tabulations.

In making estimates from the sample, two types of weighting are necessary. The returns from schools whose probabilities were less than the sampling rates for their strata had to be so weighted as to bring the probability of a student in such a school up to the stratum level. This occurred most frequently in III and IV strata schools. Many of the schools in those strata had been sampled at a rate of .0555 and it was thus necessary to weight their returns by a factor of 1.723 to bring the probability for their students up to the over-all stratum sampling rate (.096).

In addition to the above initial weighting, the returns from all III and IV schools were weighted by a factor of three to compensate for the differential sampling rates between strata. Thus, the range of weights among schools was from 1 to 5.169 and averaged 1.677.

Since the eligibility status of many of the students who were sent questionnaires but did not return them is not known, it is impossible to make a precise estimate of the survey completion rate. Assuming that the proportion of non-respondents with unknown eligibility status who were in fact ineligible was the same as the proportion of ineligibles among those who did respond, the weighted completion rate for the survey was 85 per cent. Since the non-respondents from the 1961 survey are being followed up

[8] See Question 43 of the questionnaire. A later questionnaire (spring, 1962) was pre-tested on a sample of the 1961 respondents who had not expected to be graduated in the spring of 1961. While the expectations of the vast majority had in fact been correct, some of the respondents were graduated in the spring of 1961, in spite of their pessimism in response to Question 43.

with fair success in NORC's periodic surveys of the spring, 1961, cohort, it may soon be possible to form at least a fair impression of the direction and magnitude of the non-response bias in the original survey.

Study # 431

College or University ———————————————— April, 1961

SAMPLING INSTRUCTIONS

A. *Preparing the list of seniors.*

In order to select the sample of students to whom you will distribute questionnaires, you will need a list or a file containing the name of *every eligible senior* at your school. An eligible senior is a student who is registered as an undergraduate during the spring term of 1961 and who is expected to receive his or her baccalaureate degree (A.B., B.A., B.S., B.Ed., B.Arch., B.Eng., etc.) at the end of the current term. This means that you should exclude, insofar as possible, students who had completed *all* work for their degrees prior to the current term but who will not have been formally graduated until the June convocation. The word "registered" in the first sentence of this paragraph is to be interpreted broadly as meaning "still fulfilling requirements for a baccalaureate degree." In other words, you should classify a student as "registered" even if he is no longer taking courses but is fulfilling an honors thesis or some sort of outside employment or internship requirement.

Students under five-year baccalaureate programs in fields such as engineering and architecture who are going to receive their degrees at the end of this term are to be classified as eligible seniors. Students being graduated from a professional school which requires two or more years of undergraduate work prior to admission are here viewed as receiving graduate degrees rather than baccalaureate degrees and are therefore to be *excluded* from the study. This means that students receiving Bachelor of Law degrees are invariably to be excluded while students receiving first professional degrees in fields such as divinity and social work are to be excluded if the professional school they are attending requires two or more years of undergraduate work prior to admission.

Should it turn out to be difficult to decide whether or not a certain category of students is to be included in the sample, write Mrs. Boorstin immediately describing your problem so that she can send you a ruling on the case.

Should it be difficult to distinguish students who are still registered from those who had completed all their work during a prior term, do the best you can, even if this involves distributing questionnaires to some ineligible graduating students. Err on the side of distributing too many questionnaires, if error cannot be avoided. Always write us fully describing problems of this type but, if it is unlikely that we can be of any help in solving the problem, proceed without awaiting our reply. We do wish to have complete records of such difficulties, though.

We are aware that a definitive graduation list may not yet be available at your school, so all we ask is that you assemble as complete a list as is currently possible. If it should turn out that some of the anticipated graduates fail to fulfill their degree requirements during the present term, no great damage will be done. Again, you should err on the side of distributing questionnaires to some students who may not actually be graduated this June rather than omitting any students who will be graduated. Nevertheless, you should use as accurate a list as can now be obtained and not distribute questionnaires to students who cannot possibly complete their requirements during the current term.

Your first step in selecting the sample is to assemble or gain access to a complete register of eligible seniors. Since different schools keep their records in different ways, we cannot prescribe precisely what sort of register you should use or how you should distinguish an eligible senior from an ineligible one. You might find that your school will make available to you a typed list, a set of IBM cards, a set of file cards, or some other type of record which enables you to distinguish the eligible from the ineligible seniors. Any of these, or two of them used in conjunction, may turn out to be optimum for your school. You will have to make your choice on the basis of the particular situation you find.

The order in which names appear in the register is not of great consequence. The entire graduating class may be listed in alphabetical order, in alphabetical order by type of degree to be conferred, in alphabetical order within major field, etc. If you have a choice of orderings, you should use the one involving the highest degree of substantive classification. For instance, if you have the choice between a list where the names are in alphabetical order within a B.A.-B.S. dichotomy and a list where the names are in order of grade point average, you should use the grade point list, all other factors being equal. But, if the advantage of one list over another is not clearcut, simply use the more convenient one. In general, in selecting the register from which you will draw your sample, you should give considerable weight to the simplification of your over-all task. Consider such factors as the ease of obtaining or assembling the register, the ease of drawing names from the register, and the ease of obtaining addresses once the names have been selected. If sampling from a set of IBM cards or addressograph plates will enable you to have mailing labels produced by mechanical means, it would be well to sample from such a registry in preference to a substantively more detailed list, the use of which would complicate the distribution of the questionnaires to the sample respondents.

The precise method of sampling to be used will depend on the type of register or list you decide to use. Instructions pertaining to several different types of registers appear below. But, no matter what sampling method you employ, you will need a set of "sampling numbers." These numbers appear on the IBM tabulation sheets which you should find among the materials we have sent you. There are two columns of figures listed. The left-hand column is simply a count of the sampling numbers and will enable you to check whether you have selected the proper number of names. The right-hand column contains your sampling numbers, which designate the particular students to be included in your sample.

B. *Sampling from a list.*

We shall assume you have assembled a list containing the names of all eligible seniors and no ineligible ones. If the numbers in the right-hand column of your IBM listing were:

2

5

8

12

15

19

22

etc.,

you would simply count down your list of seniors and select for the sample the second name on the list, the fifth name, the eighth name, the twelfth name, and so on. Obviously, the principle by which the names are ordered on the list should have been established in complete independence of the particular set of sampling numbers sent to you so that the sample is truly random. In other words, *chance alone* must determine who shall be asked to fill out a questionnaire—subjective considerations should in no way enter into the selection of students. If the names are listed in an arbitrary order (alphabetically within field of concentration, by grade point average, by some serial number, or what have you), the use of the sampling numbers in the manner described above will insure the selection of a random sample.

If the list contains names of particular students known to be ineligible for this study, make sure you omit counting them as you proceed down the list. It might be wise to go through the entire list crossing out the names of known ineligibles before you begin drawing the sample.

C. *Sampling from a file of cards.*

The sampling procedure to be employed with a card file is essentially the same as the one to be employed with a list. If your sampling numbers were:

4
7
11
15
19
22
etc.,

you would count through the cards of *eligible seniors* and select the name on the fourth such card, the seventh, the eleventh, etc. Since a card file is quite likely to contain cards for many students who are not eligible for this study, you must be particularly careful not to count these ineligible cards as you draw your sample. Also, should some students have two or more cards in the file, make sure you count *only one* card for each eligible senior.

IMPORTANT

Most field representatives will find that they have been sent about fifty or a hundred more sampling numbers than they will need. For instance, there may be only nine hundred eligible seniors at your school; we may be asking you to select only about one-third of these, or three hundred, but we have sent you a list containing four hundred sampling numbers. At the end of your list, there would remain unused one hundred sampling numbers ranging from 900 to 1,200. You should simply ignore all the sampling numbers greater in value than the number of eligible seniors at your school.

In a few cases, we may have grossly underestimated the size of your graduating class and have thereby sent you fewer sampling numbers than you will need. For instance, there may be 1,500 eligible seniors but the highest sampling number on your list is 1,417. In such a case, phone Mrs. Boorstin and tell her how many eligible seniors there are. She will then see that you receive additional sampling numbers or revised instructions.

After your sample has been selected, enter the name and address of each sample student to the right of his or her sampling number on the IBM sheet. There are two sheets of carbon paper and two extra copies of the sampling number list already attached. Thus, you can produce three copies of your sample list at one time.

If you have pulled a set of IBM cards for your sample members, you can either have the list of sample names and addresses machine-printed on the 3-ply IBM paper we sent or else, if you prefer, you can have it printed on other 3-ply paper.

Please send us one of the copies of the sample as soon as it has been prepared. Retain the other two copies for your own record-keeping. When you return the copy of your sample list, please send us a detailed description of the sampling procedure you employed.

D. *Sampling from a set of IBM cards.*

This section is moderately technical. Don't bother to read it unless you are seriously considering using IBM equipment. If you are using IBM equipment, it is not necessary for you to understand the *details* of mechanical selection, as long as the IBM supervisor fully understands what is to be done.

If it is possible to pull out mechanically, from your school's general file of IBM cards, the cards for all eligible seniors, there are several alternative sampling procedures available to you. Should it be difficult for you to arrange for IBM work and should a machine for addressing mailing labels from IBM cards not be available, then the simplest procedure would be to have the names and addresses of all eligible seniors listed on IBM paper. (If another list of equal accuracy were already available, you could use that and just ignore the IBM file.) The names could be listed in alphabetical order within academic majors, by grade point average, or in any other convenient order. Once you have the IBM list, you would select the sample manually as described above in the section on sampling from a list.

A second alternative would be to treat the set of IBM cards as a set of file cards and manually pull out the cards falling into the sample, as described in the section on sampling from a file. From the deck of cards you have selected for the sample, you could have a list of sample members printed and you might also be able to have address labels made up mechanically.

If you have ready access to IBM work and the graduating class is relatively large, it may be worthwhile to select the sample mechanically. There are innumerable ways in which this might be done but we shall describe the simplest, if not the most efficient, one.

For this procedure, you would need a set of IBM cards containing four blank columns (only three blank columns if there are fewer than one thousand eligible seniors at your school). If there are too few blank columns in your school's regular IBM card, the original set of cards can be reproduced, stripping columns which are irrelevant to the current task.

After you have assembled a set of cards with the proper number of blank columns, the cards should be arranged in order on the basis of some principle. (See the discussion of "order" in Section A.) This ordering of cards is done on an IBM sorter. Then, a consecutive number, running from 0001 (or 001) to the total number of eligible seniors at your school, should be punched in each card. In other words, the first card would be punched 0001, the second would be punched 0002, the third would be punched 0003, etc. This punching can be done with a reproducing punch machine from a deck of consecutive number cards, with a summary punch attachment to a tabulator wired to take progressive totals on a card count or with a calculating punch.

The next step is to have a set of cards containing the sampling numbers key-punched. Each sampling number (the *righthand* list on the IBM sheet we sent you) should be punched on a separate card. At this point, you would have two sets of cards: a set containing one card for each eligible senior and a set containing one card for each sampling number assigned to your school. These two sets should then be put into a collator wired to pull the card for each eligible senior whose consecutive number (the "order" number you had punched) corresponds to a sampling number. This is a four-pocket match. You will then have a set containing one card for each student falling into the sample. You can now use this set of sample cards for printing lists, printing mailing labels, or similar tasks.

If you wish to use an alternate mechanical procedure for selecting the sample, write Mrs. Boorstin describing the procedure you wish to employ and she will let you know by return mail whether your suggested procedure is permissible.

E. *Special sample instructions for your school (if any):* _____

_____

_____

_____

Appendix 6

The Questionnaire

NATIONAL OPINION RESEARCH CENTER

University of Chicago
5720 Woodlawn Avenue, Chicago 37, Illinois

Dear Student: April, 1961

National Opinion Research Center, a non-profit research organization affiliated with the University of Chicago, has been asked by three Federal agencies, the U.S. Office of Education, The National Science Foundation, and the National Institutes of Health, to survey the career plans of seniors in American colleges and universities.

You are one of 40,000 students in 135 schools who have been chosen by scientific probability sampling methods to participate in this study.

The research is designed to yield important information on the relationships between college experiences and career plans.

The questionnaire requires 30 minutes or so to fill out. Please answer the questions as frankly and accurately as you can. Your answers will be absolutely confidential, and no individual student's answers will be revealed in the reports, which will be based on statistical tabulations.

Almost all of the questions can be answered by drawing a circle around one or more numbers or letters in the right hand margins of the questionnaire. Thus:

> I am now—   (Circle one.)
> A student in high school   1
> A student in college   ②
> A student in graduate or
>   professional school   x

295

NOTE: After each question there are instructions in parentheses. Please follow these instructions closely as they are very important for data processing.

A. If it says "(Circle one.)," draw a circle around only the one number or letter which *best describes* your answer, even though one or more other alternatives might be relevant.

B. If it says "(Circle one in each column.)" or "(Circle one in each row.)," please look to see that you have circled one and only one number or letter in each of the appropriate rows or columns.

C. If it says "(Circle as many as apply.)," circle as many or as few numbers or letters in the columns or rows as you think are relevant.

If you are interested in the results of this study, please write a letter or card requesting a copy of the results to National Opinion Research Center, 5720 South Woodlawn, Chicago 37, Illinois, *after October, 1961*.

Thank you very much for your help.

Sincerely,

James A. Davis
Study Director

Survey 431

I. PLANS FOR THIS COMING FALL

1. What will you be doing this Fall?

Circle the number which describes what you will be doing this Fall. If you expect to be doing two things *simultaneously*, circle both. If you are considering two *alternative* plans, circle only the more probable.

Working full time at a type of job which I expect to be my long run
   career field 2   (9)
Non-career military service 3   1
Working full time at a civilian job which will probably *not* be my
   long run career field 4
Housewife 5
Graduate study in an arts and science field (physical science, biolog-
   ical science, social science, humanities) 6
Graduate study in a professional field (law, medicine, engineering,
   education, agriculture, social work, etc.) 7
Other (Circle and specify: _____) 8

2. How definite are the plans you circled in question 1? (Circle one.)

Quite definite x   (10)
Fairly definite, but subject to change 0   Y
Quite indefinite 1

3. If you are considering a set of alternative plans, different from the ones you circled in question 1, indicate them by circling the appropriate numbers below, using the categories from question 1.

If you have no alternative plans in mind, circle the number nine below. (11)
     2   3   4   5   6   7   8   9   1

4. At the time you entered college, what were your plans for study beyond the bachelor's degree? (Circle one.)

I planned to go into a line of work which requires graduate or pro-
fessional training x   (12)
I planned to go on for graduate or professional training, but I didn't   Y
have a specific field in mind 0
I planned to stop at the bachelor's degree 1
I didn't have any definite plans 2

5. Have you applied for admission to any graduate or professional school for the coming year? (Circle one.)

                                                      (13)
*No, and I do *not* expect to go to school next year 4   9
**No, but I do expect to go to school next year 5   IF 4,
***Yes, I applied to one school 6   SKIP
***Yes, I applied to 2 or 3 schools 7   TO
***Yes, I applied to 4 or more schools 8   COL.

                                                      23

    *IF "NO, AND DO NOT EXPECT TO GO TO SCHOOL NEXT YEAR": SKIP TO QUESTION 7.
    **IF "NO, BUT I DO EXPECT TO GO TO SCHOOL NEXT YEAR": SKIP TO QUESTION 6.
    ***IF "YES": PLEASE ANSWER a, b, AND c.

a. How many schools accepted you? (Circle one.)

                               None 0   (14)
                               One 1   4
                               More than one 2

b. How many schools rejected your application? (Circle one.)

                               None 5   (15)
                               One 6   9
                               More than one 7

c. Have you any applications pending? (Circle one.)

> Yes 0   (16)
>
> No 1   Y

---

6. Did you apply (or were you nominated) for financial support (scholarship, fellowship, assistantship, etc.) for this Fall? (Circle one.)

> *No . . . . •7   (17)
>
> **Yes 8   9

*IF "NO": Did you not apply because— (Circle any which apply.)

I had no intention of going to school at the time applications were
  due 0   (18)
I wouldn't need any support of this type 1   Y
The amount I could get would have been too little 2
The duties attached would have been unsatisfactory 3
I didn't think I could get any 4
It didn't occur to me to apply 5
Other (Circle and specify: _____) 6

**IF "YES": PLEASE ANSWER a, b, c, AND d.

a. To where did you apply or was your nomination sent? (Circle one or more.)

The school I will (probably) attend 0   (19)
Other school or schools 1   Y
Other source (government, private foundation, etc.) 2

---

b. Which ones *offered* you aid? (Circle one or more.)

The school I will (probably) attend 4   (20)
Other school or schools 5   9
Other source (government, private foundation, etc.) 6
No offers 7

---

c. Which of the following do you expect to *receive* next year: (Circle one or more.)

Scholarship for part tuition 1   (21)
Scholarship for full tuition 2   9
Fellowship for tuition plus an amount under $1,000 3
Fellowship for tuition plus $1,000 or more 4
Teaching assistantship 5
Research assistantship 6
No financial support of this type 7
Don't know yet 8

---

d. From which of the following source or sources do you expect to receive financial aid (scholarship, fellowship, assistantship, etc.)? (Circle one or more.)

No financial aid of this type expected 1   (22)
School I will attend 2   0
Private foundation, philanthropic organization, etc. 3
U.S. Federal government:
   National Defense Act 4
   National Science Foundation 5
   Public Health Service—National Institutes of Health 6
   Other 7
State or local government (U.S.) 8
Other (Circle and specify: _____) 9

ARE YOU SURE OR FAIRLY SURE THAT YOU WILL BE ATTENDING GRADUATE OR
PROFESSIONAL SCHOOL NEXT YEAR? (ACADEMIC YEAR 1961–1962)?   IF YES,

IF "YES": PUT A CHECK IN THIS BOX AND SKIP TO QUESTION 13 ☐   SKIP TO
   COLUMN
IF "NO": ANSWER QUESTION 7 THROUGH 12.   32

---

7. If there were no obstacles in terms of finances, grade records, getting admitted, etc., would you *like* to go on for graduate or professional study in the future? (Circle one.)

               Yes 2   (23)
               Maybe 3   5
               No 4

---

8. Do you expect to go on for graduate or professional school sometime in the future? (Circle one.)

               No 5   (24)
               Probably not 6   9
               *Probably yes 7
               *Yes 8

*IF "PROBABLY YES" OR "YES": PLEASE ANSWER a AND b.

a. Do you expect that your future employer will send you or pay for your future studies? (Do not count savings from your pay or anticipated veteran's benefits.) (Circle one.)

               Yes 0   (25)
               No 1   Y

b. When will you start your graduate or professional studies? Make your single best prediction. (Circle one.)

               Academic Year
                  '62–'63 0   (26)
                  '63–'64 1   Y
                  '64–'65 2
                  '65–'66 or after 3
             No specific date in mind . . 4

---

9. Do you have a definite job (including military service) lined up after graduation? (Circle one.)

Yes	6	(27)
No, but I intend to be working	7	9
No, I do not intend to be working	8	

10. Since you've been in college, have you at any time considered going on for graduate study or considered an occupation which would require professional training beyond a bachelor's degree? (Circle one.)

I never thought of it	2	(28)
I thought about it, but I never considered it seriously	3	1
I considered it seriously, but decided against it	4	
I do plan to go on, but not next year	5	

11. To what extent did immediate financial obstacles (not doubts about the long run economic value of further study) affect your decision regarding graduate or professional school *next year*? (Circle one.)

Financial obstacles had nothing to do with it	6	(29)
*Financial obstacles played some part in my decision	7	9
*Financial obstacles are the major reason I am not going on for further study next year	8	

* Listed below are some selected types of financial assistance. Circle *any* type which in itself (not in combination with the others) would have made it possible for you to go on to graduate or professional school next year.

Tuition Scholarship	0	(30)
Fellowship for tuition plus $1,000 cash	1	9
Loan for tuition which would not have to be paid back until I was out of school	2	
Loan for tuition plus living expenses which would not have to be paid back until I was out of school	3	
10–20 hour a week job as a teaching or research assistant	4	
Financial help from my parents	5	
Payment of all my current debts for undergraduate education . . .	6	
None of these	7	

12. Which of the following best explains why you do not anticipate going to graduate or professional school next year? (Circle any which apply.)

No desire to do so	y	(31)
Can get a desirable job without further schooling	0	SP
Financial obstacles	1	
Low grades in college	2	
Family responsibilities	3	
I would rather get married	4	
I want to get practical experience first	5	
I don't think I have the ability	6	
I lack the necessary undergraduate course prerequisites	7	
I'm tired of being a student	8	

Military service 9
I will be in a company training program which provides the equivalent X

SKIP TO QUESTION 18, "FIELDS AND CAREERS"   SKIP TO
COLUMN
38

IF YOU ARE SURE OR FAIRLY SURE THAT YOU WILL BE ATTENDING GRADUATE
OR PROFESSIONAL SCHOOL NEXT YEAR, ANSWER QUESTIONS 13 – 17.

13. Have you decided upon the specific school you will attend? (Circle one.)

Yes 7   (32)
No 8   9

---

14. Write below the name of the school that you will most probably attend next
Fall.

_____ _____ _____
(Name of School)   (City)   (State or Country)

a. Is the above school the one you are now attending? (Circle one.)

Yes , ... 4   (33)
No 5   6

---

15. If you were absolutely free to choose (ignoring finances, admissions, etc.)
would you prefer to – (Circle one.)

Go to the same school I expect to attend next year 0   (34)
*Attend a different school 1   Y

*IF "ATTEND A DIFFERENT SCHOOL": Did any of the following prevent you
from attending the school you would really prefer? (Circle any which apply.)

Wasn't offered any financial support (scholarship, fellowship, assist-
antship). 2   (35)
Was offered support, but it was too little 3   9
Was refused admission or didn't apply because I thought I would be
refused 4
Financial obstacles other than scholarship, assistantship, etc. . . . 5
Limited to schools in a particular community 6
Other (Circle and specify: _____) 7

---

16. If you were absolutely free to choose (ignoring finances, admissions, etc.)
would you prefer to – (Circle one.)

Study in the same field I will be in 0   (36)
*Study in a different field 1   Y

*IF "STUDY IN A DIFFERENT FIELD": Did any of the following prevent you from studying in the field which you really prefer? (Circle any which apply.)

Wasn't offered any financial support (scholarship, fellowship, assistantship) 2 (37)
Was offered support, but it was too little 3 9
Was refused admission or didn't apply because I thought I would be refused 4
Financial obstacles other than scholarship, assistantship, etc. 5
Limited to schools in a particular community 6
Other (Circle and specify: _____) 7

---

17. In terms of your finances during the next academic year when you are in graduate or professional school, from which of the following sources do you expect to receive $200 or more? (Circle any which apply.)

Full time job 1 (38)
Part time job other than teaching or research assistantship 2 9
Withdrawals from savings 3
National Defense Education Act Loan 4
Other Loan 5
Parents or relatives 6
Income from spouse's employment 7
Other (Circle and specify: _____) 8

IMPORTANT

The following list of fields is to be used in answering Questions 18 through 24. Read the instructions for these questions found on page 8 before using the list.

Business and Administration
92 Accounting
90 Advertising, Public Relations
9X Military Service, Military Science
97 Secretarial Science (or employed as a secretary)
72 Industrial or Personnel Psychology
91 All other business and commercial fields (Business Administration, Marketing, Insurance, Finance, Industrial Relations, etc.)
93 Public Administration (or employed as government administrator if not covered by other fields)

Engineering
10 Aeronautical
11 Civil (including Agricultural, Architectural, Civil, Sanitary)

12 Chemical (including Ceramic)
13 Electrical
14 Engineering Science, Engineering Physics, Engineering Mechanics
15 Industrial
16 Mechanical (including Naval Architecture and Marine, Welding, Textile)
17 Metallurgical
18 Mining (including Mining, Geological, Geophysical, Petroleum)
1X Engineering, General and other specialties

Physical Science (NOTE: Secondary School Science Teaching is classified under Education)
01 Astronomy, Astrophysics
02 Chemistry (excluding Biochemistry which is 32)

03 Physics (excluding Biophysics which is 34)
04 Geography
05 Geology, Geophysics
06 Oceanography
07 Metallurgy
08 Meteorology (Atmospheric sciences)
0X Physical Science, General and other specialties
09 *Mathematics and Statistics* (NOTE: Secondary School Mathematics Teaching is classified under Education)

Education (NOTE: Junior College, and University Teaching should be coded by Field of Specialization, not as Education)
50 *Elementary* (including Kindergarten and Nursery School)
Secondary — Academic Subject Fields
51 English
52 Modern Foreign Languages
53 Latin, Greek
54 History, Social Studies
55 Natural Science (General, Physics, Chemistry, Biology, etc.)
56 Mathematics
Specialized Teaching Fields
57 Physical Education, Health, Recreation
58 Music Education
59 Art Education
60 Education of Exceptional Children (Including Speech Correction)
61 Agricultural Education
62 Home Economics Education
63 Business Education
64 Trade and Industrial Education (Vocational)
65 Industrial Arts Education (Non-Vocational)
66 Counseling and Guidance
67 Educational Psychology
68 Administration and Supervision
6X Education, General and other specialties

Health Professions
20 Dentistry or Pre-Dentistry

21 Medicine or Pre-Medicine
22 Nursing
23 Optometry
24 Pharmacy
25 Physical Therapy
26 Occupational Therapy
27 Veterinary Medicine or Pre-Veterinary
28 Medical Technology or Dental Hygiene
2X Other Health Fields

Biological Sciences
30 Anatomy
31 Biology
32 Biochemistry
33 Botany and Related Plant Sciences (Plant Pathology, Plant Physiology, etc.)
34 Biophysics
35 Entomology
36 Genetics
37 Microbiology (including Bacteriology, Mycology, Parasitology, Virology, etc.)
38 Pathology
39 Pharmacology
40 Physiology
41 Zoology
3X Other Biological Science Fields

Agricultural and Related Fields
45 Agricultural Sciences (including Animal Husbandry, Agronomy, Farm Management, Horticulture, Soil Science, Soil Conservation, etc.)
46 Forestry, Fish and Wild Life Management
27 Veterinary Medicine
47 Farming (Code as occupation only, not as field of study)

Psychology (NOTE: Code Psychiatry as Medicine 21)
70 Clinical Psychology
66 Counseling and Guidance
67 Educational Psychology
71 Social Psychology
72 Industrial and Personnel Psychology

73 Experimental and General Psychology
74 Other Psychological Fields

Social Sciences
75 Anthropology, Archeology
76 Economics
04 Geography
83 History
77 Area and Regional Studies
78 Political Science, Government, International Relations
93 Public Administration
79 Sociology
96 Social Work, Group Work
7X Social Science, General and Other

Humanities
80 Fine and Applied Arts (Art, Music, Speech, Drama, etc.)
81 English, Creative Writing
82 Classical Languages and Literatures
83 History
84 Modern Foreign Languages and Literatures
85 Philosophy
8X Humanities, General and Other Fields

Other Fields and Occupations
86 Architecture, City Planning
94 Foreign Service (Code as occupation only, not field of study)
98 Home Economics (Code either as a field of study or as an occupation if you mean working as a home economist for pay)
99 Housewife (Code as occupation only, not as field of study)
87 Journalism, Radio-Television, Communications
95 Law, Pre-Law
88 Library Science, Archival Science
96 Social Work, Group Work
89 Theology, Religion (Employment as a Clergyman or religious worker)

X0 *Field of Study or Job Which has no Near Equivalent in This List* (If you use this code, please describe your field in a word or two under the questions where it applies.)

X1 *Do not expect to be either employed full time or to be a Housewife* (Code only for questions about careers, not for field of study.)

II. FIELDS AND CAREERS

On pages 6 and 7 of this questionnaire is a list of fields of study and employment. Each one can be used to describe a field of study or a type of job. Thus, for example, in questions about fields of study, "Psychology" means college courses in psychology; in questions about careers, "Psychology" means the occupation of psychologist.

IMPORTANT NOTE:
When you have chosen the field or occupation from the list which is your answer to one of the questions below, please write the two numbers or letters of that field in the double box at the end of that question. For example, if "Clinical Psychology" is now your major field, write its code number (70) in the boxes at the end of question 18 thus:

$$\boxed{7}\boxed{0}$$

18. Present major field?

If you have a joint major, give the one with the most course credits.   ☐☐ (39–40)
x   x

19. Previous major field?

If you have not shifted majors, write "yy" in the boxes.
If you have several previous majors, give the *first* one in which officially registered.   ☐☐ (41–42)
x   x

20. Future graduate or professional major?

If you do not plan to ever go to graduate or professional school, write "yy" in the boxes.
If you plan study in several fields, give the *main* one.   ☐☐ (43–44)
x   x

21. Anticipated career field?

Please give what you expect to be your long-run career and ignore any school, stop-gap job, or temporary military service which might precede it.

If you are a woman, use "Housewife (99)" only if you do not expect to work full time until your children are grown.

In addition to writing the code in the boxes, please describe your anticipated career in a few words here: _____   ☐☐ (45–46)
x   x

22. Possible alternative career field?

If none, write "yy" in the boxes.
If your alternative has the same code number as the one to question 21, write "yy" in the boxes.
If more than one alternative, give the most likely only.   ☐☐ (47–48)
x   x

23. Career preference when you started college?

Give your single strongest preference even if it was vague or or if there were several alternatives.

If absolutely no preference, write "yy" in the boxes.   ☐☐ (49–50)
x   x

24. Any alternative career field seriously considered during college which is not mentioned in questions 21, 22, or 23?

If none, write "yy" in the boxes.   ☐☐ (51–52)
x   x

NOTE: THE NEXT THREE QUESTIONS REFER TO YOUR ANSWER TO QUESTION 21 (ANTICIPATED CAREER FIELD). IF YOU CODED "99" OR "x1" AS YOUR ANSWER TO QUESTION 21, PLEASE SKIP TO QUESTION 28. OTHERWISE, ANSWER ALL THREE QUESTIONS.

25. Which of the following will be your most likely employer when you begin full time work in your anticipated career field? (If you have a definite expectation, circle one; if not, circle the most likely possibilities.)

Private company with 100 or more employees . . . . Y   (53)
Private company with fewer than 100 employees or professional   SP
    partnership X
Family business 0
Self-employed 1
Research organization or institute 2
College or University or Junior College 3
Elementary or Secondary School or School System 4
Other educational institutions (e.g. Technical Vocational School) . . 5
Federal Government (U.S.) 6
State or Local Government 7
Hospital, Church, Clinic, Welfare Organization, etc. 8
Other (Circle and specify: _____) 9

26. How do you feel about the occupation which you checked as your anticipated career field? (Circle one.)

I strongly prefer it to any other 0   (54)
I could be tempted by one or more alternatives 1   Y
I would prefer one or more alternatives 2

27. The following activities cut across a number of specific jobs. Which ones do you anticipate will be an important part of your long run career work? (Circle any which apply.)

Teaching 3   (55)
Research 4   9
Administration 5
Service to patients or clients 6
None of these 7

28. Regardless of your career plans now, when you first enrolled as a freshman in college did you have – (Circle one.)

One particular kind of work in mind 5   (56)
Two or more alternative kinds of work in mind 6   9
No specific career plans at that time 7
Planned to be a housewife 8

29. Which of these characteristics would be very important to you in picking a job or career? (Circle as many as apply.)

Making a lot of money . . . . Y   (57)
Opportunities to be original and creative X   SP

Opportunities to be helpful to others or useful to society 0
Avoiding a high pressure job which takes too much out of you . . 1
Living and working in the world of ideas 2
Freedom from supervision in my work 3
Opportunities for moderate but steady progress rather than the
    chance of extreme success or failure 4
A chance to exercise leadership 5
Remaining in the city or area in which I grew up 6
Getting away from the city or area in which I gew up 7
Opportunity to work with people rather than things 8
None of these 9

30. Listed below are six groups of occupations. The occupations within each group are similar to each other in many ways.

In Column A, circle the *two types* you would like best.

In Column B, circle the *two types* you would like least.

Consider the jobs as a group, not particular ones, and rate them only in terms of whether you would like that *type* of work regardless of whether such jobs are realistic career possibilities. Disregard considerations of salary, social standing, future advancement, etc.

Occupations	A. Two Best Liked Groups	B. Two Least Liked Groups		
Construction inspector, electrician, engineer, radio operator, tool designer, weather observer	x	x		
Physicist, anthropologist, astronomer, biologist, botanist, chemist	0	0	(58) Y	(59) Y
Social worker, clinical psychologist, employment interviewer, high school teacher, physical education teacher, public relations man .	1	1		
Bank teller, financial analyst, IBM equipment operator, office manager, statistician, tax expert	2	2		
Business executive, buyer, hotel manager, radio program director, real estate salesman, sales engineer . , ...	3	3		
Actor, commercial artist, musician, newspaper reporter, stage director, writer	4	4		

31. Please circle all the statements which describe your feelings about these specific occupations. (Circle as many or as few as apply in each column.)

	(60) SP	(61) SP	(62) SP	(63) SP	(64) SP	(65) SP
	Research Physicist or Chemist	College Professor	High School Teacher	Physician	Engineer	Business Executive
This sort of work would be very interesting	Y	Y	Y	Y	Y	Y
I don't have the ability to do this kind of work	X	X	X	X	X	X
I probably couldn't make as much money at this type of work as I'd like to make	0	0	0	0	0	0
One would have to devote too much time and energy to this work. I want to be able to spend more time with my family and friends	1	1	1	1	1	1
One would have to invest more time and money in preparing for this occupation than I feel I could afford	2	2	2	2	2	2
I know as a personal friend, or family friend, one or more people in this field	3	3	3	3	3	3
My parents would disapprove of my going into this field.	4	4	4	4	4	4
My personality isn't suitable for work in this field	5	5	5	5	5	5
People with my religious, racial, or family background don't have much chance of success in this field	6	6	6	6	6	6
Wouldn't be challenging enough for me	7	7	7	7	7	7
I wouldn't like the life I'd have to lead outside the job	8	8	8	8	8	8
This is my father's occupation . .	9	9	9	9	9	9

32. Please rate the following in terms of their effect on your career plans or decisions during college. (Circle one in each row.)

	Very Important	Fairly Important	Un-important	Never Received Any	
a. Vocational or similar psychological tests	5	6	7	8	(66) 9
b. Discussions with my academic advisor .	0	1	2	3	(67) 4
c. Discussions with faculty members other than my advisor	5	6	7	8	(68) 9
d. Advice from parents	0	1	2	3	(69) 4
e. Interviews with a professional psychological or vocational counselor	5	6	7	8	(70) 9

33. a. What is your opinion about the recently established Peace Corps? (Circle one.)

An excellent program about which I am enthusiastic 2 (71)
A good idea of which I am very much in favor 3 9
A good idea but I am not enthusiastic 4
Probably a good idea but I am not enthusiastic 5
Probably not a good idea but I am not sure 6
Definitely not a good idea 7
Don't know enough about it to have an opinion 8

b. What are you personally likely to do about the Peace Corps? (Circle one.)

Definitely not volunteer 0 (72)
Am thinking about volunteering but have not made up my mind Y
 yet 1
Have thought about volunteering but probably would not 2
Am probably going to volunteer 3
Have already volunteered 4
I am not sure what I will do 5

c. Have you filled out the Peace Corps Questionnaire? (Circle one.)

Yes 6 (73)
No, but I intend to do so . . 7 9
Definitely No 8

d. Here are some reasons young people have given for their personal reactions to the Peace Corps. Designate reasons both for volunteering and for not volunteering if both kinds seem pertinent to you. (Circle any which apply in your own case.)

(1) Reasons for volunteering:

To make a personal contribution to world peace 3 (74)
The attraction of working closely with others 4 9
The opportunity to learn about foreign cultures and languages . . 5
It would give me a chance to decide what kind of career I really
 want 6
To help the poorer nations of the world improve their economic
 conditions 7
It would further my career 8

(2) Reasons for *not* volunteering:

Family and personal obligations 1 (75)
Not eligible on physical grounds 2 9
Opposed to the general idea of a Peace Corps 3
It would interrupt my career 4
Too long a period of service 5
Low pay, undesirable working conditions, etc. 6
I don't have skills which would be useful to the Peace Corps . . . 7
My personality isn't suitable for that type of service 8

III. COLLEGE EXPERIENCE

34. Did you do all of your college work at this school? (Circle one.)

Yes x   (9)
No, transferred after freshman year 0   Y
No, transferred after sophomore year 1
No, transferred after junior year 2
No, started here, attended a year or more elsewhere, and then re-
turned 3

35. Were you regularly employed during this academic year? (Circle any which apply.)

No 4   (10)
Yes—   9

Full time job which is relevant to my anticipated career field . . . 5
Full time job which has nothing to do with my anticipated career
field 6
Part time job which is relevant to my anticipated career field . . . 7
Part time job which has nothing to do with my anticipated career
field 8

36. In which of the following have you been an active participant at this school? (Circle any which apply.)

Editorial staff of campus publication 0   (11)
Musical or dramatic group 1   Y
Business staff of campus publication or other campus group . . . 2
Campus group concerned with national or world issues 3
Inter-collegiate (varsity) athletics 4
Fraternity, Sorority (or equivalent) 5
Special interest group (e.g., Psychology Club, Outing Club) 6
Student government 7
Other (Circle and specify: _____) 8
None 9

37. Please call to mind the students of your own sex who are your closest friends here. Where did you meet them? (Circle any which apply)

Knew them before I came here x   (12)
Dormitory or rooming house 0   Y
My Fraternity or Sorority (or equivalent) 1
Campus activities 2
Classes in my major field 3
Classes in other fields 4
Other (Circle and specify:_____) 5
No close friends here 6

38. Of your close friends here, how many are going on next year for graduate or professional studies? (Circle one.)

All or almost all	x	(13)
More than half	0	Y
Less than half	1	
Few or none	2	
No close friends here	3	

39. Which of the following best describes where you lived this year? (Circle any which apply.)

Fraternity, Sorority (or equivalent) 5   (14)
Dormitory or other campus housing 6   9
Off-Campus room, apartment, house 7
With my parents 8

40. Listed below are some college courses which you might have taken. Please circle the number of any statements which describe your reactions. (Circle any which apply in each row. If none apply, leave the row blank.)

      (15)   (16)   (17)   (18)   (19)
      9   9   9   9   9

Course or Area

	Physics, Chemistry	Mathematics	Biology, Zoology, Botany	Social Sciences	English
I took one or more courses in this field or area during college	x	x	x	x	x
I *didn't* take any courses in this field or area during college	0	0	0	0	0
I found this course content very interesting . . .	1	1	1	1	1
I found this course content very dull	2	2	2	2	2
I have a flair for course work in this area	3	3	3	3	3
I found this area rough going academically . . .	4	4	4	4	4
Teachers in this area encouraged me to go on in the field	5	5	5	5	5
I admire many of the teachers in this area as persons not just as professors	6	6	6	6	6
By and large, the teachers in this area are *not* the kind of person I'd like to be	7	7	7	7	7
One or more of my close friends is majoring in this	8	8	8	8	8

41. Listed below are some purposes or results of college. Circle the one which is most important to you personally, and also circle the one which you think is most important to the typical student here. (Circle one in each column.)

	Most Important to me Personally	Most Important to the Typical Student here
A basic general education and appreciation of ideas	0	5
Having a good time while getting a degree	1	6
Career training	2	7
Developing the ability to get along with different kinds of people	3	8

(20)
4

42. Have you had any experience in original research (participating in collecting and analyzing raw data or conducting an experiment, *not* writing papers based on published sources or doing experiments from a laboratory manual) during your college studies? (Circle any which apply.)

No, I have never participated in original research 2   (22)
Yes, I have –   9

    a. Participated in research as part of a course 3
    b. Been employed by a faculty member as a research assistant   4
    c. Had an off-campus job (summer or during school year) working in research 5
    d. Participated in a summer research training program sponsored by the government or private foundation 6
    e. Conducted a research project on my own (e.g. senior thesis) 7
    f. Other (Circle and specify:_____) 8

43. What is your current academic status? (Circle one.)

Registered Spring term and studying for a bachelor's degree to be awarded at Spring commencement (May, June, July, but before Summer session commencement) 0   (23)
Registered Spring term and studying for a bachelor's degree to be awarded at Summer session commencement 1   3
Other (Circle and briefly specify your academic status: _____
_____) 2

44. When you graduate, how much personal indebtedness will you have for your education? (Count only money you owe for tuition or living costs during school not payments on car, appliances, clothes, etc.) (Circle one.)

None 5   (24)
Some, but less than $500 . . 6   9
$500 – $999 7
$1,000 or more 8

45. What is your overall (cumulative) grade point average for undergraduate work at your present college?

IMPORTANT: If your school uses letter grades (A, B, C, etc.) please circle the code number which is closest to your letter grade average.

Warning: The number which you circle probably does not correspond to the number equivalent at your school, e.g. at most schools "straight A" equals 4.0, here it equals "0".

If your school does not use letter grades, there should be special instructions accompanying your questionnaire. If, through clerical error, the instructions are missing, write your average in the margin.

(Circle one.)   *Letter Grade*   *Code Number*

Letter Grade	Code Number	
A	0	(25)
A−	1	Y
B+	2	
B	3	
B−	4	
C+	5	
C	6	
C−	7	
D+	8	
D or lower	9	

46. Listed below are a number of awards and honors. Which of these have you received during college or which are you fairly sure you will receive by the time you graduate? (Circle any which apply.)

Dean's List	Y	(26)
Phi Beta Kappa	X	SP
Other honor society based on academic achievement	0	
Graduation with honors (cum) (Magna) (Summa)	1	
National Merit Scholarship holder, Finalist, or Semi-Finalist . . .	2	
Other scholarship awarded on basis of academic ability	3	
Participation in "honors program" at this school	4	
Prize or award for scholarship or research work (e.g. "Smith prize for best biology experiment")	5	
Prize or award for literary, musical, or artistic work	6	
Took one or more graduate level courses as an undergraduate . .	7	
Other award or honor	8	
No special honors	9	

47. As best you know, how do you stand among the other people graduating in the *same major field* at your school? (Circle one.)

Top 10 per cent	4	(27)
Top quarter, but not top 10 per cent	5	9
Second quarter	6	
Third quarter	7	
Lowest quarter	8	

48. What is your emotional feeling about your college or university? (Circle one.)

I have a very strong attachment to it . . . . x (28)
I like it, but my feelings are not strong . . . . 0 Y
Mixed feelings 1
I don't like it much, but my feelings are not strong 2
I thoroughly dislike it 3

IV. PERSONAL CHARACTERISTICS

49. Your age at your last birthday? (Circle one.)

19 or younger 0 (29)
20 . . . . 1 Y
21 2
22 3
23 – 24 4
25 – 29 5
30 or older 6

50. Sex. (Circle one.)

Male 7 (30)
Female 8 9

51. Marital Status. (Circle one.)

Single, don't expect to be married before Fall, 1961 . . . . 4 (31)
*Single, expect to be married before Fall, 1961 . . . . 5 9
*Married, one or more children or expecting a child 6
*Married, no children 7
Widowed, Divorced, Separated 8

*IF "MARRIED" OR "EXPECTING TO BE MARRIED BEFORE FALL, 1961": What will your spouse or future spouse most likely be doing next year? (Circle any which apply.)

Working full time 3 (32)
Working part time 4 9
Housewife, Mother 5
Going to School 6
Military Service 7

52. Religion:

a. In which you were reared. (Circle one.)

Protestant (Circle and specify) _____ x (33)
Roman Catholic . . . . 0 Y
Jewish 1
Other (Circle and specify: _____) 2
None 3

b. Your present preference. (Circle one.)

Protestant (Circle and specify: _____) 5   (34)
Roman Catholic 6   4
Jewish 7
Other (Circle and specify: _____) 8
None 9

---

53. Your racial background. (Circle one.)

White x   (35)
Negro 0   Y
Oriental 1
Other (Circle and specify: _____) 2

---

54. How many—

a. *Older* brothers or sisters do you have? (Circle one.)

None 0   (36)
One 1   4
Two 2
Three or more 3

b. *Younger* brothers or sisters do you have? (Circle one.)

None 5   (37)
One 6   9
Two 7
Three or more 8

---

55. Are you a U.S. citizen? (Circle one.)

Yes, U.S. born x   (38)
Yes, Naturalized 0   Y
No, but I expect to stay in the U.S. 1
No, and I do not expect to stay in the U.S. 2

---

56. Please indicate your parents' (or step-parent's if parent is dead) highest educational attainment. (Circle one in each column.)

	Father	Mother	
8th grade or less	3	3	(39) (40)
Part High School	4	4	9 9
High School graduate	5	5	
Part College	6	6	
College graduate	7	7	
Graduate or professional degree beyond the bachelor's	8	8	

57 a. Which of the following categories best describes the usual occupation of the head of the household in your parental family? (Circle one.)

Professional 1   (41)
Proprietor or Manager 2   Y
Sales (Other than Sales Manager or Administrator) 3
Clerical 4
Skilled worker 5
Semi-Skilled worker 6
Service worker 7
Unskilled worker 8
Farmer or farm worker 9

  b. If the head of the household is a woman, also circle here 0
  c. If the head of the household is retired, also circle here x

58. Which of the following is the appropriate income category for your parental family? Consider annual income from all sources before taxes. (Circle one.)

Less than $5,000 per year . . 2   (42)
$5,000 – $7,499 3   9
$7,500 – $9,999 4
$10,000 – $14,999 5
$15,000 – $19,999 6
$20,000 and over 7
I have no idea 8

59. Which of the following best describes the community which you think of as your home town during high school days? (Circle one.)

Farm or open country x   (43)

Suburb in a metropolitan area of —   Y

more than 2 million population 0
500,000 to 2 million 1
100,000 to 499,999 2
less than 100,000 3

Central city in a metropolitan area or city of —

more than 2 million population 4
500,000 to 2 million 5
100,000 to 499,999 6
50,000 to 99,999 7
10,000 to 49,999 8
less than 10,000 9

60. Which of the following best describes the distance between your home town (when you were in high school) and your current college? (Circle one.)

In the same city or within commuting distance x   (44)
Within four hours automobile drive or less 0   Y

More than four hours drive, but in the same state 1
More than four hours drive, but in a different state 2

---

61. Please rate yourself on the following dimensions as you really think you are. (Circle one in each row.)

		Very	Fairly	Neither	Fairly	Very		
a.	Unfavorable toward						Favorable toward	(45)
	modern art	Y	x	0	1	2	modern art	3
b.	Politically liberal						Politically conserva-	(46)
		4	5	6	7	8	tive	9
c.	Conventional in						Unconventional in	(47)
	opinions and values	Y	x	0	1	2	opinions and values	3
d.	Religious	4	5	6	7	8	Non-religious	(48)
								9

62. Listed below are some adjectives, some of which are "favorable," some of which are "unfavorable," some of which are neither.

Please circle the ones which best describe you. Consider only those which are most characteristic of you as a person. (Most people choose five or six, but you may choose more or fewer if you want to.)

(49) SP	(50) SP	(51) SP
Ambitious x	Good Looking x	Moody x
Athletic 0	Happy 0	Obliging 0
Calm 1	Hard Driving 1	Outgoing 1
Cautious 2	High Strung 2	Poised 2
Cooperative 3	Idealistic 3	Quiet 3
Cultured 4	Impetuous 4	Rebellious 4
Dominant 5	Intellectual 5	Reserved 5
Easy Going 6	Lazy 6	Shy 6
Energetic 7	Low Brow 7	Sophisticated 7
Forceful 8	Methodical 8	Talkative 8
Fun Loving 9	Middle Brow 9	Witty 9

63. Your replies to this questionnaire are completely confidential, and absolutely no information of any kind about specific persons will be released to your school or anyone else. Your sealed questionnaire will be read only by the research staff in Chicago. However, in order to assess the statistical representativeness of the students in the sample, and because we hope to follow up some of the students in the sample next year to determine the outcome of their plans, we must ask you the following:

PLEASE PRINT

A. Your Name

Last Name	First Name	Middle Name

B. Your most likely address one year from now

Name of residence hall, department, company, etc., if any

Street Address

City or Town	Zone	State or Country

C. Name and address of someone who will know where you are or could forward a letter to you if you were not at the address you listed above

Last Name	First Name	Middle Name

Street Address

City or Town	Zone	State or Country

D. Name and address of the high school or preparatory school from which you entered college

Name of high school or preparatory school

City or Town	Zone	State or Country

IMPORTANT

You have now completed the questionnaire. Please seal it (to maintain confidentiality) and return it to the field representative at your school, according to the instructions he has provided.

WARNING: After you have sealed your questionnaire, your name will be inside. Make sure that you write your name and your return address on the outside back page, so that the field representative will know that you have returned your questionnaire.

TO SEAL: There is a gummed flap at the top of this page. Fold the questionnaire in half, and seal the folded questionnaire.

Thank you very much.

ABOUT NORC

The National Opinion Research Center is a general social research institute, founded in 1941 and affiliated with the University of Chicago since 1947. The research activities of the Center are financed through grants from and contracts with private foundations, government agencies, and universities.

Staff members of the Center are skilled social scientists, many of whom also hold appointments in the Division of Social Sciences at the University. The Center maintains a part-time national interviewing staff and has the capability of conducting surveys on a wide variety of topics using samples of populations, organizations, and institutions.

Recent studies of the Center include surveys of household medical care costs, occupational prestige, popular reactions to dramatic public events (e.g. the assassination of President Kennedy), participation in adult educational activities, and the effects on adult Catholics of attendance at Catholic schools. NORC is not-for-profit corporation governed by a Board of Trustees chosen from among prominent social scientists and laymen interested in social research.

National Opinion Research Center
5720 Woodlawn Avenue
Chicago, Illinois 60637